the book of FREE THINGS for SENIORS

by Linda & Bob Kalian

WEST ORANGE LIBRARY
46 MT. PLEASANT AVENUE
WEST ORANGE, NJ 07052
(973) 736–0198
09/05/2003

The sale of this book without a cover is unauthorized. If you purchase this book without a cover you should be aware that this book is stolen property. It was reported as "unsold' and destroyed" and neither the author nor the publisher has received any payment for this 'stripped' book. Please report any unauthorized sale to the publisher at 914-347-6671.

Library of Congress Cataloging-in-Publication Data
Kalian, Robert
Kalian, Linda

THE BOOK OF FREE THINGS FOR SENIORS

ISBN 0-934968-18-7

1. Consumer Reference   2. Catalog Free Things

This book is intended as general consumer information only and does not contain professional advice. The reader is urged to seek out and consult with a lawyer, financial advisor, health care and other professionals.

© 1999, 2000, 2001, 2002   Robert and Linda Kalian.
All rights reserved. No portion of this book may be reproduced in any form without written permission.

Quantity discounts are available. Teachers, fund raisers, premium users, contact us at the address below regarding the quantities needed.

Publisher:
Roblin Press
405 Tarrytown Road PMB 414
White Plains, NY 10607
(914) 347-6671   Fax: (914) 592-1167

Be sure to visit our Web site at: www.freethingsusa.com

If you enjoy getting something for nothing and would like to find out about our other great books of free things and amazing bargains, simply send a self-addressed stamped envelope to us at:

"I Want More Free Things"
Roblin Press
PO Box 125
Hartsdale, NY 10530

CONTENTS

What do you mean...Free?..................................... 7
Free Things For Everyone 11
Free To Help You Stay Healthy 46
Free Health & Beauty Aids 84
Free For Pet Lovers 90
Free Things For For Home & Garden 97
Free Cookbooks 112
Craft & Hobbies 144
Free For Kids 153
Learning Can Be Fun 159
Free Money For College 170
Money Matters 178
Computers & The Best Internet Sites 205
Free Things, Great Bargains & More On The Internet 213
Religion 228
Free For Cars & Drivers 232
Free For Sports Fans 244
Traveling Free Or At Big Savings 256
Traveling The USA 283
Foreign Travel 295
Free From The Government 304
Free Programs & Services From The Government ... 316
Free Legal Services 352
Nationwide Directory Of Consumer Protection Offices . 368
Free Dental Programs 385
Nationwide Helplines 399

What do you mean...Free?

We all know there's no such thing as a free lunch...right?

WRONG!!!

About 20 years ago we made a startling discovery...Unknown to most people, we are all surrounded by a dazzling array of thousands of valuable no-strings-attached free things of every type and description.

It doesn't matter if you're young or old, rich or poor....there are tons of great things yours absolutely FREE for the asking. But to take advantage of all these terrific free things, you must first know about them. That's why we researched and wrote this book. In it you are about to discover that you are floating in an ocean of free things, exciting programs and amazing discounts that you never knew existed. Simply keep your eyes and ears open and follow these few tips:

1. Use this book as your first and most valuable resource. It is chuck full of great stuff of every kind. Some are in this book to save you money, others will solve problems or bring you benefits. But there are also a ton of fascinating freebies that are here mostly for fun.

2. Keep it simple. No need to write if you can pick up the phone and call. We've included the phone numbers (many are toll-free) throughout the book along with web sites wherever they're available.

3. If you have a computer, make life even simpler by 'surfing the net'. If you don't yet have one, visit your local library which is almost certain to have computers you can use. You'll be amazed at how easy it is to use and just how much valuable information you can get off the Internet in no time.

4. Near the back of the book we've included a number of important directories you'll find useful in getting answers, solving problems and getting important benefits that are coming to you.

So if you need legal help, or dental care or if you have a consumer complaint, or need medications you can't afford, keep in mind that help is often just a phone call away. And if you need assistance and aren't sure exactly who to call for help, start by checking the directory. It is a great resource for an instant referral to the right agency or department.

5. If a listing calls for a 'SASE' that means that

when you write in for your free item, include a long (#10) Self-Addressed Stamped Envelope that you've written your return address on.

6. Teachers, civic and religious groups: If you'd like quantities of any item, ask for it and mention what it's for. Usually you'll get the quantity you need.

7. Ask for the items you want by name. Often companies will have several gifts available and won't know which one you're asking for unless you specify.

8. While we've done our best to put together the most complete and up-to-date information possible, once the book is in print addresses and phone numbers can and will change. Offers may be withdrawn (although in our experience the offers are generally replaced with a new and often even better one. But if you do come across a change or deletion that should be made in the next edition, we would really appreciate it if you would let us know by writing to:

Revisions Editor
Roblin Press
P.O. Box 125
Hartsdale, NY 10530

9. Hope you enjoy the book. If you can think of anything that would make the next edition of the book better for you, please let us know at the address above. We'd love to hear from you. Thanks. .

10. Remember, you work your tail just to pay for all the necessities of life. Now it's your turn to enjoy all the very best life has in store for you....for FREE!

Enjoy!

Free Things For Everyone

Let's jump right in to the world of free things by looking at three things that are yours for the asking right from the White House

Free Gift From The President

Can you imagine how exciting it would be to actually get a personal card from the President of the United States! Actually the President will send a congratulatory card signed by the President and the First Lady and embossed with the Presidential seal to any couple celebrating their 50th anniversary (or beyond) or to any citizen celebrating their 80th (or later) birthday. At the other end of the age spectrum, the President will also send a congratulatory card

to any newborn child. If you'd like, you can also have the card sent to you so you can frame it and give it as a unique one-of-a-kind gift! Send your requests at least 4 weeks in advance to:
THE GREETINGS OFFICE
THE WHITE HOUSE
WASHINGTON, DC 20500

Free Photo Of The President

How would you like a full color autographed photo of the President and First Lady? To get your photo simply request it by mail or fax from:
GREETINGS OFFICE
OLD EXECUTIVE OFFICE BUILDING, ROOM 39
WASHINGTON, DC 20502
FAX: 202-395-1232

Free From The White House

The President would like you to have a beautiful full color book, *The White House, The House of The People*. It features a room-by-room photo tour and history of the White House. For your free copy write to:
THE WHITE HOUSE
WASHINGTON, DC 20500

Tell The President What You Think

Yes, your opinion really does count. That's one of the great things about our country. And whether

Free Things For Everyone

you agree or disagree with his policies, the President would like to hear what you have to say. In fact there's a phone number you can call that will connects right into the White House where you you will be asked to express your opinion on the subject that concerns you most. So if you always wanted to give them a piece of your mind, now you can just be calling: **202-456-1111**

Free For The Asking –All Around You

One important thing to remember is that there are lots of things all around you that are free for the asking. All you have to do is be aware of them and to *ASK*. Let's take a look at a few examples:

Free For Consumers

Check supermarket bulletin boards for free items that neighbors want to get rid of or trade.

Credit card companies offer free month trials on discount shopping clubs, travel, insurance and offer all kinds of specials. The one thing you have to remember is if you don't want it, after the month is up, cancel it.

You can even get free magazine trial subscriptions, tapes and CD's just for asking. Always remember to look in your local paper for deals at the supermarkets for buy one item, get one free.

Free Things For Everyone

Free TV Show Tickets

If you enjoy watching TV shows, you'll enjoy it that much more when you're watching it live right at the TV studio. Now there's an easy online way to get free TV tickets for yourself and your guests to almost any show that has a live audience. On your computer (if you don't have a computer, use the one at your local library) log onto this web site and you will not only get instant tickets to your favorite TV show for up to 6 people but you'll also get a detailed map to the TV studio – all printed out on your printer. Visit their web site at:
www.tvtix.com

More Free Tickets To TV Shows

The TV networks will provide you with free tickets to any of their shows that have audiences. If you plan to be in Los Angeles or New York and would like to see a TV show write to the network (care of their 'Ticket Department') before your visit. Generally you will get a letter you can exchange for tickets for any show open at the time of your visit. Write to:

ABC, 415 PROSPECT AVE., LOS ANGELES, CA 90028

CBS TICKET DIV., TELEVISION CITY 7800 BEVERLY BLVD., LOS ANGELES, CA 90036

NBC, 3000 WEST ALAMEDA AVE.. BURBANK, CA 91523 (OR 30 ROCKEFELLER PLAZA, NEW YORK, NY 10020)

Free Things For Everyone

Free Scented Sachet

Now you can freshen your home with a beautiful lace sachet filled with sweet smelling potpourri. Use it in a drawer to freshen lingerie or even in a closet to refresh your linens. It makes a great gift. Send six first class stamps postage and ask for a *Scented Sachet*. Send to:

SWEET SCENTS
2431 BUCK RD.
HARRISON, MI 48625

Free Pets

Your local paper may have ads for free kittens and pups when their cats have litters and dogs have pups. Animal shelters also have free pets. Most often they will only ask you to pay for the shots.

Free Land Fill/Fire Wood

Some contractors offer free land fill and free top soil when they want to get rid of it. The only catch might be that you have to remove it (or pay a nominal delivery charge.) Check out construction sites. You can often get free fire wood when they are clearing the land.

Free Computer Services

There are tons of offers to try different things before you buy. For example computer online services

offer a variety of *free trials* just to get you to try their service and to surf the Internet. Call:
AMERICA ON LINE (CURRENTLY OFFERING 700 FREE HOURS JUST FOR SIGNING ON): 1-888-265-8002
PRODIGY: 1-800-776-3449
COMPUSERVE: 1-800-848-8990

Free Haircuts

Free haircuts are available through some of your local beauty and barber schools. Check your phone book and give them a call. Some may ask a small fee or a tip for the trainee. Some of your larger hair designers may offer free style and cuts certain months or certain times of the year. Call your favorite salon and find out when they are training their students. You benefit by getting the designer him/herself for free. (In their salon they may charge anywhere from $50.00 and up.) Companies like Clairol often offer free hair coloring when they are testing new products. Don't hesitate to give any of them a call. Remember, if you don't ask you'll never know.

Want to try free perfume or have a makeover? Try any one of your larger department stores. You are never obligated to buy and some of the companies will even give you free product samples. You could have a ball going from store to store. Next time you need a new look, try your local department store.

Free Travel

There are lots of options around for free or almost

free travel.

The airlines offer you free tickets for changing your flight if they are overbooked. So next time you are at the airport ready to take a flight, volunteer to be 'bumped'. Typically you'll be put on a flight leaving an hour or so later and get a free ticket for a future flight. Frequent flyer fares are still a good deal as long as they are offered. Make sure you are a member of the airline's frequent flyer club if you plan on doing any airline travel. They usually don't put a time restriction on them.

If you have a unique specialty, many cruise lines will give you a free trip when you give a lecture about your specialty on one of their cruises. They often have theme cruises you might fit in with. For example, if you are a fitness specialist they often look for people to teach aerobics on board. So if you have a special skill, the cruise line might feel it is special enough to give you a free trip if you spend a few hours instructing others while on the cruise. Check the toll-free directory information (800-555-1212) for the phone numbers of the cruise lines.

There are some courier services that will ask you to carry a package anywhere in the world they travel to. With that you get a free trip for carrying the parcel. Sometimes you can get to stay a few extra days as long as you can catch their plane on the return flight.

When they travel, some families look for housesitters. In return for watching their home, you get a free place to live. If you like to travel, you can might even trade apartments and homes with people in other parts of the country (or the world) through different real estate exchanges. Check the classified section of your local newspaper.

Free For Using Your Credit Card

The credit card war is heating up...and you stand to benefit. Today more and more banks and companies are offering credit cards that come with added bonuses for using it. For example, some banks offer credit cards that give you one frequent flyer mile for each dollar you charge on their card. You can use the miles to get free airline tickets. Also, many larger chain stores offer you free dollars to spend in their store just for opening a charge account with them. There is no obligation to use the card and you can cut it up if you don't plan to use it.

Free Concerts

Don't overlook all the free concerts and theatre productions in all community parks outdoors especially in the summer months. Check with your local parks and recreation department.

Many movie theatres have deals on slow nights. Our local movie theatre offers a special on Tuesday nights: Buy one ticket, get one free. Many also offer half price tickets for seniors. Check it out.
If you like concerts and drama some theatre and opera companies offer ushers (if you are willing to

work a shift) free tickets in exchange for your work.

These are just a small handful of the tons of free and practically free offers all around you all the time. The important thing is to keep an eye out for them and take advantage of them where they are of interest to you.

Free Dinner

Don't forget that there are quite a few restaurant chains that offer you a free dinner on your birthday. All you have to show is a license or some proof of your birthdate.

Also check the ads for local restaurants that offer those great coupons for buy-one dinner get-one free.

Free Long Distance Calls

Because of all the competition between phone companies, if you are willing to switch they'll offer you all kinds of deals from $100.00 checks to several hours of free calls. Shop around for the best deal before you sign up with another phone company. First, take advantage of the free offers. Don't be hesitant about switching phone companies...you can always switch again to another company that offers you an even better deal.

Free Things For Everyone

Never Pay More Than 5¢ A Minute For Any Long Distance Call

After you've used your free calls, shop around for the best deal before you sign up with another phone company. Companies like IDT now offer long distance service for as little as 5¢ a minute, 24 hours a day, 7 days a week. Companies like IDT are called 'resellers' since they buy time from long distance companies and resell this time to you at low prices. For more information on their 5¢ a minute plan call IDT at: **1-800-CALL-IDT** (that's 1-800-225-5438)

Back Talk

Back talk and how to deal with it constructively is some handy advice Covenant House offers you for dealing with your child. These helpful tips will open lines of communication and help keep you in touch with your child before he/she gets out of hand. If you need expert advice or support, call their NINELINE at **1-800-999-9999**. They will put you in touch with people who can help you right in your own town.

Free Fridge Magnets

If you collect fridge magnets this miniature teddy bear magnet is for you. It's hand made out of wood and comes with a brightly colored bow around his neck. It makes a great addition to any refrigerator. You'll enjoy attaching that special message to one of these mini magnets. Send a long self addressed

envelope to: (limit one per household)
TINY TEDDIES
2431 BUCK RD.
HARRISON, MI 48625

Book Bargains

Catalog of Book Bargains is for all book lovers that want to save 90% or more off original prices. Recent best sellers are sold in this 50 page catalog at very sharp discounts. The catalog is free from
P. DAEDALUS BOOKS INC.
BOX 9132
HYATTSVILLE, MD. 20781
OR CALL: 1-800-395-2665

Get Rich At Home

Have you ever dreamed of starting your own business from your home? If so you will want to get the *Mail Order Success Secrets report*. Learn how to start in your spare time with little money and grow rich in the most exciting business in the world. Send a SASE to:
ROBLIN-LFT
405 TARRYTOWN RD. PMB 414
WHITE PLAINS, NY 10607

Keeping Your Breath Fresh

These great *Fresh Breath Capsules* will help you

cure your bad breath internally. Dont worry...the next time you eat garlic or spicy food, pop one of these Breath Fresh capsules. They also have other great products like Retinol A, Ultramins plus Vitamins and Thigh Cream. To try the Breath Freshener, send $1.00 to cover postage and handling to:
21ST CENTURY GROUP
10 CHESTNUT STREET
SPRING VALLEY, NY 10877

Free For Cigar Lovers

If you are a cigar smoker or know someone who is, this catalog is a must. Not only will you find every cigar you can think of, but all the accessories that go with them. There is a Cigar Hall of Fame and even some unusual and interesting gifts for people who don't smoke. Drop a card to:
THE THOMPSON COMPANY
5401 HANGAR COURT
P.O. BOX 30303
TAMPA, FL 33630-3303

Put Your Best Foot Forward

When your feet ache and you are looking for some kind of relief what can you do? The Podiatric Association of America has a toll-free number you can call to get assistance. Call:
1-800-FOOT-CARE

Free Things For Everyone

Free Help For Older People

Getting help and information about services for older people anywhere in the United States is now easy. There is a new national *Eldercare Locator* service. Dial: **1-800-677-1116** between 9 a.m. and 5p.m. Monday through Friday. Have the name and address of the person who needs assistance, the zip code and a brief description of the service or information needed. The *"Eldercare Locator"* provides information about adult day-care centers, legal assistance, home health services and more. This service taps into a nationwide network of organizations familiar with state and local community services throughout the country.

Surprise Gift Club

We've all faced the problem of what to give someone as a gift. Finally there's help. The Surprise Gift of the Month Club has developed an innovative solution. They will offer you a broad selection of items from kites, iron ons, coasters, stickers, records, crewel and needlepoint kits and many more items to select from. Anyone young or old will be delighted to receive a gift each month. It's a nice way to say "I'm thinking of you" to someone special. For a sample of the assorted crewel and needlepoint kits, send $1.00 for postage and handling to:
SURPRISE GIFT OF THE MONTH CLUB
55 RAILROAD AVE.
GARNERVILLE, NY 10923

Before Your Buy A Home

Are you considering buying a house? This 160 page book from Lawyers Title Insurance Corp. is a must for you. It will help answer all those questions you have about owning your own home. Ask for *The Process of Home Buying*. Send 75¢ postage & handling to:

LAWYERS TITLE INSURANCE CORP. DEPT. CW
6630 WEST BROAD ST.
BOX 27567
RICHMOND, VA 23230

Take An Elderhostel Vacation

Elderhostel offers moderately priced learning vacations across the United States and Canada as well as 45 nations abroad for senior citizens who enjoy adventure and travel but who have a limited amount of money to spend. The subjects taught on these vacations range from astronomy, to zoology. For a catalog of courses and travel itineraries, write:
ELDERHOSTEL
75 FEDERAL ST., THIRD FLOOR
BOSTON, MA. 02110-1941
OR CALL 1-617-426-7788

Consumer Gem Kit

Buying a valuable gem can be a tricky affair unless you are prepared. Have you ever wondered what makes one diamond more valuable than another that looks the same to the naked eye? Before buying any gemstone it is essential to learn exactly what to look for. For example do you know the 4 'C's' that determine a diamond's value? They are... Cut... Color... Clarity... Carat (weight). To learn more about what to look for when buying a diamond, send for a free consumer kit from the American Gem Society. Send a card to:

THE AMERICAN GEM SOCIETY
8881 W. SAHARA AVE.
LAS VEGAS, NV 89117

House Of Onyx

If you like gems and gemstones...whether in the rough or finished into fine jewelry or artifacts, this catalog is for you. You will find some fabulous close-out buys on some fantastic gemstones, geodes even Mexican onyx and malachite carvings. If you are just a collector or need some great gifts, send for this catalog. Write:

HOUSE OF ONYX
THE AARON BUILDING
120 MAIN ST.
GREENVILLE, KY 42345

Before You Discipline Your Child

Parenting has never been easy. Next time you feel like hitting your child, try another approach... start by taking a few minutes to calm down. For example you might do something like making an origami paper hat, or any game that gives you the time you need to cool off. Remember the time it takes to make a paper hat could keep you from hurting your child. For an excellent free book on this subject, write:
"PREVENTING CHILD ABUSE"
PO BOX 2866 P
CHICAGO, IL 60690

Sleep Tight

A healthful good night's sleep makes for a very productive, pleasant person. Learn all the facts on how to get a healthful sleep, by selecting the right bedding pillows and positions. The makers of Simmons will send you this free book *Consumer Guide To Better Sleep* plus several others including *It's Never Too Early To Start Caring For Your Back* and tips for shopping for the right bed. Send a business-sized SASE to:
SIMMONS BEAUTYREST
ONE CONCOURSE CENTER, SUITE 600
BOX C-93
ATLANTA, GA 30328

Free Parenting Web Site

If you have questions about parenting, now you can

get help 24 hours a day from experts like Dr. Bill and Martha Sears, Dr. Spock and Dr. Nancy Snyderman. It's all customized for your child's age and interests. Best of all it's free on the new online parenting site:
WWW.PARENTTIME.COM

Knife Showplace

This catalog with hundreds of knives, swords specialty and novelty knives, sharpening systems, accessories and lots more will help you find that special carving knife for apples, cheese or fruitcake. If you are a collector of swords and sheaths there are a quite a few to choose from. Write to:
SMOKY MOUNTAIN KNIFE WORKS
BOX 4430
SEVIERVILLE, TN 37864

Saving Time And Money

The publishers of *Quick, Easy, Cheap and Simple* newsletter would like to send a sample issue. It's loaded with information in the form of handy, easy-to-understand tips, on the all important topics of saving both time and money. You'll also find an assortment of quick and easy recipe ideas. For your free newsletter, mail a SASE to:
QUICK, EASY, CHEAP AND SIMPLE
4057 N. DRAKE-RP5
CHICAGO, IL 60618-2219

Free Love Letter Newsletter

Love guru, Greg Godek, author of the bestselling book, *1001 Ways To Be More Romantic*, would like to give you a free one year subscription to LoveLetter Newsletter, chuck full of great romantic ideas. Put the spark back in your love life. Call Source Book at: **1-800-727-8866**

Free Help To Improve Your Reading Skills

This freebie is for adults whose reading levels is grade 4 to 6, and is a great way to help improve their skills. Each issue contains articles covering important international news as well as features on education, health, leisure, law, etc. To get a free issue, ask for *News For You Sample Copy*. Write to:
NEW READERS PRESS
DEPT. 100, PO BOX 888
SYRACUSE, NY 13210

Clothes For People With Handicaps

Fashion Ease specializes in clothing for elderly, arthritic or handicapped people. Styles wrap and close easily with Velcro or snaps. There are wheelchair accessories and items for the incontinent. To get a copy of their free catalog write to:
FASHION EASE
1541 60TH ST
BROOKLYN, NY 11219

Discounted Wigs

For the best prices on the finest wigs, send for this free catalog. You will be amazed at the beautiful selection of wigs from Revlon, Adolfo and many more. So if you are in the market for a wig write to:
BEAUTY TREND
PO BOX 9323, DEPT. 44002
HIALEAH, FL 33014

"Bridal Toasting Tips"

Martini & Rossi Asti Spumante share with you all the traditions of the bridal toast from around the world. Included in your freebie are suggested toasts for nervous members of the wedding party; also a wine serving guide and ideas for starting new traditions. Ask for *Bridal Toasting Tips*. Send a SASE to:
THE ALDEN GROUP
DEPT. M, 52 VANDERBILT AVE
NEW YORK, NY 10017

Free Videos On Loan

To help bring art appreciation to a wider audience The National Gallery of Art would like to send you a video without charge. They have dozens of videos and slide programs to lend to individuals, community groups, schools, etc. Your only obligation is to pay the postage when sending the materials back. For a complete *catalog and reservation card* send a

postcard to:
NATIONAL GALLERY OF ART
EXTENSION PROGRAM
WASHINGTON, DC 20565

Free For The Large Or Tall Woman

Lane Bryant offers a stunning collection of dresses, coats, jeans, sportswear, lingerie and shoes to the woman who wears half size or large size apparel. You'll find name brands and designer fashions in their free *catalog*. If you are 5'7" or taller also ask for their *Tall Collection catalog*. Write:
LANE BRYANT
DEPT. A
INDIANAPOLIS, IN 46201

Home Buying

If you are thinking of buying a home any time in the near future, there are certain things you should do to protect yourself. For example before buying a home, it is a good idea to hire a trained inspector to check for defects you might not see such as termites or a roof in need of repair. But first be sure to get a free copy of *American Homeowners Foundation Top Ten Home Buyers Tips*. Call them toll-free at: **1-800-489-7776**
Or visit their web site at:
www.americanhomeowners.org

Easy Shopping

Relax and shop at home. Lillian Vernon's *free catalog is* full of affordable treasures from around the world. Drop a postcard to:

LILLIAN VERNON
VIRGINIA BEACH, VA 23479

Unique Gift Catalog

Harriet Carter has provided distinctive gifts since 1958. This fun-filled catalog is chuck-full of unique gifts you will find fascinating. Write to:

HARRIET CARTER
DEPT. 14
NORTH WALES, PA 19455

Free From Cooperative Extension

Your local cooperative extension office offers an amazing range of free information and services to all who request them. Soil analysis, 4-H information, home economics classes and money-management workshops are just a few of the services available. Call your local Extension Service. It's listed under "County Government" in the phone book.

Get That Bug

The makers of Raid bug sprays would like you to have a highly informative chart, *Raid Insecticides - What to Use For Effective Control.* Learn how to deal with crawling, flying and biting pests both inside

and outside your home (including plant pests). You'll also receive a money-saving coupon. Send a postcard to:
"INSECT CONTROL"
JOHNSON WAX
RACINE, WI 53403

Effective Consumer Action

If you ever wanted to complain to a company about one of their products but didn't know how to go about it, this is for you. *How To Talk To A Company And Get Action* should help you get your problem solved—fast. You'll also receive the "Story of Coca Cola". Write to:
CONSUMER INFORMATION CENTER
COCA-COLA CO.
DEPT. FR, P.O. DRAWER 1734
ATLANTA, GA 30301

Gerber Baby

Whether you are a new parent or just looking for some helpful tips Gerber has a great book *Feeding Your Baby*. This handy guide gives you practical tips for feeding your baby from birth to age three. So your baby will learn healthful eating habits right from the start. You'll also receive some money savings coupons to get you started. Ask for the Gerber baby care package. Call:
1-800-4-GERBER

Finding The Right Camp Or School

Choosing the right sleepaway camp or private school can be very confusing. To help take the confusion out of camp or school shopping here's a helpful booklet, *How To Choose A Camp For Your Child*. Send a SASE to:
AMERICAN CAMPING ASSN.
5000 STATE RD.
67 NORTH
MARTINSVILLE, IN 46151

Fly Your Flag Over The Capitol

Your Congressman will provide a unique service for you free of charge. If you'd like to have your own flag flown over the U.S. Capitol Building write to your congressman. The flag itself is not free (prices range from $8.00 to $17.00 depending upon size and material) but the service of having the flag purchased, flown and sent to you is free. This also makes a unique gift for someone special. Write to your own Congressman,
CONGRESS OF THE UNITED STATES
WASHINGTON, DC 20515

Words of Wisdom

If you need words of encouragement to keep going in the face of adversity (and who doesn't), *Portrait of An Achiever* is an inspirational addition to any home. This beautiful parchment reproduction is

suitable for framing and makes an excellent gift. Send $1.00 s&h to:
ROBLIN PRESS
405 TARRYTOWN RD PMB 414 - POA
WHITE PLAINS, NY 10607

Boys & Girls Clubs

Give your boys and girls things to do and a place to go to develop their character. The Boys & Girls Clubs of America have been doing this for over 100 years. They have 1100 local chapters in 700 towns. Ask for the *Boys & Girls Club Information Package*. Write to:
BOYS & GIRLS CLUBS OF AMERICA
3 WEST 35TH ST.
NEW YORK, NY 10001

Safe Mail Order Buying

Here is a practical and informative guide detailing the protection you have under the F.T.C.'s Mail Order Merchandise Rule. A free copy of *Shopping By Phone & Mail* is yours for the asking by writing to:
SHOPPING BY PHONE AND MAIL
DEPARTMENT P
FEDERAL TRADE COMMISSION
WASHINGTON, DC 20580

Keeping Warm

If you are looking for a superior blend of hand selected white goose and duck down feather comforters, pillows or outerwear this is the place for you. Drop a card for their *free catalog* to:

THE COMPANY STORE
500 COMPANY STORE ROAD
LA GROSSE, WI 54601

Are You Sensitive To Milk?

If you are allergic to milk you will want to get a copy of *'Ross's Educational Materials Catalog'* designed specifically for those with a lactose intolerance. Write to:

EDUCATIONAL SERVICES
ROSS LABORATORIES
COLUMBUS, OH 43216

Preserve Our History

If you'd like to participate in the preservation of sites, buildings and objects that are important to American history and culture, there is something you can do. Drop a card asking for the *Historic Preservation package* to:

NATIONAL TRUST FOR HISTORIC PRESERVATION
1785 MASSACHUSETTS AVE. N.W.
WASHINGTON, DC 20036

Free Things For Everyone

Free Consumer Handbook

A problem everyone has at one time or another is who to turn to when he has a complaint. Now with the *Consumer Resource Handbook* you will know the best non-government and government sources to contact for help. This is something no one should be without. Send a card to:

CONSUMER RESOURCE HANDBOOK
CONSUMER INFORMATION CENTER
PUEBLO, CO 91009

Your Own Moneytree

Can you imagine how great it would be to have your very own moneytree growing in a corner of your kitchen? Well maybe you can. American companies give away billions of dollars of gifts, cash, sweepstakes and freebies every year. The editors of *MoneyTree Digest* will show you how to get your share of the Great American Giveaway. To get a sample issue of this terrific magazine, send $1.00 postage & handling to:

MONEYTREE DIGEST DEPT. LFT
648 CENTRAL AVE. PBM 441
SCARSDALE, NY 10583

Popcorn Pandemonium

Love popcorn? Ready for something different? Why not try rum butter toffee, peanut butter, fruit salad or cinnamon flavored popcorn? The Popcorn Factory has everything you ever dreamed of in popcorn, jelly beans, pretzels, nuts and home poppers. For a free

catalog, write to:
THE POPCORN FACTORY
801 TECHNOLOGY WAY SUITE 100
LIBERTYBILLE, IL 60048
OR CALL: 1-800-223-2676

Buying Life Insurance

Buying the right amount and the right type of life insurance is one of the important decisions you must make. Before you make any decision, be sure to get your copy of *How To Choose A Life Insurance Company*. To get your copy of this informative booklet, simply send a postcard to:
OCCIDENTAL LIFE
BOX 2101 TERMINAL ANNEX
LOS ANGELES, CA 90051

Caring For Elderly Parents

Are you faced with the dilemma of possibly caring for elderly parents - then you have lots of questions about medicare, medicaid, power of attorney and making or planning medical decisions. The National Academy of Elder Law Attorneys offers free brochures that address these complicated issues: *Medicaid, Medicare, Durable Power of Attorney* and *Planning for Medical Decision Making*. To receive all four, send a long SASE and request them by name. Write to:
NATIONAL ACADEMY OF ELDER LAW ATTORNEYS
1604 N. COUNTRY CLUB RD. DEPT. FC
TUCSON, AZ 85716-3102

If you need an attorney devoted to elder law, call your local state bar association or check out NAELA's web site:
www.naela.org

Free For Flag Lovers

If you are looking for any kind of flags, poles and accessories, custom designs states, nations, historic and nautical, this *free catalog* has them all. Write to:
CHRIS REID
P.O. BOX 1827SM
MIDLOTHIAN, VA 23113

Do You Suffer From Chapped Lips?

If you suffer from dry chapped lips or mouth sores, this is especially for you. You will receive sample packets of Blistex Lip Ointment plus two informative brochures and a 25¢-off coupon too. Send a long SASE to:
BLISTEX SAMPLE OFFER
1800 SWIFT DR.
OAK BROOK, IL 60521

Love Fragrances

If you love all those expensive perfumes and co-

lognes advertised on TV, radio and magazines but don't want to pay the high prices, this is a must for you. For your free list and scented cards, drop a card to:
ESSENTIAL PRODUCTS CO.
90 WATER ST.
NEW YORK, NY 10005

Helping Your Child Learn

If you are a parent, you want to help build a solid foundation of important basic skills for your child. This *free catalog* will help you encourage learning and prepare your child for the future. Write:
SCHOOL ZONE PUBLISHING
PO BOX 777
GRAND HAVEN, MI 49417

Keep Warm

Stay warm this winter with insulated clothing, outdoor equipment and toasty down comforters that you make yourself — with the help of a Frostline kit. For a copy of their free catalog, send a postcard to:
FROSTLINE KITS
2525 RIVER ROAD.
GRAND JUNCTION, CO 81505

Before You Move

Mayflower has a nice packet of moving materials

free for the asking. It includes labels to mark your boxes with plus tips to make your move run smoother and faster. Ask for your *"Moving Kit"* from your local Mayflower mover or send a card to:
MAYFLOWER MOVERS
BOX 107B
INDIANAPOLIS, IN 46206

Have You Decided To Move?

How To Stretch Your Moving Budget – The Interstate Moving Guide is a useful booklet that will help you make your interstate move run smoothly. It tells you how to prepare for moving day, how moving costs are calculated, a glossary of moving terms and lots more. It's your free from:
ATLAS VAN LINES
1212 ST. GEORGE RD.
EVANSVILLE, IN 47703.

Free Help With Your Next Move

To help you with your next move United Van Lines has set up a toll free number you can call. They will provide you with the phone number of the United Van Line office nearest you. Your local office is set up to answer any specific questions you may have. For example, they can answer your questions about employment, educational facilities, housing, and more, in 7,000 cities and towns throughout the 50 states (and foreign countries too). Your local United Van Line can also provide you with guides which

make preplanning a lot easier. Call:
1-800-325-3870
Or write to:
CUSTOMER RELATIONS
UNITED VAN LINES
ONE UNITED DR.
FENTON, MO 63026

Carpet Care

If you are thinking of adding or changing carpets in your home but are confused by the many choices you have to make, call The Carpet and Rug Institute toll-free information line for answers to your questions related to carpeting your home:
1-800-882-8846

Making Your Home Safe

If you would like to make your home a safer place to live, be sure to get *Don't Be A Victim* and also *Danger In The Home--How To Make Your Home A Healthy Home For Children*. You'll find a checklist which will show you how to make every room of your home, from the kitchen to the bedroom safer. You will also find useful toll-free numbers you can call for help with health problems like respiratory illnesses, childhood lead poisoning and safe drinking water. To get your free safety poster, call:
1-800-HUDS-FHA

Free Things For Everyone

If You Love Ships...

This 100 page *catalog is* full of decorative nautical ideas for the home. If you're looking for a ship model, marine painting or ship's wheel you'll find it here. Drop a postcard to:
PRESTON'S
174-A MAIN ST. WHARF
GREENPORT, NY 11944

Hair Removal

If you're a woman with unsightly body hair, this is for you. Nudit's helpline allows women to discuss with experts the sensitive issue of hair removal treatments. Their toll-free hotline number is:
1-800-62-NUDIT

Children and Violence

In today's society children are exposed to the media's hype of violence and horror stories. There are several warning signs to help us recognize and prevent any violence children may be exposed to. The American Psychological Association and MTV, publish an excellent guide called *Warning Signs*, to help us discuss these issues with our children before they get out of hand. For a free copy of *Warning Signs*, call:
1-800-268-0078

Free Guide To Internet Safety

Parents know to buckle up their kids before driving on the highway but what can they do to keep them safe on the information highway...the Internet? The U.S. Department Of Education publishes a great guide to help you set rules for your children's Internet use and to be aware of their activities online. The Internet can offer an invaluable source of information for your child if he or she is looking for specific information, however there may also be offensive and off-limit sites that you should be aware of. Today computer technology changes so fast that the more informed parents are the better equipped they are to point out safe sites for their kids. Ask for *Parents Guide to the Internet*. To get your free copy, call:
1-800-USA-LEARN

Pet Allergies

If you are allergic to pets there may be a new way to eliminate those allegies around the house with a new vacuum by Nilfisk, Inc. of America. Call toll-free:
1-800-241-9420 Ext 2

HERE ARE A FEW TOLL-FREE HOTLINES YOU CAN CALL FOR SPECIAL UP-TO-THE MINUTE INFORMATION ON IMPORTANT TOPICS

Free Headache Hotline

The American Council for Headache Education may offer a solution on how to lessen your pain and discomfort
1-800-255-ACHE

Asthma Information

If you suffer from asthma, you will want to get a free copy of *Making The Most of Your Next Doctor Visit*. You will discover what you can do to assist your doctor in helping you relieve your asthma suffering. Call:
1-800-727-8462

Peace Corps

The Peace Corps can give you the chance to immerse yourself in a totally different culture while helping to make an important difference in other people's lives. If you like helping people and want to get involved, be sure to get the *Peace Corps Information package*. Call toll-free:
1-800-424-8580

Free Things For Everyone

Free Retirement Guide

If you are planning to retire any time soon, you will definitely want to get a copy of *Making The Most Of Your Retirement*. This new 87 page retirement guide features information about finance, health and lifestyle option. It comes to you free from State Farm Insurance. To get you copy, call them toll-free at:
1-888-733-8368

Free To Help You Stay Healthy

Health Answers Online

Dr. Koop, the former Surgeon General has an outstanding web site you will want to visit for the latest news on all health-related subjects. At this site you will find a wealth of information on wellness, nutrition, fitness and prevention as well as current information on over 50 health topics ranging from Alzheimer's disease to cancer, diabetes, heart disease and migraine. You can also sign up for their free Newsletter which they will e-mail directly to you. You will also find links to prescription drug sites where you can purchase medicine and vitamins quickly, easily and at terrific savings. Visit their web site at:
www.drkoop.com

Free Headache Relief

We all live in a fast-paced, stress-full society and trying to balance work, family and social life can take its toll. If you suffer from

stress related headaches, the folks at Excedrin would like to help. First, there's their free colorful newsletter, *Excedrin Headache Relief Update.* You'll learn the warning signs and some common foods that trigger migraines. There's also a readers corner where experts answer your questions. You'll even receive a coupon towards your next purchase of Excedrin. They also have a toll-free customer service number you can call for help and an excellent web site. For help with your persistent headache problems, contact them at:
EXCEDRIN HEADACHE RESOURCE CENTER
PO Box 687
WILTON, CT 06897
Or call them toll-free at:
1-800-468-7746
You can also visit their web site at:
www.excedrin.com

Healthy, Happy Kids

If you're a parent or about to become one, here are three free publications you will want to get:

Sneak Health Into Your Snacks put out by the American Institute For Cancer Research, will show you how to get your kids to eat healthy meals without them knowing that it's good for them. For your free copy, send a long SASE to:
AICR
1759 R STREET NW
WASHINGTON, DC 20009
Or better yet, call them toll-free at:
1-800-843-8114

Especially For Teens: You And Your Sexuality is a free brochure that will help your teens better understand and deal with their budding sexuality. To get a copy, send a long SASE requesting publication # APO42 to:
**ACOG RESOURCE CENTER
PO BOX 96920
WASHINGTON, DC 20090**

Your Child And Antibiotics will tell you more about the important role antibiotics can play in keeping your child healthy. To get your free copy, send a long SASE to:
**AMERICAN ACADEMY OF PEDIATRICS
PUBLICATIONS DIVISION
141 NORTHWEST POINT BLVD.
PO BOX 747
ELK GROVE VILLAGE, IL 60009**

Are You Having A Baby?

If you are about to have a baby or if you've recently had a newborn, this one's for you. It's called *The Mayo Clinic Complete Book of Pregnancy & Baby's First Year* and it's yours free from the 'good neighbor' folks at State Farm. This beautiful 750 page book covers all aspects of pregnancy and baby care through age one. It is not only one of the most comprehensive guides to baby care but also an excellent resource book you'll use over and over again. The book is divided into 4 sections...pregnancy, childbirth, living and understanding your baby and there's even a section 'from partners to parents: a

family is born.' This beautiful book is a must for anyone starting a family. It also makes an excellent gift. To get your copy, contact your local State Farm Insurance agent or call them toll free at:
1-888-733-8368

Child Safety

Hidden Hazards II spotlights potential family safety risks. Every parent is interested in the safety of their child and the products that are around that are safe and hazardous. Ask for *Hidden Hazards II*. For your free copy, send a SASE to:
COALITION FOR CONSUMER HEALTH AND SAFETY
PO BOX 12099
WASHINGTON, DC 20005-0999

Breast Feeding Guide

If you are a new mother or soon to be one, this handy *Breast Feeding Guide* will answer most of the questions you may have about breast feeding. Write for this excellent information to:
MEDELA, INC.
PO BOX 660
MC HENRY, IL 60051-0660

Free Guide To Child's Ear Infections

Anyone with a child knows the trauma involved when your child suffers an earache. Learn the causes, symptoms and cures of ear infections before the suffering begins. This handy guide will explain everything. Ask for:

Free Medical Care & Health Information

A PARENT'S GUIDE TO CHILDREN'S EARACHE
C/O CHILDREN'S TYLENOL
1675 BROADWAY, 33RD FL.
NEW YORK, NY 10019

Free Help To Lower Your Cholesterol & Blood Pressure

Call the National Heart, Lung and Blood Institute for recorded information on cholesterol and high blood pressure. When you call leave your name and address for written information. Call:
1-800-575-WELL

Young At Heart

The National Institute on Aging would like you to have a copy of *"For Hearts and Arteries: What Scientists are Learning About Age and the Cardiovascular System."* Learn how the latest research can help keep your heart running younger no matter what your age.
NIA INFORMATION CENTER
PO Box 8057
GAITHERSBURG, MD. 20898-8057
OR CALL 1-800-222-2225
or visit their web site at:
www.nih.gov/nia

Free Newsletter For Healthier Eyes

Keep yourself informed of the latest information on eye care with the free *Looking Ahead* newsletter

from Merck. In this quarterly newsletter you'll find news encompassing a wide spectrum of eye care from prevention of eye disorders like glaucoma to the latest in contact lens wear – all designed to protect the health of your eyes. For a free subscription, write to:
LOOKING AHEAD NEWSLETTER
SUITE 1200, 100 CRESCENT CENTRE PARKWAY
TUCKER, GA 30084-9862

Free Lung Disease Guide

If you or someone you know has a lung disease, one essential guide you will want to get is a free copy of the *Lung Disease Resource Guide*. In it is a wealth of helpful information, resources and contacts including video tapes, books, organizations and toll-free health lines...even a glossary of terms. To get your free copy, call:
1-800-356-2982

News On Nails

Healthy nails are gorgeous nails. But if you've noticed that your nails are discolored or getting thick or brittle, you may have what millions of people have – fungus-ridden nails. Fortunately there is something you can do. The first step should be to get the free brochure and video called *Barefoot Without Embarrassment: Uncovering The Inside Story On Nail Fungus*. Write to:
NOVARTIS PHARMACEUTICALS
PO BOX 29201
SHAWNEE MISSION, KS 66201-9669

Free Medical Care & Health Information

Free Help With Skin Problems

If you suffer from red, itchy, scaling skin, you owe it to yourself to get help. Now there's a toll-free number you can call. It's called the *Exorex National Psoriasis and Eczema Helpline.* To help you achieve and sustain long-lasting remission, when you call you'll receive a mail-in rebate & coupon book providing you with savings on Exorex products. Call:
1-888-551-6300

Teen Smoking

Centers for Disease Control's Offices on Smoking and Health will help you tackle questions on how to curb teen smoking. If you have a teenager and would like some specific advice, call:
1-800-CDC-1311
You can also visit their web site at:
www.cdc.gov/tobacco

Stop That Itch

If you're bothered by an itching problem that is linked to hot weather, the makers of Lanacane have prepared a helpful brochure called, *A Guide To Summer Itching* you'll want to get. For your free copy, write to:
LANACANE ITCH INFORMATION CENTER
PO BOX 328-LC
WHITE PLAINS, NY 10602
Or you can visit their web site at:
www.lanacane.com

Free Medical Care & Health Information

Discover the World of Natural Medicine

If you are interested in learning about natural remedies and natural products and their effect on your body send for this *catalog of homeopathic remedies*. Enzymatic Therapy and Leaning offer you some of their natural methods of feeling better. They will even send you a $3.00 coupon to try Herpilyn, a cold sore remedy. To get answers to your questions, you can call their consumer information line.
1-800-783-2286

Tension & Depression

The National Mental Health Association has lots of information on how to handle tension and depression. If you have any questions, they have a toll-free number and will send you helpful information. Write or call them:
THE NATIONAL MENTAL HEALTH ASSOCIATION,
ALEXANDRIA, VA
1-800-969-6642

The Men's Maintenance Manual

Did you know that women go to the doctor almost three times as often as men? Did you also know that women on average live 7 years longer than men? A recent survey showed that a huge percentage of men have not been to the doctor in years. That means that many diseases that could be prevented if caught early enough will go undetected in men until it's too late. To educate people about preventable disease, the National Men's Health Foundation has a

Free Medical Care & Health Information

free copy of *Men's Maintenance Manual,* a guide with advice on diet, stress and health risks plus a list of resources. To get your free copy, call:
1-800-955-2002
Or visit their web site at:
www.menshealth.com

Keeping Your Heart Healthy

The American Heart Association would like to help you take care of your heart. When you call their toll-free helpline, your call will be routed to your local AHA office for information on heart disease, strokes, high blood pressure and diet. Some offices can tell you about local support groups or low-cost or free screenings for blood pressure and cholesterol.

You can also get free copies of a variety of booklets dealing with your heart. Topics include blood pressure, CPR, cholesterol, diet, exercise, heart disease and strokes to mention just a few. Learn the best ways to eat smart and healthy by reducing fat in your diet. You'll also learn how to read the new food labels to help you shop for healthier foods. Ask for *How to Read the New Food Label,* and *Save Food Dollars and Help Your Heart* and other heart-related topics you may be interested in. Write to:
THE AMERICAN HEART ASSOCIATION
NATIONAL CENTER
7272 GREENVILLE AVE.

DALLAS, TX 75231
1-800-AHA-USA-1 (that's 1-800-242-8721)
or visit their web site at:
www.americanheart.com

Sleep Hotline

If you suffer from chronic sleeplessness, the sleep experts at Searle would like to help. They have set up a shuteye hotline you can call. When you call ask them for their full package of information on overcoming sleeplessness. Call them toll-free at:
1-800-SHUTEYE

Free Help With Bladder Problems

Did you know that nearly half a milliom people suffer from interstitial cystitis an often misdiagnosed chronic bladder disorder. The National Institutes of Health has published a free booklet that gives basic information in layman's terms on the disease. Ask for *Interstitial Cystitis* by writing to:
IC BOOKLET
NATIONAL KIDNEY AND UROLOGIC DISEASES INFORMATION CLEARINGHOUSE
3 INFORMATION WAY
BETHESDA, MD. 20892-3580

Joint Replacement

If you or anyone you know ever needs joint replacement you will want to read this valuable information. You will learn Why and when it is necessary... how it is performed.. benefits...risks. Ask for *Total Joint Replacement*. Send a SASE to:

AMERICAN ACADEMY OF ORTHOPEDIC SURGEONS
BOX 2058
DES PLAINES, IL 60016

The Facts About Prostate Cancer

Early Detection of Prostate Cancer answers the most often -asked questions about prostate cancer. Although the disease is of prime concern to men over 55, it explains that the disease can often exist without symptoms and that men over 40 should tested annually. The National Cancer Institute also includes a list of problems that might indicate prostate cancer. It also covers the specifics of diagnosis, treatment, and prognosis- which is excellent if the condition is caught early enough. For your free copy or to speak with a specialist call:
1-800-422-6237

Now Hear This

If you are experiencing hearing loss and your doctor has recommended a hearing aid, you may need help in determining what kind of device you need. First, visit the Miracle-Ear web site where you will find helpful information on hearing loss. You'll also find a large number of links to other sites of interest to those with hearing loss including the location of the Miracle-Ear center nearest you.
Visit their web site at:

WWW.MIRACLE-EAR.COM

Free Medical Care & Health Information

Cancer Hotline

The National Cancer Institute's Information Service provides the latest information about cancer, including causes and medical referral to low-cost clinics, medical consultation, referral to patient support groups and publications on request. They can provide you with literature and answer questions concerning various types of cancer and the standard treatment. Send a postcard to:
NCI, CANCER INFORMATION SERVICE
NCI BUILDING 31, ROOM 10A1B
BETHESDA, MD 20205
OR CALL **1-800-4-CANCER**

A Healthier You

Research shows that eating fresh fruits and vegetables help put more fiber in your diet and helps make for a healthier you. Information about the vitamins, minerals and fiber in fruits and vegetables are essential to a healthier you. This booklet from the American Institute for Cancer Research includes healthy recipes. Just send a SASE to:
THE AMERICAN INSTITUTE FOR CANCER RESEARCH
DEPT. AP
WASHINGTON, DC 20069

Free Parent Resource Guide

It's important for children to develop good eating habits when they are young so that they can grow up to be healthier, more active adults. The Ameri-

can Academy of Pediatrics has some important nutrition information just for the asking. Send a business sized SASE to:
NUTRITION BROCHURES DEPT., C
AMERICAN ACADEMY OF PEDIATRICS
PO BOX 927
ELK GROVE, IL 60009

Back Troubles?

The BackSaver catalog has a wonderful assortment of all types of products for your back, including chairs, seat and back support cushions, sleeping supports, reading tables and more. It's free from:
BACKSAVER PRODUCTS CO.
53 JEFFREY AVE.
HOLLISTON, MA 01746

Allergies And Asthma

If you have questions about allergies or asthma, now you can find answers. The Asthma and Allergy Foundation has a toll-free phone number and will answer questions you have regarding the symptoms of allergies to different substances, foods and how all these can be related to asthma.
CALL: 1-800-7-ASTHMA

ABC's Of Eyecare

The Better Vision Institute has some worthwhile information on your eyes and how to take the best

care of them. Topics include everything from the proper selection of eyeglass frames, to eye care for children & adults, tips on correct lighting, correct type of sunglasses and more. Send a business-sized SASE to:
BETTER VISION INSTITUTE
PO BOX 77097
WASHINGTON, DC 20013
OR CALL **1-800-424-8422**

Depression Awareness

Today we are very aware of everything around us and yet we sometimes blot out or deny the signs of depression in ourselves and those around us. This very informative information on depression is published by the National Institute of Mental Health. To learn the facts and become more aware about what you can do about depression and anxiety disorders including obsessive-compulsive disorders, call them toll-free at:
OR CALL: **1-800-421-4211**

Healthy Teeth

Teeth: we get one set of permanent healthy adult teeth so it's essential to learn how to keep them strong and cavity free. Dental care is also a very important career opportunity that also allows you to help others take care of their teeth. If you think you may be interested in finding out more about career options, ask for a copy of *Dental Hygiene - A Profession of Opportunities* and also *Facts About*

Free Medical Care & Health Information

Dental Hygiene. Send a SASE to:
AMERICAN DENTAL HYGIENISTS' ASSOCIATION
444 N. MICHIGAN AVE.
CHICAGO, IL 60611
ATTN: NUTRITION DEPT.

Wellness Guide For Older Adults

The purpose of this *Wellness Guide* is to offer you advice on health issues and preventive care. It is designed to provide practical information on matters such as sensory changes, diet, exercise, legal and financial matters as well as common health problems - all designed to help you remain vibrant, active and independent throughout life. Write to:
MARKETING SERVICES
PENNSYLVANIA HOSPITAL
800 SPRUCE STREET
PHILADELPHIA, PA 19107

Hiking Safety

Whether you are walking to lose weight, exploring a tourist attraction, or hiking to enjoy scenic trails, there are a number of guideline your should follow. Send a SASE and ask for *"Hiking Safety"* from:
AMERICAN HIKING SOCIETY
DEPT T, PO BOX 20160
WASHINGTON, DC 20041

Free Medical Care & Health Information

Do You Really Need A Hysterectomy?

The American College of Obstetricians and Gynecologists has published a free pamphlet *Understanding Hysterectomy* which outlines what constitutes a medically necessary hysterectomy and describes what the surgery involves. Request a free copy from:
ACOG
409 12TH ST. SW
WASHINGTON, DC 20024

Massage Therapy

Stress got you down? The *Massage Therapy* booklet will give you detailed information about different methods of massage and benefits of each. It will also answer some of your questions. Write:
AMERICAN MASSAGE THERAPY ASSOCIATION
820 DAVIS ST., SUITE 100
EVANSTON, IL 60201

Nutrition Hotline

Find out how your diet is affecting your health. Call the American Institute for Cancer Research, Nutrition Hotline and ask a registered dietician your personal questions on diet, nutrition and cancer. When you call you can leave your question with an operator and a dietician will call you back within 48 hours with an answer to your question.
CALL BETWEEN 9AM -5PM, EST MONDAY-FRIDAY:
1-800-843-8114

Free Medical Care & Health Information

Asthma Relief

Asthma patients who use inhalers may be masking the physical cause for their symptoms. Doctors have come up with a checklist for asthma patients who rely on those inhalers to open their airways. If you use the inhaler more than three times a week, if you go through more than one canister a month, and if your asthma awakens you at night, you may be suffering from an inflammation of the airways that is the real cause of your symptoms and may need drug treatment to clear it up. To receive a copy of the list, write to:

ASTHMA INFORMATION CENTER
BOX 790
SPRINGHOUSE, PA 19477

Free Child's Health Record

This easy to use health record log is great for parents and kids alike. Keep your child's vital health records in this handy easy-to-read log. With it you will keep track of illnesses, allergies, health exams, immunizations and tests, family history and health insurance, It features the ever popular peanuts gang (Charlie Brown, Snoopy and friends) and is sure to be popular with the little ones. Ask for *Your Child's Health Record*. Send a long SASE to:

MET LIFE INSURANCE (16UV)
BOX HR
ONE MADISON AVE.
NEW YORK, NY 10010

Free Medical Care & Health Information

Free Health Publications

The AICR also has a variety of free publications detailed to help you live a healthier lifestyle. A small contribution gets you a very informative newsletter and you can ask for the following booklets by name: *Get Fit, Trim Down* - lose weight sensibly. *Alcohol and Cancer Risk: Make the Choice For Health.* - find out how alcohol affects your cancer risk. *Diet & Cancer* - are you eating enough fiber, something that's been linked to lower cancer risk? *Reducing Your Risk of Colon Cancer* - learn steps you can take that may reduce your risk of one of the most common cancers in the United States. Also ask for *Everything Doesn't Cause Cancer* which will calm many of the concerns you may have about what causes cancer. You can ask for one of these or all. Write to:
AMERICAN INSTITUTE FOR CANCER RESEARCH
WASHINGTON, DC 20069

Home Health

This Home Health catalog is the official supplier of Edgar Cayce products for health, beauty and wellness. You'll find over 50 products to help you feel and look your best. There is everything from juices, vitamins, even minerals and salts from the Dead Sea. Write to:
HOME HEALTH
949 SEAHAWK CIRCLE
VIRGINIA BEACH, VA 23452

Free Medical Care & Health Information

Iron - Essential Mineral

In order to understand the effect that iron and iron deficiency on health development of your baby, this free brochure on iron from Carnation, makers of Good Start Infant Formula, and Follow-Up Formula can answer those questions. Ask for *Iron Brochure*. You'll also learn that although iron is essential for your baby, it is just as essential to a mature adult. Send a SASE to:

CARNATION NUTRITIONAL PRODUCTS
IRON BROCHURE OFFER
PO BOX 65785
SALT LAKE CITY, UT 84165

Family Health Record

Every member of the family should keep a medical record. The family's medical record will be useful to you in filling out insurance forms, as well as school and travel records. It can also be vital in helping a physician diagnose a medical problem a family member might have. If you would like they will also send you information on prenatal & natal care, guide to healthy pregnancy and information on how your baby grows. They also have informative brochures for teens about drugs and sexually transmitted disease. Write to:

MARCH OF DIMES
1275 MAMARONECK AVE.
WHITE PLAINS, NY 10605

Free Medical Care & Health Information

Help For Visually Handicapped

A great series of publications are free to those with Impaired vision. Printed in very large type are instructions for knitting, crocheting, gardening, children's books, etc. Also available are guides for the partially sighted including a dial operator personal directory. There are also 2 free newsletters—*IN FOCUS* for youths and *SEEING CLEARLY* for adults. For a complete listing write:
NATIONAL ASSOCIATION FOR VISUALLY HANDICAPPED
305 E. 24TH ST.
NEW YORK, NY 10010
(IN CALIF—3201 BALBOA ST., SAN FRANCISCO, CA 94121)

Johnson & Johnson Hotline

Who can a consumer turn to for answers to their questions concerning hygiene, personal care and baby care? To help you with these questions Johnson & Johnson has set up a toll-free consumer information hotline you can call. Call them with your questions Monday thru Friday between the hours of from 8:00am to 6:00pm EST.
THEIR TOLL-FREE HOTLINE IS:
1-800-526-3967

Hearing Loss

Straight Talk About Hearing Loss, is a fact-filled book about hearing loss and hearing aids. If you're concerned about hearing loss, get the facts about Miracle-Ear. For your free book, call:
1-800-582-2911

Help For The Deaf

Every year over 200,000 children are born deaf or suffer hearing loss in their first years of life. *Speech and Hearing Checklist* tells parents how to detect possible deafness in their children. Another nice booklet, *Listen! Hear!* is for parents of children who may be deaf or hard of hearing. Both are free from:
ALEXANDER GRAHAM BELL ASSOCIATION FOR THE DEAF
3417 VOLTA PL. N.W.
WASHINGTON, DC 20007

Stay Healthy and Save Money Too

While vitamins and supplements can help you maintain the nutrients your body needs to stay healthy, they can also be expensive too. Now you can check out the prices of the vitamins and other health-related products you need at the WebRx web site. You'll find that you cn often save as much as 50%. Visit them at:
WWW.VITAMINS.COM

Medicare Hotline

If you have questions or problems regarding Medicare, now there's a toll-free number you can call for help. When you call you can get additional information regarding a Medicare claim you may have, general information about Medicare and the services it provides. They can also help you with information regarding insurance supplements to Medi-

care, mammograms and lots more. Call:
1-800-638-6833

Heart Diet

If you would like a copy of the American Heart Association recommendations including lists of good and bad foods, and practical suggestions for cutting out the bad stuff. Ask for *Exercise Your Heart; An Eating Plan For Healthy Americans; Cholesterol & Your Heart* and *Recipes For Low-Fat, Low Cholesterol Meals*. Send a SASE to:
AMERICAN HEART ASSOCIATION, NATIONAL CENTER
PO BOX UCB
7320 GREENVILLE AVE.
DALLAS, TX 78531

Help With Bedwetting

Bedwetting— What It's All About and How To End It is a report written by two medical doctors that will help you end this serious problem before it causes complicated psychological problems. Write to:
CASE DIRECTION CENTER
555 BIRCH ST.
NEKOOSA, WI 54457

Free Medical Supply Catalog

You can order your medical supplies from your home

by phone and save up to 60%. Send for this free catalog from America's leading mail order medical supply catalog. Drop a postcard to:
BRUCE MEDICAL SUPPLY
DEPARTMENT 712
411 WAVERLY OAKS RD.
WALTHAM. MA 02154

Free Family Planning Assistance

For years Planned Parenthood has provided important information dealing with making intelligent family planning decisions. Ask for *Planned Parenthood Guide, Your Contraceptive Choices* and *Sex & Disease - What You Need To Know."* Send a card to:
PLANNED PARENTHOOD
810 7TH AVE.
NEW YORK. NY 10019

Infant Care Hotline

Being a new parent can be quite unsettling. Now there is someone you can call for help. Beech Nut Baby Foods has set up a toll-free hotline you can call. You will receive expert advice on infant care from a pediatrician, child psychologist, dentist or nutritionist. If you are about to have a child or have recently had one be sure to ask for the *"new parent packet"* and also for information about their label-saving program where you can exchange product UPC labels for discount coupons. Call between the hours of 9am and 8pm E.S.T. weekdays:
1-800-523-6633

Free Medical Care & Health Information

Sexually Transmitted Diseases Hotline

If you suspect you may have contracted a sexually transmitted disease, there's a toll free hotline you can call for help and for information. Their specialists will answer your questions concerning STDs and tell you the symptoms that are the warning signs of disease and how to get help. You'll be referred to free or low-cost public health clinics or doctors in your area. They will also send you free brochures concerning STDs. Call Monday thru Friday between 8AM and 8PM. at:
1-800-227-8922

Skin Protection

Prevention is always far better than a cure. For a free booklet *Skin Cancer: If You Can Spot It You Can Stop It,* send a long SASE to:
THE SKIN CANCER FOUNDATION
BOX 561
NEW YORK, NY 10156

HIV & AIDS Hotline

If you have or suspect you may have contracted HIV, there's a toll-free number you can call in confidence for help and for information concerning HIV and AIDS. Call toll-free:
1-800-342-2437

Free Medical Care & Health Information

Free Help For Alcoholics & Their Families

Alcoholism is a disease and can be cured. AA wants to help anyone who has (or suspects they have) a drinking problem. Find out what AA is and how it can help - ask for their *information package*. All literature comes in an unmarked envelope. Write to:
A A
BOX 459
GRAND CENTRAL STATION
NEW YORK, NY 10163

And if you're in a disfunctional relationship with an alchoic or know a teen whose parent is an alcoholic, be sure to contact:
AL-ANON FAMILY GROUP HEADQUARTERS
1600 CORPORATE LANDING PARKWAY
VIRGINIA BEACH, VA 23454-5617
Website: www.al-anon-alateen.org

Treating Strokes

For up-to-date information on strokes and effective treatment and therapy for those who fall victim to a stroke, ask for your free copy of *Guide To Strokes,* write:
STROKE
NINCDS-W
9000 ROCKVILLE PIKE, BLDG 31, RM 8A16
BETHESDA, MD 20892

Get In Shape !

As part of a program initiated by the President's

Free Medical Care & Health Information

Council on Physical Fitness and Sports, The Hershey Company has a number of helpful and informative resources that are yours free for the asking. They are geared to young people ages 6-17. There's even a motivational message from Arnold Schwarzenegger. Learn how to get in shape to meet the presidents challenge. A few of the free items include:

Hershey's Field of Fun - helpful tips for running a field day at school, camp or any other group program.
Official Rule Book of Hershey's Track & Field
New Softball Rules
National Track & Field Youth Program - information about this great program including rules and regulations.
The Story Behind The Chocolate Bar - The Story of Milton S. Hershey
Send a long SASE to:
HERSHEY'S YOUTH PROGRAM
HERSHEYS CHOCOLATE
19 EAST CHOCOLATE AVE.
PO BOX 814
HERSHEY, PA 17033

Free Contact Lenses

If you wear contact lenses or are thinking of getting them, Johnson & Johnson would like you to try their Acuvue contacts. They have made arrangements with local optometrist throughout the country to supply you with a your first pair. Just ask an optometrist in your area who carries Acuvue contacts for a free pair.

Health Hotlines

To help answer various health questions you may have there are a number of toll-free hotlines you can call:

CALCIUM INFORMATION CENTER:
1-800-321-2681
MILK CONSUMER HOTLINE:
1-800-WHY-MILK
NATIONAL CENTER FOR NUTRITION & DIURETICS
1-800-366-1655
NATIONAL OSTEOPEROSIS FOUNDATION
1-800-223-9994
FOOD ALLERGY NETWORK
1-800-929-4040
CONSUMER NUTRITION HOTLINE
1-800-366-1655

THE BLOCH NATIONAL CANCER HOTLINE
They will put you in touch with someone who has had the same type of cancer and will help you deal with the initial fear. Call:
1-800-433-0464

National Cancer Institute

To help you keep informed about the most up-to-

date information about cancer, the National Cancer Institute has a toll-free number you can call. When you call you can ask for free publications, or ask for help locating FDA-approved mammography facilities or talk with cancer specialists.
1-800-422-6237

Cancer Care

Cancer Care provides a wide range of programs for cancer patients and their families. They will also provide pamphlets and *A Helping Hand: The Resource Guide for People with Cancer.* Call:
1-800-813-HOPE

Breast Cancer

Women need to be fully aware of the signs of breast cancer. The Susan G. Komen Breast Cancer Foundation can help anyone who needs referrals to certified mammography centers, clinical trials and other programs about breast cancer. They will even supply you with free shower cards on breast self-exam to hand out at a baby or wedding shower. What a way to show you care about every one of your guests. They can even supply you with large print pamphlets and cards *Taking Charge: Breast Health for Older Women*. If you have any questions or want specific information, call them at:
1-800-IMAWARE

Free Medical Care & Health Information

American Cancer Society

They offer referrals to cancer centers across the country, plus free informative booklets on cancer risk reduction and early detection and treatment. Call them toll-free at:
1-800-ACS-2345

National Alliance of Breast Cancer Organizations

This is a helpful organization if you need referrals to physicians, support groups, speakers and minority health advocates. They also help groups plan breast cancer awareness events. Call:
1-888-80-NABCO
Web site: www.nabco.org

Beating The Silent Killer

Ovarian cancer is a silent killer and very often a woman doesn't have a warning sign that she has symptoms until it's too late. That's why it is important to have a check up and learn to identify those warning signs. Send for your free copy of *It Whispers... So Listen, What Every Woman Should Know About Ovarian Cancer*, send a self addressed stamped envelope to:
NATIONAL OVARIAN CANCER COALITION
2335 EAST ATLANTIC BLVD., SUITE 401
POMPANO BEACH, FL 33062

Free Medical Care & Health Information

Stopping Skin Cancer Before It Starts

Skin cancer can lead to disfigurement or even death once it has spread to other parts of the body. But if treated early, it is almost always curable. Self examination of your skin every three months is the best way to detect any abnormalities. To help you look for unusual marks, growths or changes on your skin, the Skin Cancer Foundation will send you a free brochure that includes a body map and warning signs of all major skin cancers. Send a long self addressed stamped envelope to:

THE SKIN CANCER FOUNDATION
BOX 561 DEPT. SE
NEW YORK, NY 10156

Protecting Your Skin

Remember that being out in the sun is a healthy thing to do, as long as you protect your skin from the damaging rays of the sun.

The American Academy of Dermatology has some valuable tips for you next to you venture out. Ask for *Protect Your Skin From the Sun*. Call toll-free:
1-888-462-3376 OR WRITE:
AMERICAN ACADEMY OF
DERMATOLOGY
930 N. MEACHAM RD.,
SCHAUMBURG, ILL, 60173
Web site: www.aad.org

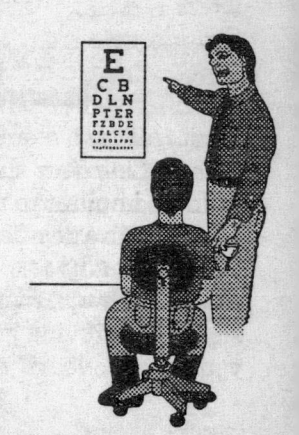

Free Medical Care & Health Information

Cancer Clinical Trials Info

The American Society of Clinical Oncology has extensive information about cancer on its web site that covers everything from local resources to clinical trials. For more information, log onto:
www.asco.org

Protect Yourself From Drug Interactions

Some times when someone is taking more than one prescription drug, the particular combination of drugs may produce an adverse reaction. If you suspect a you may have problem coming from drug interaction, let your doctor know. You can report adverse interactions to the Food and Drug Administrations MedWatch by calling:
1-888-463-6332
For a reporting forum or to download information online go to:
www.fda.gov/medwatch.

Clearing Up Cataracts

A cataract is a clouding of the eye's natural lens. In cataract surgery the lens is removed and replaced with an implant to restore vision. For the most part, implants are designed to give good vision at one distance, usually far, so you would need glasses for reading. Now, Array Multifocal lens implant is designed to provide good distance and near vision. If you want to learn more about this procedure, visit

their web site at:
www.arraylens.com

Pesticides and Food Safety

Did you ever wonder what makes that delicious red apple so shiny and slick? Well if it looks as if it's been sealed with a shiny coat of wax, maybe it has been. Fruits and vegetables in some instances (unless they are organically grown) go through processes where they are coated to protect them against insects and other pests until they are harvested and shipped to market. If you want to learn more about pesticides and food safety write and ask for this very informative guide: *A Consumer's Guide to Pesticides and Food Safety*. Send a SASE to:

INTERNATIONAL FOOD INFORMATION COUNCIL FOUNDATION
100 CONNECTICUT AVE., NW, SUITE 430
WASHINGTON, DC 20036

High Blood Pressure

Learn about high blood pressure and its effects on the body. The National Kidney Foundation has a free book just for the asking. Ask for *High Blood Pressure and Your Kidneys*. Write to:

NATIONAL KIDNEY FOUNDATION
30 E. 33RD ST.
NEW YORK, NY 10016

Snack Time

Do you like to snack but are worried about what

those sweets do to your teeth? If so you'll want to send for this free copy of *Snack Smart for Healthy Teeth*. Learn more about tasty snacks that won't harm your teeth. Ask for *Snack Smart for Healthy Teeth*. Write to:

NATIONAL INSTITUTE OF DENTAL AND CRANIOFACIAL RESEARCH
31 CENTER DR. MSC 2290
BETHESDA, MD 20892-2290

Free For Allergy Sufferers

Over 40 millions people suffer from annoying seasonal nasal allergies with symptoms that include sneezing, running nose and congestion. If that describes you, you might want to ask your doctor about Nasonex spray. If he prescribes it, you can get a free one month trial offer directly from the manufacturer. This is a limited time offer so write today to:

NASONEX TRIAL OFFER
SCHERING LABORATORIES
KENILWORTH, NJ 07033

Life Without Allergies

If you are bothered by allergies you know how that fact can dominate your life. The American College of Allergy, Asthma and Immunology has a free brochure for you called, *You Can Have A Life Without Allergies*. To get your copy simply call:

1-800-842-7777

Or visit their web site at:
http://allergy.mcg.edu

Free Medical Care & Health Information

Answers To Your Surgery Questions

If you are considering having any type of non-emergency surgery, be sure to get your free copy of *Questions to Ask Your Doctor Before Surgery*. It will help you be informed about the options and risks involved. Call toll-free:
1-800-358-9295

How Good Is Your Doctor?

Want to check your doctor's track record? It's important to find out if the specialist or doctor you search out is board-certified in his specialty. Here are several web sites that will help you with this search. On the Internet, to find if the doctor is actually certified in his specialty, search:
www.certified-doctor.com
Also to get biographies and malpractice information, check with DocFinder at:
www.docboard.org
There is also a huge resource called 16,638 *Questionable Doctors* put out by the Public Citizens Health Research Group. It lists doctors who have lost their licenses, or who have been fined or suspended. Check this out on the Web at:
www.citizen.org

Allergy Relief

Do you suffer from seasonal or year round nasal allergies? Then you'll want to learn more about na-

sal allergies and how you can get relief. The makers of Flonase want you to know the facts by sending your their brochure, *Feel-Better Facts About Nasal Allergies*. Along with this important information you will receive a $5.00-off coupon your first prescription. They will also send you a free allergy newsletter, *Allergy Talk,* to keep you more informed. If you suffer from nasal allergies don't wait, call:
1-800-FLONASE
Or visit their website at:
www.glaxowellcome.com

Free Prescription Drug Programs

It's a well known fact that prescription drugs can cost a fortune. In many cases the costs may be a lot more than you can afford.

Most people don't know it but the pharmaceutical industry has had a long tradition of providing prescription medicines free of charge to people who might not otherwise be able to afford to have the important medications they need. You (or your doctor will need to check with the individual pharmaceutical manufacturer for the specific requirements to qualify for their free prescription drug program (generally referred to as Indigent Patient Drug Programs.)

COMMON QUESTIONS

Q. I need medication but can not afford to pay for it. Why hasn't my doctor told me about these programs?

A. Believe it or not even many doctors themselves don't know about these programs until you mention it to them.

Q. What are the steps I should take if I need a medication and can't afford it?

A. First, find out from your doctor the name of the drug you need and the manufacturer. Next, ask your physician to contact the company and request any forms needed to enroll you in their program. As a general rule, the application for free medication must be filled out and returned by your doctor.

Q. Who determines whether a medication is covered?

A. The individual pharmaceutical company determines which drugs are covered.

Q. Who's eligible for the program and how do you apply?

A. Once again each company makes the determination as to who is eligible for its program. Often they will rely on the doctor's opinion as to whether he/she feels you are needy enough to qualify for free medication.

Since virtually every pharmaceutical company has an Indigent Patient Drug program, it's very likely that with the help of your physician you will find that the medicine you need but can't afford is covered by a free-drug program.

Free Prescription Drugs Programs For Seniors

If you're a senior living on a fixed income in one of the following eleven states and you do not have Medicare or private insurance, you could be getting all of your prescription drugs free or for as little as a dollar or two. All you do is make a phone call to your state's office at the numbers listed. If you live in a state not listed here there still may be a program that can assist you. Check the white pages of your phone book for your state's Office Of The Aging for assistance.

CONNECTICUT: **800-423-5026**
DELAWARE
  WILMINGTON COUNTY: **800-292-9538**
  KENT OR SUFFEX COUNTIES: **800-763-9326**
ILLINOIS: **800-624-2459**
MAINE: **207-626-8475**
MARYLAND: **800-492-1974**
MICHIGAN: **517-373-8230**
NEW JERSEY: **800-792-9745**
NEW YORK: **800-332-3742**
PENNSYLVANIA: **800-225-7223**
RHODE ISLAND: **800-322-2880**
VERMONT: **800-250-8427**

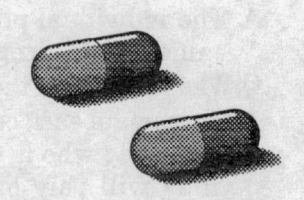

Free Medical Care

How would you like to have the finest medical care money can buy...and not spend a cent for it? That's exactly what thousands of people are doing every year thanks to the National Institutes of Health Clinical Center. The NIH is funded by the federal government and is one of the nation's leading medical research centers.

At any one time they have as many as 900 programs under way in dozens of hospitals throughout the country studying the newest procedures in the treatment of every imaginable disease including all types of cancer, heart disease, and Alzheimer's to mention just a few.

And if your condition is one that is being studied you may qualify for free medical care at their 540 bed hospital in Bethesda, Maryland. To find out about their ongoing research projects and clinical trials and whether you qualify for treatment, call their toll-free hotline:
1-800-411-1222
NATIONAL INSTITUTES OF HEALTH CLINICAL CENTER
BETHESDA, MD 20292

Free Hospital Care

If you don't have insurance coverage, even a very brief hospital stay can easily cost you tens of thousands of dollars and put you on the edge of bankruptcy. Fortunately now there is something you can do. If you need hospital care but can not afford it and have no insurance or if you already been in the hospital and can't afford to pay the bill, try calling the *Hill-Burton Hotline*. With this program over 1,000 participating hospitals and other health facilities provide free or low-cost medical care to patients who can't afford to pay.

You can qualify for this program even if your income is double the poverty income guidelines and even if the bill has already been turned over to a collection agency. For more information, call the Hill-Burton Hotline at:
1-800-492-0359

Free Health & Beauty Aids

For many large companies the best way to promote their products is directly to the consumer. And what better way of doing it, than by giving you a free sample. You'll like it, pass it on to your friends and family and the company will have more loyal customers. Everyone comes out ahead!

Some of the free samples listed below may have limited availability, so call now!

Free Earrings

Do your ears sting, turn black or just kill you when you put on your favorite gold earrings? Here's the answer to those sensitive ear woes. Once again you'll be able to wear those fashionable earrings you always dreaded to put on because you were allergic. Simply Whispers will not only send you a catalog of their quality earrings made of top-quality surgical steel with the look of silver or 24-karat electroplated for gold lovers, but a free pair to try as well. Best of all they are guaranteed for life. You have a choice of pierced or clip. Write to them at:

SIMPLY WHISPERS
430 COURT ST.
PLYMOUTH, MA 02360
OR CALL THEM TOLL-FREE AT: **1-800-445-9088**

Free Health & Beauty Aids

10 Steps To Healthy White Teeth

The makers of Rembrandt toothpaste want you to be aware of how you can keep your teeth healthy and white and to show you how to do that they want you to have, *Top Ten Oral Care Problems Have One Solution- Rembrandt*. They also have valuable information they will send you on aging teeth. Along with your free sample of Rembrandt whitening toothpaste they will also send you $1.00 off coupons for all of their products. To get your free sample and money-off coupons call toll-free:
1-800-548-3663

Plus, if you have canker sores in your mouth, call this toll-free hotline for information on a toothpaste specifically designed to relieve your problem.
1-800-433-6628

If You Suffer From Migraine Pain

For anyone who suffers from the excruciating pain of a migraine headache, *Chart Your Route To Relief,* is a personal migraine management program that actually helps you find relief. It includes a comprehensive chart that will help you and your doctor pinpoint the cause. To get your free chart simply request it by name when you write to:
CHART YOUR ROUTE
BOX 816
MEDFORD, NY 11763

Free Health & Beauty Aids

Taking Care Of Your Skin

Alpha Hydroxy will be happy to send you information about all their skin products and how they will work for you. They also have a consumer hotline updated monthly that tells about their products and where they are available. If you are interested in finding out about their facial, body care and foot care products, call toll-free:
1-800-55-ALPHA

Ask The Hair Coloring Experts

Are you thinking of changing your hair color? Having trouble finding the right shade? Can't cover that problem gray? The experts at Clairol have a toll-free hotline you can call for answers to all your hair coloring questions. Their color consultants will also provide you with helpful tips that will help you look your very best. Call them Monday-Friday 8:30am-8:30pm or Saturday 9am-6pm EST at:
1-800-223-5800
You can also visit the Clairol Women's Link site on the Internet at: **www.womenslink.com**

Migraine Relief

If you suffer from migrane headaches, you will want to get the *Excedrin Migraine Tablets and Relief Guide.* When you request it, you'll also receive a free sample of their new migraine tablets plus helpful information on dealing with migraine headaches.

Free Health & Beauty Aids

Call them toll-free:
1-800-580-4455
Or visit their web site at: **www.excedrin.com**

Milk Sensitive?—Now You Can Enjoy A Milk Shake

Do you have trouble digesting milk and milk products? Now for the first time you can enjoy a big glass of milk or even a delicious ice cream sundae with the help of Lactaid Ultra tablets. To have your questions answered and to receive a free sample plus a coupon to save money on your next purchase, call:
1-800-LACTAID (that's 1-800-522-8243).

Pantyhose Problems?

The National Association of Hosiery Manufacturers would like to help you overcome your fear of stocking runs, snags and droops. They will provide you with valuable information and helpful tips on how to determine your correct size, stocking care and how to make your hosiery last. When you call them you can also ask them any specific questions you may have about stockings. Call:
1-800-346-7379

Leg Talk

Has this ever happened to you…you're down to your last pair of stockings and late for an important meeting when, for no apparent reason, the stockings

Free Health & Beauty Aids

'run'? Would you like to find out why this happens and what you can do about it? Write for your free copy of *Sheer Facts About Hosiery* to:
NATIONAL HOSIERY ASSOCIATION
200 N. SHARON AMITY BLVD.
CHARLOTTE, NC 28211

Keep It Clean

The makers of Oil of Olay would like you to see just how clean and beautiful your skin can be. When you visit their web site, you'll find a wealth of information including cosmetic tips and tips on body and face care. You can also sign up to receive free product samples. Visit them at:
www.oilorolay.com

Healthy Diet-Healthy Looks

We've all heard the expression, 'you are what you eat.' Well it's true, the basics of looking good and feeling good, start with healthy eating habits. The American Dietetic Association is making a concerted effort to get us back on a healthy eating track. They have a toll-free phone line you can call weekdays for more information on healthy eating and for a referral to a local dietician. Call the Consumer Nutrition Hotline at:
1-800-366-1655

Hair Care Guidance & More

If you would like advice on how to manage your hair,

Free Health & Beauty Aids

how to color it or just how to keep it looking good, L'Oreal has the answers for you. Next time you can't decide which shampoo or conditioner is best for your hair type, visit their web site at:
www.loreal.com
Or you can write to them at:
**L'OREAL CONSUMER AFFAIRS
PO BOX 98
WESTFIELD, NJ 07091**

Free For Pet Lovers

Being Kind To Animals

If you care deeply for animals, The American Society For The Prevention of Cruelty to Animals...the ASPCA has an information packet including booklets about caring for or traveling with your pets. To get a full list of their helpful information, write to:
AMERICAN SOCIETY OF PREVENTION OF CRUELTY TO
ANIMALS
PUBLIC INFORMATION DEPT.
424 E. 92ND ST.
NEW YORK, NY 10128
Or visit them on the Internet at: **www.aspca.org**

You And Your New Puppy or New Kitten

Are you thinking of getting a new puppy or kitten? If so, this freebie from Iams Company is for you. *You & Your New Puppy* and *You & Your New Kitten* will give you useful advice on feeding, house-training, health care, grooming, training of a new pet and lots more. Write to:
THE IAMS COMPANY
PUPPY/KITTEN INFORMATION CENTER
BOX 1475, DAYTON, OHIO 45401

Free For Pet Lovers

How Would You Like A Free Pet?

If you have ever stopped by a pet shop in the mall to play with the delightful puppy they had sitting in the window, you learned that to take that puppy home would make a deep dent in your wallet. There's no reason to spend hundreds of dollars when your local newspaper and supermarket bulletin boards may have ads giving away free kittens and pups when their pets have litters. Also, don't forget that animal shelters also have delightful free pets dying for a home. Usually they'll only ask you to pay for the shots. Call your local animal shelter for more information.

Taking Special Care Of Your Cat

Special Care for Special Cats is a cat chow that helps maintain the urinary tract health for your cat. It's made with real chicken for a great taste. For information call toll-free:
1-800-CAT CARE

Caring For A Dog With Arthritis

Does your dog have difficulty getting up after a nap or a hard time climbing? Most people just assume that it's old age and that nothing can be done about it. The problem may very well be osteoarthritis which afflicts 1 dog in 5. Pfizer Dog Care has a toll-free number you can call for information on what you can do for your dog if it suffers from this problem. Call them toll-free:
1-800-720-DOGS

Free Animal Calendar And Datebook

For pet lovers everywhere, The Animal Protection Institute has a handy informative *Animals Calendar and Datebook*. In addition to being a datebook and calendar it is full of hundreds of fascinating facts about animals plus a listing of important animal events. If you love animals, this is definitely for you. Write to:

ANIMAL PROTECTION INSTITUTE
2831 FRUITAGE ROAD
SACRAMENTO, CA 95820.
OR CALL TOLL-FREE: **1-800-348-PETS**
Internet: **www.onlineapi@aol.com**

Breath Friend For Your Pet

Did you know that regular dental care may actually prolong a pet's life? Breath Friend is a pet oral cleanser that cleans teeth and eliminates bad breath without brushing. You will receive absolutely free a *Breath Friend* sample and information about the importance of oral health in pets. You'll even get a $1.00 rebate on your first purchase. Send a long SASE to:

AMERICAN MEDIA GROUP
7300 W. 110TH ST., SUITE 960
OVERLAND PARK, KS 66210
Or visit their website: **www.breathfriend.com**

Free Vet Care For Your Pet

Remember if you live near a university that has a Veterinary school, you may be able to get free vet care for your pet especially if you are a senior citizen. Call them and ask about the services they offer.

Also, if you need help with an ailing pet, contact:
CENTER FOR VETERINARY MEDICINE
U.S. FOOD AND DRUG ADMINISTRATION
7500 STANDISH PLACE
ROCKVILLE, MD 20855
301-443-1544

Caring For Your Pet

If you have a dog or are planning to get one, make sure you write for *free pet information* from the folks at Ralston Purina dog food products. They have an excellent freebie that will not only give you a brief history of dogs, but also give you tips on feeding your dog, grooming, obedience training, keeping your dog healthy and traveling with your dog. They may also include discount coupons and a Purina dog food guide to balancing nutrients to meet your dog's needs. Also ask for *Guide To Caring For Your Dog* and *Help...My Pet Refuses To Eat*. These freebies

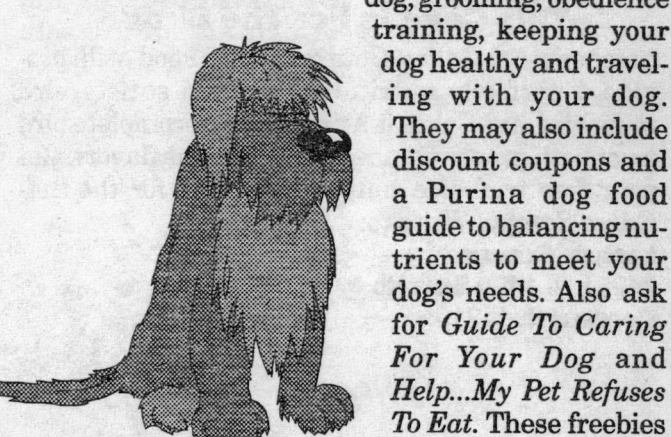

are a must if you've ever thought of getting a dog for a pet. Write to:
RALSTON PURINA
DOG FOOD DIVISION
CHECKERBOARD SQUARE
ST. LOUIS, MO 63164

Raising A Healthy Pet

If you have a cat or dog, Gaines Foods has a number of useful and informative publications that will show you how to care for and raise a healthy pet. They are yours just for the asking. Just ask for the free publications list from:
QUAKER PROFESSIONAL SERVICES
585 HAWTHORNE COURT #14
GALESBURG, IL 61401

This Cake Is For The Birds

Lafeber's Avi-Cakes Gourmet Bird Food will provide a perfectly nutritious snack to satisfy bird munchies. Avi-Cakes is a nutritionally complete bird treat with proper vitamins and delicious flavors. Get your free trial size sample now. Ask for the *Avi-Cakes Sample* Write to:
LAFEBER COMPANY
24981 N. 1400 EAST RD
CORNELL, IL 61319

Free For Pet Lovers

Fish Are Fun

Fish are educational, fun and something the whole family can enjoy. Now you can learn step-by-step how to set up a year round backyard pond and stock it with hardy fish. Send for your free *We Are The Water Garden Experts*. Drop a postcard to:
TETRA POND
3001 COMMERCE ST.
BLACKSBURG, VA 24060-6671

Better Pet Care And Nutrition

If you'd like any information about proper pet care and pet nutrition, the makers of Kal Kan pet food would like to help you. They will send you *Understanding Your Dog* and *Understanding Your Cat*. Write to:
KAL KAN CONSUMER ADVISORY SERVICE
3386 EAST 44TH ST.
P.O. BOX 58853
VERNON, CA 90058

Caring For Your Pets

The American Humane Association has a whole series of informative booklets available for pet owners. These booklets tell how to care for dogs, cats, horses, birds and fish. For a complete listing, write for their free *catalog of publications*. From:
AMERICAN HUMANE ASSOCIATION
P.O. BOX 1266
DENVER, CO 80201

Free For Pet Lovers

More Than A Friend

To millions of people their pet is a real member of the family. And love of animals has inspired many to follow a career path to becoming a veterinarian. For these people, the American Veterinary Association has an interesting booklet called *Today's Veterinarian* about the opportunities available today in this interesting field. For your free copy, send a postcard to:

AMERICAN VETERINARY ASSOCIATION
1931 NORTH MEECHAM RD. SUITE 100
SCHAUMBURG, IL 60196

For Home & Garden

Light Up Your Garden

Like to add a colorful look to your garden? Consider using Holland or domestic bulbs. For a full color catalog write to:
VAN BOURGONDIEN
PO BOX A, 245 FARMINGDALE RD.
ROUTE 109
BABYLON, NY 11702

Burpee Gardens

This catalog is packed with everything you can imagine to start your vegetable, flower or fruit garden. They have seed starter kits and plants. You'll even find garden helpers, bird houses and fun seed kits for kids. Grow your

Free Things For Home & Garden

own herb garden right on your kitchen window sill. When you call or write mention OFFER #82 and in addition to their new *Flowering Bulb and Perennial Catalogue*, you'll also receive a special $5.00-off coupon. Free from:
W. ATLEE BURPEE & CO.
WARMINSTER, PA 18974
OR CALL 1-800-888-1447

Why Your Plants Don't Grow

The question of why some plants fail to grow even when they are carefully tended to, has always been somewhat of a mystery. Now Gurney Seed and Nursery would like to throw some light on the subject so you can have a more beautiful garden. They will also send you the new *Gurney Catalog*. It features over 4000 items—many shown in full color. You'll find how-to-grow-it tips plus planting charts and moisture guides along with many special offers. If you'd like a packet of giant sunflower seeds, include a quarter. Write:
GURNEY SEED & NURSERY CO.
DEPT. 84, 1130 PAGE ST.
YANKTON SD 57079

Grow Your Own Organic Food

How To Grow An Organic Garden will get you started raising your own delicious and naturally pure vegetables. It even includes a plan for a sample garden. Get your free copy and let Mother Nature do her thing. Write to:

Free Things For Home & Garden

ORGANIC GARDENING & FARMING
33 E. MINOR ST.
EMMAUS, PA 18049

Growing Ideas

In the last few years backyard community gardens have been popping up all over the nation. Bring your community together and save money too - start a community garden. You'll also receive teaching tools to help young minds grow. Ask for the free *Growing Ideas package* from:
NATIONAL GARDEN ASSOCIATION
180 FLYNN AVE.
BURLINGTON, VT 05401

Exotic Imported Plants

If you enjoy unusual and out-of-the ordinary type plants this one's for you. The new *Stokes seed catalog* features 1300 varieties including many imported from England, Europe, and Canada. Get your free catalog from:
STOKES SEEDS INC.
BOX 548
BUFFALO, NY 14240

Miller's Nursery Guide

In this new catalog you'll find a new seedless grape, virus-free berries and several pages of tested recipes and a whole lot more. Miller Nurseries has put together a broad selection of their most popular

Free Things For Home & Garden

nursery items. Ask for their new *Catalog & Planting Guide*:
J. E. MILLER NURSERIES
DEPT. 706
WEST LAKE RD.
CANANDAIGUA, NY 14424

Free Lawn Care Help

Here's a super 5-star special for anyone with a lawn or garden. To help improve lawn, flowers, vegetable garden, trees and shrubs - call the experts at Scott Lawn Products on their toll-free phone. They have the answers to any and all questions about lawn growing, disease, fertilizing, problem areas etc. They'll give you a free subscription to *"Lawn Care"* with loads of useful information (plus money saving coupons). They'll be happy to send you any of the dozens of booklets, magazines and brochures that will help you grow the perfect lawn or garden. Excellent. Call toll free:
800-543-TURF OR WRITE:
SCOTT LAWN PRODUCTS
14111 SCOTTS LAWN RD.
MARYVILLE, OH 43041
Or visit their web site at:
www.scotts.com

Free Fertilizer

Free manure is available to gardeners through Extension Services located throughout the country. To find the one nearest you, call your local U.S. De-

Free Things For Home & Garden

partment of Agriculture Extension Service. You'll find their number in your local phone book.

Full-size Fruit From Dwarf-size Trees

If your yard is too small to grow as many fruit trees as you'd like, take a look at this free catalog. These dwarf trees grow only 8 to 10 feet tall but grow full size apples, peaches, pears, cherries, and nectarines. This catalog features almost 400 varieties of fruit, shade and nut trees plus shrubs, vines, ornamentals, and award-winning roses. Send a postcard for the catalog and special offers to:
STARK BROTHER NURSERIES & ORCHARD CO.
BOX A12119
LOUISIANA, MO 63353

Great Gardens

The Burreil Seed Growers have a nice seed catalog every home gardener will want to have. Before you get ready to plant your next garden be sure to get a copy of this catalog. Send a postcard to:
D.V. BURREIL SEED GROWERS
PO BOX 150H
ROCKY FORD, CO 81067

Gardener's Handbook

If you want to learn how to have a beautiful fruitful garden, be sure to get a free copy of *The Park Gardener's Handbook*. In it you will find all kinds

Free Things For Home & Garden

of useful information that will help you to get more productive results from your gardening efforts. You can also choose from over 3000 new and rare varieties of flowers and vegetables as well as the more familiar types—all available in the full color Park catalog you'll receive. Send a postcard to:

GEORGE W. PARK SEED CO. INC.
254 COKEBURY ROAD
GREENWOOD, SC 29647

Potpourri Bonnets

These delightful miniature straw hat bonnet magnets are filled with potpourri and ready for your refrigerator or bath room. They are yours for two first class loose stamps. Send to:

VALERIE'S HATTERY
4494 POLK
DEARBORN, MI 48125

"Tips For Energy Savers"

Saving energy not only makes America less energy dependent on other nations - it will save you a tidy sum of money too. The Department of Energy would like you to have a useful energy-saving package. Ask for the *"Energy Saver Booklets."* It's yours free from:

D.O.E. TECHNICAL INFORMATION CENTER
BOX 62
OAK RIDGE, TN 37830

Free Things For Home & Garden

Home Security Tips

There are many ways to protect your property from burglars. If you don't have a security system in your home, there are still things you can do. The Newent Co., will send you an authentic appearing sample alarm warning sticker along with all kinds of "Home Security Tips." Don't wait, protect yourself and your property from criminals today. Ask for: *Warning Sticker & Security Tips.* Send a SASE to:

THE NEWENT COMPANY NEWSLETTER
PO BOX 40
CANTERBURY, CT 06331

Solar Energy & Your Home

One day your home may be heated and powered with free energy from the sun. Here are the answers to many of the most frequently asked questions about putting solar and other kinds of renewable energy to work for you. Write to:

RENEWABLE ENERGY INFORMATION
BOX 8900
SILVER SPRINGS, MD 20907

Also, if you have a computer you can access the Department of Energy and Renewable Resouces, on the Worldwide Web. At their web site you will find a comprehensive resource for DOE's energy efficient and renewable energy information and also access to over 600 links and 80,000 documents. They can be found on the Internet at:
www.eren.doe.gov

Free Things For Home & Garden

What Does Fiberglas Do?

All About Insulation and *Owens-Corning Fiberglas* are two of the useful guides found in the "Fiberglas information series". You'll find out how Fiberglas is made and how it's used for insulation, dust-stops and air filters. Free from:
OWEN CORNING FIBERGLAS
FIBERGLAS TOWER
TOLEDO, OH 43659

Home Remodeling Ideas

Are you getting ready to build or remodel? The *Insider's Look At Building Your Home* and *Insider's Look At Remodeling Your Home* are an absolute must. Your creative juices will begin to flow as you thumb through these beautifully illustrated idea books. The answer books will provide help in solving your remodeling problems whether adding a room or simply changing a window. Write to:
ANDERSEN CORP.
BAYPORT, MN 55003
1-800-426-4261 EXT 2837
Web address: www.andersenwindow.com

Let The Sun Shine In

If you're planning on building or remodeling a house, have you thought about which windows and doors are right for you? *Window Scaping* tells all about the many types of windows and doors available to help you to decide for yourself. It's free from:
ROLSCREEN CO.
PELLA, IA 50219

Free Things For Home & Garden

Beautify & Protect Your Home

Red Devil would like to show you the right way to beautify your home with wall coverings and protect it with caulk. Ask them for the free "wallcovering and caulk booklets." Write to:

RED DEVIL INC.
CONSUMER RELATIONS
PO BOX 3133, UNION, NJ 07083

Get Rid Of That Trash

If you're considering a garbage disposal, trash compactor or hot water dispenser check out In-Sink Erator. Ask for their *information package* and then decide which is best for your needs and budget. Write to:

IN-SINK ERATOR
4700 21ST ST.
RACINE, WI 53406

Free Spot Removal Guide

This helpful *Emergency Spot Removal Guide* will help you get rid of some of the trickiest stains you may get on your carpets or draperies. It is free for the asking and will come with discount coupons. Drop a postcard to:

COIT DRAPERY & CARPET CLEANERS
DEPT. ABJ, 897 HINKLEY RD.
BURLINGAME, CA 94010

Free Things For Home & Garden

Free Samples of Wood Stain

If you are planning on staining any wood in, on or around your home, one of the finest products you can use is Cabot Stains. But often it is difficult to tell just what a particular color stain will look like before you actually put it on your wood and try it out. To get sample cans of up to 4 different color stains, first get a color chart from a paint store and select the colors you would like to try. Then call Cabot's Consumer Hotline and request free sample cans and a paint brush. Call them toll-free at:
1-800-US-STAINS

Wallpaper By Mail

This great *catalog* offers you an excellent selection of high quality wall covering products at low prices. To make your selection easier, they will send you free swatches of the paper and even matching fabrics. Send a postcard to:
ROBINSON'S WALLCOVERINGS
225 WEST SPRING ST.
TITUSVILLE, PA 16354

"Story Of Hardwood Plywood"

If you are a handyman you will enjoy this informative booklet which gives the whole story of plywood. Best of all you'll receive a set of 4 different plans showing you how to build a bookcase, room divider, saddle seat desk and TV trays (planter/desk/stereo,

Free Things For Home & Garden

etc.) All free from:
HARDWOOD PLYWOOD MANUFACTURERS
PO Box 2789
RESTON, VA 22090

Guide To Paint & Varnish Removal

In this handy guide you will learn some great and easy ways to improve the appearance of your house. There are quick and easy methods for removing mildew and mildew stains from both interior and exterior surfaces. These helpful hints are a must for any tough cleaning job. Send for your free guide to:
SAVOGRAN COMPANY
P.O. BOX 130
NORWOOD, MA 02062

"Stain Removal"

Most stains can be removed by following certain procedures. The folks at Maytag have an excellent stain removal guide they will send to you just for the asking. Remember, once you master the steps it's easy to remove just about any stain by referring to this handy guide. You'll also receive *Facts of Laundry.- Choosing The Right Laundry Additives*. Send a postcard to:
MAYTAG COMPANY
CUSTOMER EDUCATION DEPT.
ONE DEPENDABILITY SQUARE
NEWTON, IA 50208
Or you can download these guides at their web site:
www.maytag.com

Free Things For Home & Garden

Stain Out Hotline

Do you have questions about problem stains on those favorite garments What do you do if it's an unknown mystery stain and you don't know where to begin? The Dow Stain Experts, the makers of Spray'N Wash, have the answers for you. Give them a call at:
1-800 260-1066

Building A House

Even though the prices of homes have skyrocked, you may still be able to afford the home you've always wanted. For the past quarter century DeGeorge Homes has helped over 15,000 people enjoy home ownership with their step-by-step instructions and pre-cut materials. For a free copy of their 80 page *color catalog* with 50 exciting models to choose from, write to:
DEGEORGE HOMES
55 REALTY DRIVE
CHESHIRE, CT 06410
OR CALL THEM AT: 1-800-342-7576

Carpet Cleaning

Hoover will send you a free guide to carpet care. The *Consumer Guide to Carpet Cleaning* is loaded with carpet care tips and facts, cleaning alternatives, a stain removal chart and more. This 16 page booklet provides important information you should know. Ask for *Consumer Guide to Carpet Cleaning*.

Free Things For Home & Garden

Send a SASE to:
THE HOOVER COMPANY
CONSUMER EDUCATION, DEPT. FC
101 E. MAPLE ST.
NORTH CANTON, OH 44720

Choosing Carpeting

Dupont Company offers you this free booklet *"Consumer's Guide To Choosing Carpets"* to help answer all your questions about carpet care. Drop a card to:
DUPONT CO.
ROOM G 40284
WILMINGTON, DE 19898

The All Purpose Wonder

Want to save money and look good too? Send for *This Little Box With A House Full of Uses*. In it you will learn how to use baking soda in ways you never thought of...in the kitchen, bathroom, basement, even on your pet. Write to:
ARM & HAMMER
CONSUMER RELATIONS
CHURCH & DWIGHT CO.
PRINCETON, NJ 08547

Amgard Security

To protect your family and home, a home security alarm system is essential. To help you decide on

Free Things For Home & Garden

what type of protection is best for you and your family ask for the free *Amgard Security Planning Guide*. Drop a card to:
AMGARD SECURITY OFFER
AMWAY CORPORATION-33A-2J
ADA, MI 49355

Glistening Silver

If you would like to keep your silverware shining like new, try storing it in Hagerty's Tarnish Intercept Bags. Once the silverware is placed inside and the bag zipper is closed, it locks out tarnish. The inside of the bag will blacken when it has absorbed all the corrosion-causing gases. You then remove the silver and place it in a new bag. For information on their line of precious metal care products, call: **1-800-348-5162** x137
W. J. HAGERTY SONS, LTD.
P.O. BOX 1496
SOUTH BEND, IN 46624.
OR VISIT THEIR WEB SITE AT: **www.hagerty-polish.com**

Colors & Clorox

Here are lots of helpful tips from Clorox on keeping your clothes clean, bright and stain free. Ask for *Emergency Spot Removal Guide*. Drop a card to:
THE CLOROX CO.
PO BOX 24305
OAKLAND, CA 94623

Free Things For Home & Garden

Shingle It

Lots of remodeling ideas are contained in this great *Red Shingle & Shake package*. It shows how to use shingles and shakes outside and inside your house. These guides also show how to do-it-yourself and save. Drop a card to:

CEDAR SHAKE & SHINTLE BUREAU
#2 7101 HORNE STREET
MISSION, BC V2V 7A2 CANADA

Free Cookbooks

Companies give away terrific recipe collections and cookbooks as their way of showing you new and exciting ways of using their products to create meals both you and your family will love. It is always a nice idea to mention, however briefly, how much you enjoy using their products.

Recipe For Health

We've long known that an important key to good health is a combination of good eating habits and regular exercise. The folks at Stonyfield Farm would like to show you how to be strong and well by adding calcium-rich yogurt and proper exercise into your life. For a free *Wellness Kit* including Stonyfield Farm money-saving coupons plus their Health & Nutrition Guide and a special video offer, send a long SASE to:
STONYFIELD FARM WELLNESS KIT
10 BURTON DRIVE
LONDONDERRY, NH 03053

A Dash Of Health

If you are looking for healthy meals but don't want to compromise taste, you've got to try a recipe or

two from Mrs. Dash and Molly McButter. When you call this toll-free number you will get the delicious recipes of the month using these two great tasting and healthy food additives. Call:
1-800-622-DASH

Better Than Butter

Do you like the flavor of butter but can't take the fat and cholesterol? Then you'll want to try Butter Buds These are natural flavor granules made from real butter with no artificial ingredients. Try your free sample on vegetables, rice, noodles, potatoes or anything you want to add butter flavor to. With your free sample you will also receive a money-off coupon towards your next purchase, and a handy carrying case to carry your Butter Buds with you. To get your free sample of Butter Buds, write to:

CUMBERLAND PACKING CORP.
2 CUMBERLAND STREET
BROOKLYN, NY 11205

Holiday Cooking Help

Holiday times are family fun times and that means food. That also means cooking crises. Fortunately now there's a variety of sources you can turn to for help solving your holiday cooking problems. The following companies are there for you to answer your cooking questions:

Free Cookbooks

Butterball Turkey Talkline

During the holiday season of November and December, Butterball offers you round the clock assistance in person from 7am to 5pm plus automated service after hours. They offer you solutions to virtually every turkey-related need. They also offer free recipe cards with tips and money-saving coupons to every caller. Call them toll-free at:
1-800-323-4848
During the rest of the year, you can visit their web site at:
www.butterball.com

Reynolds Turkey Tips Line

Call this 24-hour automated hotline for professional advice on turkey defrosting, preparation and cooking. They also offer you a free Holiday Solutions brochure and a packet of holiday recipes and tips. Call them at:
1-800-745-4000

Perdue Helpline

Let's say it's Thanksgiving Day and you have a cooking problem. Try calling the Perdue Helpline where there are Consumer Representatives on hand to coach you through your cooking dilemmas. They also have a free booklet containing tips on safe handling of poultry. Call them at:
1-800-473-7383

Ocean Spray Consumer Helpline

This service is available year-round, Monday to Friday 9am to 4pm (including Thanksgiving). Their staff will answer questions on cranberries. They also offer recipes, cooking tips, nutritional information, menu planning worksheets and product information. Call them toll-free at:
1-800-662-3263

Free Holiday Bakeline

during the months of November and December, Land O'Lakes offers you personal help from 7am to 5pm with baking advice from the experts. They can also help you with your home baking emergencies and will send you a free booklet with baking tips and recipes. For help, call their toll-free helpline at:
1-800-782-9606
During the rest of the year you can visit their web site at:
www.landolakes.com

Is Fish Really Good For You?

For years folklore has held that eating more fish will help you stay healthy. Now research has proven that eating fish really is good for you. According to a study by the National Fisheries Institute, the average person eats a total of about 15 pounds of fish a year, or 4 1/2 ounces per week. Among the top 10 choices are salmon and catfish. The Catfish Institute has three recipe brochures waiting for you. In

them you'll find a variety of ideas besides traditional high-fat frying. They're yours free just by calling:
1-888-451-FISH

Safe Food Preparation

Summertime is barbecue and picnic time. There are some basics you need to follow when grilling meats safely outdoors. For tips on safe food preparation and safe food handling call the USDA Meat and Poultry Hotline: Call weekdays 10am -4pm EST:
1-800-535-4555

Low Fat

Today we are all conscious of what we eat to stay healthy. Low fat meals and lots of fresh fruits and vegetables are an essential part of healthy living. This great *Fast Low-Fat Fresh* collection comes with some great ideas for healthy low-fat meals. For your free copy ask for *Low -Fat Fresh* write:
CALIFORNIA TABLE GRAPE COMMISSION
PO BOX 27320
FRESNO, CA 93729-7320
e-mail: info@tablegrape.com

Simple And Tasty Recipes

The folks at College Inn Broth have a great recipe book that will help you enhance all your dishes by using their chicken, beef & vegetable broths. Call:
1-800-55-BROTH

Free Cookbooks

Meat & Poultry Hotline

The USDA has a meat and poultry hotline to help you with questions dealing with food safety. There are a full series of recorded answers to the most commonly asked question or if you have specific questions, you can speak with a food safety expert. Call weekdays from 10:00am–4:00pm EST to speak to a specialist. For recorded messages, you can call 24 hours a day.
1-800 535-4555

Steak Sauce Recipe

Learn all the great tasting meals you can make by using A-1 Steak sauce in new and innovative ways. Ask for *A-1 Steak Sauce Recipe Book* from:
NABISCO FOODS, INC.
PO BOX 1928
EAST HANOVER, NJ 07936-1928

Changing Courses

To stay healthy it is important to reduce the amount of fat you eat. For great recipes using reduced fat sour cream, ask for the *Changing Courses* recipe collection. Call toll-free:
1-800-782-9602

Kerr Kitchen Pantry

The Kerr Kitchen Pantry has a wonderful newsletter that they will send to you just for the asking.

Free Cookbooks

This informative newsletter will give you all kinds of great tips for canning, freezing fresh vegetables and fruits. There are great recipes of the season as well as some helpful hints for homemakers. You'll also find some great canning recipes for relish, sauces and jelly. Ask for the *Kerr Kitchen Pantry Newsletter*. Write to:
CONSUMER PRODUCTS DIVISION
KERR GROUP
1840 CENTURY PARK EAST
LOS ANGELES, CA 90067

Hot Potato

Are you constantly wondering what you can do to make dinner more interesting? Learn why potatoes are America's favorite vegetable and new ways to prepare and serve this healthy vegetable. Ask for *Dinnertime Dilemma. Answers to That Age-Old Question*. Send a long SASE to:
"DINNERTIME DILEMMA,"
DEPT PA, 55 UNION STREET
SAN FRANCISCO, CA 94111

Prize-Winning Beef Recipes

If you would like to sample some of the best beef recipes in the nation, be sure to get a copy of the *National Beef Cook-Off Prize Winning Recipes*. You will find a host of delicious easy-to-prepare meals ranging from Chile Pizza to Gecian Skillet Ribeyes. Send a SASE to:
NATIONAL BEEF COOK-OFF RECIPES

Free Cookbooks

DEPT NBCO-1997
444 N. MICHIGAN AVE 18TH FLOOR
CHICAGO, IL 60611
OR CALL TOLL-FREE: 800-848-9088

Deli-delicious

Simply Sensational Suppers Recipes contains a slew of recipes for perfect party platters. Preparation times and even calorie counts accompany the recipes. This wonderful freebie comes to you from the National Live Stock and Meat Board. Ask for *Simply Sensational Suppers*. Just send a SASE to:
NATIONAL LIVE STOCK AND MEAT BOARD
444 N. MICHIGAN AVE., DEPT. EE
CHICAGO, IL 60611

When In Rome

History shows that the Romans used clay cookware centuries ago. Clay retains moisture which is released slowly during cooking resulting in savory self-basted food. For a terrific collection of recipes using clay Brique Ware, ask for *Brique Ware Recipes and Microwaving with Nordic Ware.* Free from:
CUSTOMER SERVICE NORDIC WARE
HIGHWAY 7 AT 100
MINNEAPOLIS, MN 55416

Just For Dessert Lovers

The ultimate cookie is here. Saco Foods will send

Free Cookbooks

you these ten delicious recipes plus a 20 cents off coupon. Create a chocolate sensation today with these delicious chocolate chunks. Remember it's the chocolate that counts. Now it's easy to get more sweet satisfaction in each bite! They even have a *Bake Your Best Hot line:* **800-373-SACO.** Or send a SASE to:
**SACO FOODS
FREE COOKIE OFFER
PO BOX 616
MIDDLETOWN, WI 53562**

Hot Stuff

Red Devil Hot Sauce is a zesty hot sauce that has dozens of uses—in soups, stews, sandwiches and just about anywhere you want to add a lively taste to your food. For a compact collection of dozens of recipes, send a postcard asking for *Seasoning With Trappey's Red Devil Hot Sauce* to:
**B. F. TRAPPEY'S SONS
DRAWER 400
NEW IBERIA, LA 70560**

Bakers Hotline

Fleishmann's Yeast Bakers Help Line, specializes answering your questions about yeast and breadbaking, including advice on using bread machines. Call weekdays between 10 am and 8pm.
1-800-777-4959

Free Cookbooks

Cooking Light

We all know that what we eat affects our health. But exactly what foods are the best for our health? How do you prepare foods that are good for you? Now there's a toll-free number you can call for answers to these and other questions you may have. This hotline sponsored by the Healthy Cooking magazine will put you in touch with registered dietitians who will answer your questions about cooking light. Call toll-free between 9 a.m. and 5:30 p.m. weekdays:
1-800-231-3438

Snap, Crackle &...Nutrition

When is a Rice Krispie more than a Rice Krispie? When it's part of a well-balanced nutrition program. The people at Kellogg's would like to show you how to serve your family more nutritious meals. Send for *Kellogg's Favorite Recipes* free from:
DEPARTMENT OF HOME ECONOMICS
KELLOGG CO.
BATTLE CREEK, MI 49016

Rice So Nice

Are you always in a hurry to prepare a new nutritious main dish. Call the Rice-A-Roni Main Dish Helpline. Call this computerized phone service will help you put together a great meals in less than 30 minutes. You will also receive quick to prepare rice and pasta recipes. Call **1-800-421-2444** Or write to:

GOLDEN GRAIN CO.
PO BOX 651230
SALT LAKE CITY, UT 84165

Poppin' Fresh Dough

Pillsbury brings you some prize winning recipes…cakes from scratch, easy yeast baking…all kinds of refrigerated dough ideas. All this to help make your next dessert a sweet and tasty delight. Yours free from:

PILLSBURY CO.
CONSUMER RESPONSE
P.O. BOX 550
MINNEAPOLIS, MN 55440

"Golden Blossom"

Many say that Golden Blossom Honey is the tastiest honey there is. To show you how to use their sweet necter in new ways they will send you a nice collection of recipes. Just call and ask for the free Golden Blosssom recipes collection. Call:
1-800-220-2110

Grill-out

If you love to barbacue, call The Weber Grill Hotline at **1-800-GRILL-OUT** and get answers to all your barbecue questions including cooking methods, fat trimming tips and clean up to recipes, steak cooking hints and food safety tips. You'll also receive a free guide with loads of great barbecue recipes. Ask

Free Cookbooks

for *More Backyard Barbecue Basics*. Or write to:
WEBER
BOX BAH
200 EAST DANIELS RD.
PALATINE, IL 60067

Popcorn Lovers

If popcorn is a favorite of yours *Favorite Popcorn Recipes* is a must. It features mouth-watering popcorn balls, zesty treats and sweet 'n munchy snacks. Drop a postcard to:
AMERICAN POPCORN CO.
BOX 178
SIOUX CITY, IA 51102

Cheese Recipes

Six cheese recipes on file cards are available free from Marin French Cheese Company. Also included will be a mail order price list for their fine line of cheeses. Free from:
MARIN FRENCH CHEESE CO.
7500 RED HILL RD.
PETALUMA, CA 94953

Food Fasts

The Department of Agriculture has a large package of fascinating and educational materials including a handy food pyramid guide waiting for you. Learn exactly what the USDA does in the areas of

consumer services, food safety, nutrition and lots more. Excellent teaching and learning tool. Write:
U.S. DEPARTMENT OF AGRICULTURE
PUBLICATIONS DIV.
WASHINGTON, DC 20250.
OR YOU CAN ACCESS THEIR HOME PAGE ON THE WORLDWIDE WEB AT INTERNET ADDRESS: http://www.usda.gov

Eating Healthy

AARP has a nutrition guide with information on dietary guidelines, the food pyramid, the new food labels and special diets for a better quality of life. To get a free copy of *Healthy Eating For a Healthy Life* (stock #D15565), send a postcard to:
AARP FULFILLMEMNT EE0924
601 E STREET N.W.
WASHINGTON, D.C. 20049

Pasta - A Food For Today

Here are three excellent booklets for the health conscious. There are great recipes and lots of things you can add to pasta. There are even quick microwave dishes you can make. Ask for *Hershey Pasta Recipes* from:
HERSHEY PASTA GROUP
CONSUMER RELATIONS
PO BOX 815
HERSHEY, PA 17033

Free Cookbooks

Delicious De-light Tortillas

To help you add a 'south of the border' touch to your next meal, the folks at Mission Foods would like to send you *The Art of Light Tortillas*. Learn how to make a delightful Spanish Pizza, Strawberry Breakfast Crepes, Fiesta Crab Crisps and lots more.
CALL TOLL FREE: **1-800-600-TACO**
Or visit their web site at:
www.missionfoods.com

Do You Have A Sweet Tooth?

Looking for new dessert ideas your whole family will enjoy? You'll find lots of yummy dessert recipes and also learn how to cut the fat from sweets with *Plum Good* recipe. For your free copy and discount coupon, write to:
SOKOL & CO.
5315 DANSHER RD.
COUNTRYSIDE, IL 60525

Breakfast & More

Roman Meal Company makes an excellent line of whole grain breads. The *Roman recipe collection* will show you how to make meals your family will love—like Porcupine Meatballs or Sloppy Joe's. You'll also receive budget stretcher ideas and low-fat diet menus. Free from:
ROMAN MEAL CO.
PO BOX 11126
TACOMA, WA 98411

Free Cookbooks

Free Apple Sauce Recipes

This great cookbook has some of the most delightful recipes using Lucky Leaf Apple Sauce. You will find recipes for everything from entrees to desserts. It's yours free from:
KNOUSE FOODS
PEACH GLEN, PA 17306

Sausage Recipes

Discover a ton of tasty new ways of enjoying sausages with the *Hillshire Farm Sausage recipes*. For your free copy send a postcard to:
MARKETING DEPARTMENT
HILLSHIRE FARMS
3241 SPRING GROVE AVE.
CINCINNATI, OH 45225
Or else you visit Hillshire's web site at:
www.hillshirefarms.com

Dinner Pancakes

From the makers of Mrs. Butterworth's buttered syrup, comes a nice collection of budget recipes that will appeal to any palate. Send a postcard asking for *"Mrs. Butterworth's Inflation Fighting Recipes"* to:
LEVER BROTHERS CO.
390 PARK AVE.
NEW YORK, NY 10022

Free Cookbooks

Not For Dieters

Here's a yummy collection of *Centennial Classics Recipes.*" Selections like Chocolate Peppermint Whirlaway Pie will make your mouth water just thinking about it. Your diet can wait 'til next month. Also ask for *A Profile Of Hershey Foods.* Drop a card to:

CONSUMER INFORMATION
HERSHEY FOODS
HERSHEY, PA 17033
OR CALL: 1-800-468-1714

If you'd like to visit their web site, it's at:
www.hersheys.com

Seafood Delight

This compact collection of seafood recipe ideas comes to you from Lassco Smoked Salmon. You'll find tasty delights that'll make your next barbecue more fun, and gourmet delicacies to liven up any meal. When you write, ask for Seafood Recipes from Lassco." It's your free from:

LASSCO
778 KOHLER ST.
LOS ANGELES, CA 90021

V.I.P. From Idaho

Heart Healthy recipes will provide you with some tasty recipe plus handy tips on buying and storing Idaho Potatoes. Write to:

IDAHO POTATO COMMISSION
P.O. Box 1068
BOISE, ID 83701

You can also check out their web site at:
www.idahopotato.com

Butter It Up

One visit to the Best of Butter web site will reveal a world of ideas, recipes and tips on how to use Kellers Hotel Bar Butter in delighful new ways. At the web site you will be taken step-by-step through the special recipe for that month. To find out more about their new recipes, cooking tips and product information, visit Keller's/Hotel Bar Foods Web site address at:
www.butter1.com

Georgia Peach

Like peaches? You're gonna love Georgia Peach Cobler, Peach Salsa, and other low fat recipes using peaches. Send a long SASE and ask for *Enjoy Georgia Peaches: A Southern Tradition* to:
GEORGIA PEACH COMMISSION
BOX 38146
ATLANTA, GA 30334

Deliciosa

If you are afraid to enjoy pasta meals just because you're on a diet— this one's for you. With *Super Solutions For Super Suppers* you'll enjoy delicious Italian meals that are nutritionally balanced and still allow you to lose weight. You'll also receive a discount coupon. Send to:

Free Cookbooks

RAGU FOODS, INC.
33 BENEDICT PL.
GREENWICH. CT 06830

Spice Up Your Life

Grey Poupon Dijon Mustard has a terrific book that features a host of different ways to spice up your menu with Grey Poupon Dijon Mustard. Here are tasty recipe ideas for red meat, chicken, pasta, fish and more. Ask for *Grill Recipes Using Dijon Mustard*. Write to:

NABISCO FOODS GROUP
GREY POUPON
PO BOX 720
HUDSON, WI 54016

Bees & Honey

Here's a double-barreled special. Fascinating facts about bees and honey plus a collection of taste tempting recipes using golden honey. Just ask for *Cook It Right With Honey*. Send a card to:

DADANT & SONS
HAMILTON, IL 62341

Sweet As An...Onion?

An onion is probably the last thing you think of when you think of sweet foods. Vidalia Onion would like to change your mind. These special onions are mild and tasty. They're grown only in a small section of Georgia where weather and soil conditions blend to make the World's Sweetest Onion. Send today for

Free Cookbooks

the Vidalia Onion recipe collection which will also show you how to freeze and store these unique onions. Send a SASE to:
VIDALIA ONION COMMITTEE
P.O. Box 1609
VIDALIA, GA 30474

Birthday Party Planner

Before you plan your child's next birthday party, be sure to send for this freebie. Skippy has put together some great party ideas from invitations to decorations and activities. Ask for *Skippy Peanut Butter Party Planner* from:
SKIPPY PEANUT BUTTER
DEPT. SPP, BOX 307
COVENTRY, CT 06238

Basket Of Fresh Ideas

This collection of strawberry recipes will show you how to use this tasty fruit to make mouth watering desserts and drinks. Send a card to:
CALIFORNIA STRAWBERRY ADVISORY BOARD
P.O. Box 269
WATSONVILLE, CA 95077

Young At Heart

If you are one of the 60 million Americans with high blood pressure, you should learn how to eat right. Send for the free booklet, *So You Have High Blood Cholesterol* from:

Free Cookbooks

INFORMATION CENTER
NATIONAL HEART, LUNG, & BLOOD INSTITUTE
7200 WISCONSIN AVE., PO BOX 30105
BETHESDA, MD 20824

Nuts About Nuts

If you're crazy about nuts, *All The Goodness of Hawaii is* the catalog for you. You can order anything from Macadamia Nuts to Kona Coffee. For your free copy, send a postcard to:
MAUNA LOA
MAINLAND GIFT CENTER
PO BOX 1772
PEORIA, IL 61656

Top Hits From Frito Lays

This new recipe collection *Baked Low Fat - Taste The Fun Not The Fat* will provide you with a host of innovative new ways to enjoy Tostitos Tortilla Chips. Enjoy Chicken Curry Nachos or Italian Nachos. You'll also learn the story of Frito-Lay. It's free from:
FRITO-LAY,
PO BOX 35034
DALLAS, TX 75235

A Touch Of Tabasco

Add a little zest to your next meal with these recipes using Tabasco sauce. Send a card asking for *From The Land of Tabasco Sauce*. This cookbook features dozens of tangy and tasty meal ideas and recipes for everything from Holiday Turkey to Cream Onion Dip. Put a little spice in your life and your meals. Write to:

MCILHENNY CO.
AVERY ISLAND, LA 70513

Adventures in Good Eating

Looking for new meal ideas your whole family will enjoy? Meals such as Stuffed Pork Chops and Tangy Chicken are among those you'll find in the *Heinz Recipe Collection*. Also ask for the *Heinz Cooking With Beans*. All free from:

H. J. HEINZ
PO BOX 57
PITTSBURGH, PA 15230

Hot Stuff

If you like your food red hot, you'll definitely want to send for this. *Tempting Recipes With Red Devil Hot Sauce* will show you some great ways to spice up your meals. You will also receive a Red Devil discount coupon and a Tabasco catalog. Send a card to:

B. F. TRAPPEY'S SONS. INC.
BOX 400
NEW IBERIA, LA 70560

Simply Sweet Recipes

NutraSweet Company has a nice package of easy to prepare recipes. Some of the things you will receive include, *Home Sweet Home With Equal* -

Free Cookbooks

NutraSweet Spoonful Recipes, plus some simple tips for making food label information easy to understand and discount coupons. To get your free package, write to:
E-Z SURVIVAL KIT
THE NUTRASWEET COMPANY
PO BOX 830
DEERFIELD, IL 60015

Yam It Up

How would you like to enjoy a marshmallow yam dessert or yam orange cookies? These are just two of the tasty treats you'll find featured in the *Sweet Potato recipe* collection with dozens of prize winning yam recipes. Free from:
LOUISIANA DEPARTMENT OF AGRICULTURE
P.O. BOX 3334
BATON ROUGE, LA 70821

Cookouts Are Fun

Grill Lovers Catalog has something every barbecue chef will enjoy having. It yours free from:
W. C. BRADLEY
BOX 1240
COLUMBUS, GA 31902

Cooking With Sweet Potatoes

Here's a collection of 28 tasty meals using sweet potatoes. You'll enjoy the main dishes and colorful casseroles featuring sweet potatoes in combination

with other vegetables and meats. For your free copy write:
SWEET POTATO COUNCIL
P.O. BOX 14
1475 MARSH HILL RD
MCHENRY, MD 21541

Sherry, Sherry

The makers of the original cream sherry – Harvey's Bristol Cream have a great recipe collection just for the asking. You'll find Peachy Cranberry Sauce for pork, Millionaire's Manhattan plus lots more. Send a long SASE and ask for *HBC's Recipes* to:
HBC RECIPE COLLECTION
PO BOX 767
HOLMDEL, NJ 07733

Salad Dressing

This small collection gives you 5 recipes using Uncle Dan's Salad Dressing and shows how it can be used as seasoning, for party dips and even as a sandwich spread. Write to:
UNCLE DAN'S
PO BOX 980
YAKIMA, WA 98907

Garden Of Eden

The fig has been with us ever since Adam and Eve decided that fig leaves made nifty apparel. Now

Free Cookbooks

Buyers Guide To Dietary Fiber along with *Fabulous Figs - The Fitness Fruit* and *This Fig Can Teach You A Lot About Nutrition* will give you delicious new ways to use this delightful and nutritious fruit. Free from:
DRIED FRUIT ADVISORY BOARD
BOX 709
FRESNO, CA 93712

Ummm ... Good

Campbell has a special collection of recipes along with a discount coupon waiting for you. They feature their tasty line of soups. When you write ask for the *Golden Corn Soup Chronology*. Write to:
CAMPBELL SOUP CO.
HOME ECONOMICS DEPT.
CAMPBELL PLACE
CAMDEN, NJ 08101

Texasweet Citrus Recipes

This collection of mouth-watering citrus recipes comes to you from TexaSweet. Their Ruby Red grapefruit has a sweet, juicy flavor. The recipes cover breakfast, dinner, dessert and drinks using this delectable citrus. Send a postcard to:
TEXASWEET
P.O. BOX 2497
MCALLEN. TX 78501

Almond Specialties

For a change of pace try using almonds to flavor

Free Cookbooks

your next meal. The *Fast & Fabulous* collection will show you how to use almonds in everything from chocolate-almond apricot bread, turkey tetrazzini almondine and almond-blueberry fruit cake. Free from:
ALMOND BOARD OF CALIFORNIA
12TH STREET, BOX 31307
MODESTO, CA 95354

Olive Oil Recipes

When dinner's done you may receive a standing ovation from your family for the meal you just made with the help of this recipe collection. *How To Change Your Oil & Recipes* will give you a couple of dozen creative meal ideas using olive oil. You will also receive a store discount coupon. Send a card to:
POMPEIAN OLIVE OIL
4201 PULASKI HIGHWAY
BALTIMORE, MD 21224

Sweet 'N Low Samples

For an envelope full of Sweet 'N Low samples plus a handy carry case, just send a SASE and request *Sweet 'N Low Samples*. Send to:
SWEET 'N LOW, CUMBERLAND PACKING CORP
2 CUMBERLAND ST.
BROOKLYN, NY 11205
Or you can visit their web site at:
www.sweetnlow.com

Free Cookbooks

Fresh From Florida

What a wonderful package this is—an outstanding collection of recipes and information on seafood and aquaculture. Discover how to make a Seafare Saute & lots more. Send a long SASE to:

BOB CRAWFORD
COMMISSIONER OF AGRICULTURE & CONSUMER SERVICES
BUREAU OF SEAFOOD & AQUACULTURE
2051 EAST DIRAC DR.
TALLAHASSEE, FL 32310-3760

Soup To Nuts

The *Light & Elegant Cookbook* includes recipes of all kinds with everything from soups to nuts. All these exciting meals feature Lea & Perrins Sauce. There's even a nice index to help you easily find the recipe you want. Free from:

LEE & PERRINS SAUCE
POLLITT DR.
FAIRLAWN, NJ 07410

Thomas' Promises..

If you like Thomas' English Muffins plain—you'll love 'em fancy. To get their *English Muffins Recipes* plus a discount coupon, send a postcard to:

S.B. THOMAS. INC.
930 N. RIVERVIEW DR.
TOTOWA, NJ 07512

Free Cookbooks

"Nutrition Facts"

Oscar Mayer sandwich spreads are easy and versatile to use. Try the spreads on crackers, breads and in other recipes. For a nice collection of recipe ideas, send a postcard to:
OSCAR MAYER
DEPT. ST, P.O. BOX 7188
MADISON, WI 53707

A Sweet Way To Cheat

If you love sweets (and who doesn't) but must watch your weight *26 Ways To Get Back To Nature* is for you. For your free copy of this booklet plus four others including *Cakes For All Occasions*, send a postcard to:
SUGAR FOODS CORP.
9500 EL DORADO AVE., P.O. BOX 1220
SUN VALLEY CA 91352

Creole Cooking

If you enjoy the unique taste and flavors of cajon and creole food, this one's for you. Tony Chachere's Creole Foods, featured in Oprah Winfrey's cookbook *In The Kitchen With Rosie* would like to send you a free cookbook showing you how to use their creole seasoning to create old-fashioned Louisiana taste delights. Write to
TONY CHACHERE'S CREOLE FOODS
533 NORTH LOMBARD ST.
PO BOX 1687
OPELOUSAS, LA 70571

Free Cookbooks

Eight For Dinner

The American Lamb Council several recipe collections that will show you exciting ways to make your dinners more delightful. The collection includes *Make It Simple, Make It Sizzle,* and *Festive Lamb Recipes,* plus several others. You'll find wine-basted, marinated, grilled, roasted and broiled recipes using fresh American lamb. Send a long SASE to:

THE AMERICAN LAMB COUNCIL
6911 S. YOSEMITE ST.
ENGLEWOOD, CO 80112

Bring Home The Bacon

If you like bacon, be sure to get your copy of *Savor The Flavor, Round The Clock With Oscar Mayer Bacon.* In it you'll discover tasty recipes and cooking ideas featuring bacon. They will also include party & cookout recipes using Oscar Mayers Little Wieners & Little Smokies plus Nutrition Facts. Send a postcard to:

BACON BOOKLET
OSCAR MAYER CONSUMER CENTER
PO BOX 7188
MADISON, WI 53707

How To Comfort

Now you can make some great desserts, drinks even coffee using that versatile liquor from Kentucky — Southern Comfort. If you want more delicious recipe ideas, write:

SOUTHERN COMFORT COMPANY
DEPT. GT, BOX 1080
LOUISVILLE, KY 40201

Delicious Skinny Beef

Looking for something easy but delicious for your family's meals? How about meals that are perfect for anyone watching their weight? Try something different... like 'beef, pasta & artichoke toss' or 'quick steak & vegetable soup'. Send a SASE and ask for *Delicious Easy Beef Recipes From Skinny Beef*. Send to:

MEAT BOARD TEST KITCHENS
DEPT. DEBR, 444 N. MICHIGAN AVE
CHICAGO, IL 60611

Wine And Dine

The Gallo recipe collection will provide you with dozens of palate pleasing ways of using Gallo to enhance your next meal. Included is a delightful recipe for Goumet Pizza and lots more. These recipes will let you turn everyday cooking into an adventure. Write to:

E & J GALLO WINERY
MODESTO, CA 95353

"White Wine Recipes"

Wine lovers delight in trying new wines and new ways to enjoy familiar wines. With this compact collection of recipes you'll create tasty new meals using the fine wines of Widmer. Free from:

WIDMER WINE CELLARS
NAPLES, NY 14512

Wine Lovers

"Beaulieu Vineyards" describes and pictures the Beaulieu line of fine wines. Also includes a card for a free wine tasting tour of their vineyard. Write to:
BEAULIEU VINEYARDS
PO BOX 329
RUTHERFORD, CA 94573

Cordial Recipes

Hiram Walker has put together a selection of over 30 famous food and drink recipes from around the world. These recipes all feature their fine line of cordials. Just ask for their free *The Best Of Kahlua*. Pink Chinchilla Pie anyone? Write to:
HIRAM WALKER
P.O. BOX 33006
DETROIT, MI 48232

Chambord Recipes

Chambord is a liqueur made with small black raspberries plus other fruits & herbs combined with honey. For new ways to enjoy this magnificent liqueur, send for the free *Chambord Recipe Book* from:
CHAMBORD RECIPES
LA MAISON DELAN ET CIE
2180 OAKDALE DR.
PHILADELPHIA, PA 19125

Free Cookbooks

Virgin Island Rum

Cruzan Rum is an exceptionally clean tasting rum that works well with mixers or on its own. For your copy of the free *Imported Rum Recipes,* write:
CRUZAN RUM DISTILLERY
PO BOX 218, FREDERIKSTED
ST. CROIS, VI 00840

A Touch Of Mexico From Your Computer

If you're looking for a tasty change in your usual dinner fare, why not try a novel Mexican meal. It's called *Mexican Meals Made Easy* and it's brought to you by the folks at Ortega. At their web site you will find interesting recipes for Mexican dinners using just the ingredients you have on hand. Visit them at their web site:
www.ortegafoods.com

What's In Your Cupboard?

If you have a computer, Uncle Ben's has a terrific idea to help you make a quick and simple dinners using just the ingredients you have on hand. When you visit their web site you'll have over 1,000 recipes from Uncle Ben's kitchen right at your fingertips. Simply input the ingredients you have in your cupboard and they'll supply you with a delicious dish you can whip up in no time. This unique cooking site also offers helpful shopping lists, product information, healthy lifestyle tips and more. Visit their web site at:
www.unclebens.com

Free Cookbooks

More Cooking Help Via The Internet

Here are three sites you can visit for cooking help, tips and ideas:

Better Homes and Gardens

At this site you'll find menu plans, cooking tips and interesting decorating ideas.
www.bhglive.com

Epicurious

Here you'll find tips, theme menu ideas, vegetarian recipes as well as beer and wine suggestions. Visit them at:
www.epicurious.com

Cooking.com

If you've looking for interesting traditional and alternative menu ideas and products, you must visit this Internet site at:
www.cooking.com

Craft & Hobbies

Free Celebrity Autograph

Have you always wanted to collect a celebrity's autograph but didn't know how to get it? Now there's someone who will teach you how. When you write, you'll receive a free address of a celebrity and instructions on how to request an 8x10 autographed celebrity photo. The first time you write, the celebrity's address you receive will be Mr. Greenhill's choice. He's been doing this for 10 years so he knows what he's doing. To get on the celeb bandwagon, send a long SASE to:
DAVID GREENHILL
2306 CEDAR WAY
DALLAS TX 75241

Star Search

Do you have a favorite recording artist or special movie star? Well here's your chance to get an autograph of that famous star. You'll receive a listing of over 100 superstar names and addresses along with a brief bio as well as helpful hints on making your star search productive. Send a long SASE to:
JIM WEAVER'S AUTOGRAPHS IN THE MAIL
322 MALL BLVD., #345,
MONROEVILLE, PA 15146-2229

Crafts & Hobbies

Who Wouldn't Love This

You're going to love this adorable fuzzy pom pom teddy bear. This cutey makes a nice little gift for anyone or you can add it to your stuffed animal collection. Just send 3 first class stamps and ask for the *pom pom teddy bear*. Write to:

TEDDY BEARS
2431 BUCK ROAD
HARRISON, MI 48625

Fun With Ribbons

Learn to create colorful and fun projects with ribbons. You'll be amazed at what you can create using ribbons of all sizes, colors and textures. This is a great rainy day project and you can even use the finished projects to raise money for a special cause. Write to:

CON OFFRAY & SON
ROUTE 24
BOX 601
CHESTER, NJ 07930

Free Bead Supply Catalog

Are you looking for an interesting and challenging hobby? The Frantz Bead Company has put together an informative newsletter and supply catalog to help teach you the art of bead making. You'll get the free newsletter plus a catalog with a full assortment of terrific bead supplies. Simply send a postcard to:

FRANTZ BEAD COMPANY
1222 SUNSET HILL ROAD
SHELTON, WA 98584

Crafts & Hobbies

You might like to check out their web site at:
www.frantzartglass.com

Beautiful Christmas Ornament

If you love to collect truly unique Christmas ornaments, you will definitely want to get this one. It's a beautiful hand-made angel that will quickly become the centerpiece of your holiday decorations. Simply send $2.00 (or 7 loose first class stamps) for shipping and handling and request the *'Christmas Angel'* from:
ANGELIC CREATIONS
PO Box 4620
TRAVERSE CITY, MI 49685

If You Like Duplicate Bridge

Do you enjoy playing duplicate bridge? If so you'll want this *catalog and product source guide* with just about anything you might want or need for this game. Write to:
AMERICAN CONTRACT BRIDGE LEAGUE
2990 AIRWAYS BLVD.
P.O. Box 161192
MEMPHIS, TN 38116

10 Ways To Play Better Chess

Learn the official rules of this challenging game of chess and also receive another publication to join the U.S. Chess Federation. Chess helps you develop your ability to think analytically. Ask for *Ten Tips To Winning Chess*. Send a long SASE to:

Crafts & Hobbies

U.S. CHESS FEDERATION DEPT. 17
186 ROUTE 9W
NEW WINDSOR, NY 12553.
OR CALL: **1-800-388-KING**

Crocheting A Doll

If you love to crochet you'll want this free pattern for a pair of Raggedy Ann and Andy dolls. Crocheting these dolls are just half the fun ...giving them as a gift and seeing the joy they bring is the rest. Send a long SASE and $1.00 postage and handling to:
NP PATTERNS
341 4TH TERRACE
EGG HARBOR, NJ 08215

Help From Kodak on How To Take Great Photos

This 48 page guide in full color shows you how to take the best snapshots under any circumstances. It's easy to understand and deals with topics such as lighting, flash photography, action and more. So start taking better pictures now. Ask for *Hot Shots With Any Camera*. Call them toll-free: **1-800-242-2424.**

Crochet Time

These free crochet instructions will show you how to make some beautiful hand made ornaments, that you could sell, give as gifts or enjoy yourself. You

Crafts & Hobbies

can make seven simple thread snowflakes and 10 easy yarn ornaments. So get started now and send for your free instructions. Ask for: Crochet Tree-Trim Pattern, SASE to:
LORRAINE VETTER-SR
7924 SOPER HILL ROAD
EVERETT, WA 98205

Blackjack Strategy Card

A free Black Jack Strategy Card is yours for the asking. This pocket-sized card gives you invaluable strategies, based on what you are dealt and what the tester is showing. Various combinations of hands and dealer show cards are printed right on an easy to read chart. Gambling, blackjack in particular, can be fun if you're able to combine luck with a little strategy. Ask for *Black Jack Strategy Card*. Write to:
THOMAS GAMING SERVICES
PO BOX 1383
GOLETA, CA 93116

Are You Having Problems With Your Polaroid?

Have your Polaroid photos been coming out the way you'd like? If not there's a toll-free hotline to call where an expert will answer any questions you may have. Call toll free 8AM -8PM Monday through Saturday at: **800-343-5000.** Polaroid has a wonderful policy of complete customer satisfaction. Your problem may lie with defective film which they'll replace at no charge. Send defective film or photos to:

Crafts & Hobbies

Polaroid Customer Care Service
784 MEMORIAL DR.
CAMBRIDGE, MA 02139

Would You Like To Become A Ventriloquist?

Do you remember Howdy Doody, and Edgar and Jerry Mahoney? Well now you can learn all the same techniques they used. Here is your chance to learn about what a ventriloquist is and how to become one. You will also learn how to build a puppet and even put together and market a show. You will learn how to start the show, the direction to go in and lots more. To receive this 32 page booklet on *How To Become A Ventriloquist,* write to:

THE NORTH AMERICAN ASSOCIATION OF VENTRILOQUISTS
Box 420
Littleton CO 80160

Just For Knife Collectors

This catalog is packed with hundreds of knives, swords, specialty and novelty knives, sharpening systems, accessories and more. Now you can find that special carving knife for meat, cheese or fruitcake. If you are a collector of swords and sheaths there are several to choose from. Write:

SMOKY MOUNTAIN KNIFE WORKS
Box 4430
SEVIERVILLE, TN 37864

Crafts & Hobbies

Taking Better Photos

Kodak has a terrific freebie for anyone who wants to take perfect (or at least better) photographs. Call their toll-free phone number and ask for the beautifully illustrated book, *How To Take Great Pictures*. Call them toll-free:
1-800-599-5929.

Can You Picture This?

Kodak has a great web site that will help you take better photos. You will find… Top 10 techniques for good photos; Problem-pictures remedies; Picture taking tips for any situation plus a host of other topics and chat rooms relating to digital, general and professional photography. Visit their web site at:
www.kodak.com

Enjoying Play Clay

Did you know you can create your own unique gifts, decorations and jewelry with 'play clay'? You'll learn how to make play clay from Arm & Hammer Baking Soda. To get this freebie. Send a postcard and ask for *Play Clay* to:
ARM & HAMMER CONSUMER RELATIONS
DIVISION OF CHURCH & DWIGHT CO.
PRINCETON, NJ 08543-5297
OR CALL: **1-800-524-1328**

Crafts & Hobbies

Creating Beautiful Letters

If you are interested in learning how to create handcrafted lettering, this is for you. With the *Hunt Lettering Charts* you will receive a super collection of Roman Gothic, Old English and Manuscript lettering charts plus helpful hints. Send a card to:
HUNT BIENFANG PAPER CO.
2020 W. FRONT ST.
STATESVILLE, NC 28677

Just For Comic Book Collectors

While rumaging through the attic many people have stumbled across comic books they've had since they were kids bringing back wonderful memories of their childhood. For some that is the beginning of an enjoyable hobby of collecting old comic books. If that describes you, you'll want to send for a *giant list of back issues of Marvel comics*. Send 50¢ postage to:
R. CRESTOHL
4732 CIRCLE RD.
MONTREAL, CANADA

Old-Time Stamp Collection

There's an old-time collection of 26 different stamps waiting for you. Each stamp is 50 to 100 years old. The stamps are worth $2.00 at catalog prices but are yours for only 50¢ postage. You'll also receive other stamps on approval but there's no obligation to buy anything. Write to:
FALCON STAMP CO. 072 ST.
FALCONER, NY 14733

Crafts & Hobbies

Start A Stamp Club

If you're interested in collecting stamps, you will probably enjoy the hobby more in the company of other stamp collectors. If this sounds like something you might be interested in, ask for your free copy of *You Can Start A Stamp Club*. Write to:

AMERICAN PHILATELIC SOCIETY
P.O. Box 8000
STATE COLLEGE, PA 16801

Free Numismatic News

Here's a newspaper every coin collectors will want to have. Simply write and request a free copy of *'Numismatic Weekly.'* You'll enjoy its many interesting articles on all aspects of this fascinating hobby. Send a card to:

NUMISMATIC NEWS WEEKLY
IOLA, WI 54990

Free For Kids

Money Management For Teenagers

Consumer Federation of America has a helpful guide that will help you to teach your teenager responsible money management. This is a must for every parent. Send a SASE to:
CONSUMER FEDERATION OF AMERICA
TEACHING YOUR CHILD HOW TO SAVE AND SPEND"
1424 16TH ST. NW, SUITE 604
WASHINGTON, DC 20036

Free Circus Tickets

If your child was born in the U.S. since 1993, he or she is entitled to a free ticket to a Ringling Brothers & Barnum & Bailey Show redeemable any time in his/her lifetime. To get their free ticket, parents only need send their newborn's name, address, and date of birth to:
RINGLING BROTHERS & BARNUM & BAILEY
PO Box 39845
EDINA, MN 55439

Free For Kids

Free Spiderman Comic Book

The American Cancer Society would love to send you a free SpiderMan comic book. SpiderMan and his webbed buddies battle the evil villain Smokescreen in a vivid, and exciting antismoking comic. To get this free comic book ask for the *Spiderman Comic Book*. Call The American Cancer Society at:
1-800-227-2345

Free Coloring Book

If you've ever wanted to know more about your lungs, and have fun while doing it this free offer is for you. You have your choice of three books, an activity book, a coloring book, or a crossword puzzle book. Specify the books you want or ask for the *"facts about smoking"* package: *Smoking...Lungs At Work* #0840; *Second-Hand Smoke; Let's Solve The Smokeword* puzzle-book, #0043. Send it on a postcard to:
AMERICAN LUNG ASSOCIATION
BOX 596
NEW YORK, NY 10116

Free Science Weekly

An introduction to the wonderful world of science. Science Weekly, will send you a free sample copy of their newsletter- written specifically for kids. It's an easy read and touches on important topics involving science and is written for kids (grades K -

8th) in order to bring them a better understanding of the sciences, languages and even mathematics. Write and specify which grade level you want when you write to:
SCIENCE WEEKLY
SUBSCRIPTION DEPT.
PO Box 70154
WASHINGTON, DC 20088

Free Coloring Books

The makers of Triaminic cough and cold medicines is giving away two free educational coloring books. These two books are great and help kids to learn and understand about illnesses such as Alzheimer's, epilepsy and diabetes. They offer descriptions and excellent explanations. Ask for: *Kid's Educational Coloring Books* (specify English or Spanish). Write to:
JEFF'S COMPANION ANIMAL SHELTER
C/O SANDOZ PHARMACEUTICALS
59 ROUTE 10
E. HANOVER, NJ 07936

Make A Badge

This great kit is not only fun but can be a profit-maker too. If you like collecting buttons, you'll love making your own. Send for

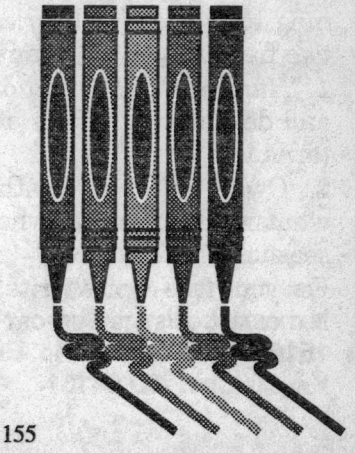

your *free catalog and free idea book* today. Write to:
**BADGE A MINIT
348 NORTH 30TH RD.
LA SALLE, IL 61301**

Learning Yo Yo Tricks

This easy to understand, illustrated pamphlet teaches you the "ancient -art" of *Yo Yo Trickery.* Learn some of the same tricks that made the Yo Yo famous, like Walking the Dog, the Spinner, The Creeper, Loop the Loop and lots more. You'll be learning the fun tournament tricks in no time. Ask for "Yo *Yo Trick Pamphlet."* Send a SASE to:
**DUNCAN TOYS CO.
PO BOX 5
MIDDLEFIELD, OH 44062**

Owlie Skywarn

What can you do to make yourself safe from lightning, tornadoes and hurricanes? Owlie Skywarn has two freebies you will want to have:

1. "Hurricanes & Tornados - tells about the causes and devastating effects of storms, hurricanes and tornados.

2. "Owlie Skywarn Weather Book" - learn exactly what weather is and what causes the changes in seasons.

For your free copies write to:
**NATIONAL LOGISTICS SUPPORT CENTER
1510 EAST BANNISTER RD. BLDG. #1
KANSAS CITY, MO 64131**

Energy Information

Everyone must do their share to save energy. The Conservation & Renewable Energy Inquiry & Referral Service (CAREIRS) has a nice information package any youngster would love to have: Learn what you can do to conserve energy. Excellent! Free from:

CAREIRS
PO Box 3048
MERRIFIELD, VA 22116

Fun-Filled Catalog

If you'd like a copy of what is probably the most unusual and funfilled catalog in the world, send for the *Johnson Smith Catalog*. It is filled with 1600 novelties, gadgets and fun-makers of every type. Send a postcard to:

JOHNSON SMITH CO.
4514 19TH COURT E.
BRADENTON, FL 34203

Don't Get Hooked

The Office on Smoking and Health has a variety of colorful posters and interesting material explaining the real dangers of smoking. Ask for their free catalog of informative materials on smoking and your health. After you receive the catalog you can request the specific free materials you want. Send a postcard to:

OFFICE ON SMOKING AND HEALTH
PARK BLDG., 1-58
ROCKVILLE, MD 20857

Free For Kids

Take A Bite Out Of Crime

The crime detective dog, McGruff will show you what you can do to fight crime. McGruff and his nephew, Scruff will send you a fun comic/activity book that will show your children how to make themselves and their friends safer. They also have a *Parent's Streetwise Kids Guide*. Ask for *Scruff McGruff Take a Bite Out of Crime*. Call toll-free: **1-800-627-2911.** OR WRITE TO:
NATIONAL CRIME PREVENTION COUNCIL
1700 K STREET N.W. 2ND FLOOR
WASHINGTON, D.C. 20006-3817

Also, for a free action kit packed with ideas and real life experiences of what neighbors working together can do to prevent crime and make you and your family safer, call:
1-800-WE-PREVENT

Learning Can Be Fun

Free Parent's Guide To Cyberspace

The internet has opened us all to a new world. At the touch of a keyboard you can watch a volcano come to life, read a story to your child, view an original copy of Lincoln's Gettysburg address or instantly send a letter to a friend across the country or on the other side of the world. For a free copy of the *Librarian's Guide to Cyberspace for Parents & Kids,"* request it from:

AMERICAN LIBRARY ASSOCIATION INFORMATION OFFICE
50 EAST HURON ST DEPT P
CHICAGO, IL 60611
web site: www.ala.org/parentspage/greatsites

Free Cotton Poster

Here's a huge wall poster with colorful illustrations showing the development of cotton from seed to clothing. Also included will be an interesting book on cotton. The kids will love this. *The Story of Cotton* poster is yours free from:

NATIONAL COTTON COUNCIL
PO BOX 12285
MEMPHIS, TN 38112

Learning Something New

Understanding Stocks & Bonds

Getting Help When You Invest and *Understanding Stocks and Bonds* and two fascinating guides that tells all about how the stock market works and the important role it plays in our nation's economy. The New York Stock Exchange also has an excellent series of educational aids, huge wall posters, ticker tape, teacher guides and more. Incidentally teachers can get a package tailored to the grade level they're teaching. Quantities of books will be supplied for each student. Write to:

N.Y. STOCK EXCHANGE
EDUCATIONAL SERVICES
11 WALL ST.
NEW YORK, NY 10005

KEEP IN MIND: If you don't have a computer or Internet access at home, most libraries have computers you can use and educational programs for children and adults to teach you how to use them.

Australia Today

What is life like 'down-under'? *Australia Now* will give you a look—in full color-at what's happening in Australia today. You'll also receive vacation planning, travel tips and information on locations, tours and accommodations. Drop a postcard to:

AUSTRALIAN CONSULATE GENERAL
630 FIFTH AVE. SUITE 420
NEW YORK NY 10111

Learning Something New

U.S. Monetary System

How much do you really know about how the U.S. economy works? Do you know what the Federal Reserve System is or how it helps our monetary system work? For answers to these and other questions, get a copy of *Too Much, Too Little*. Put out by the Federal Reserve and geared to high school grade levels, itexplains in comic book format just how the Federal Reserve helps keep out economy strong. Free from:
FEDERAL RESERVE OF NY–PUBLICATIONS DEPT.
FEDERAL RESERVE PO STATION
NEW YORK, NY 10045-0001

Sky Gazers

If you enjoy studying the heavens, you will want to get a copy of *Essential Magazines of Astronomy* with a catalog of some of the finest astronomy books that will delight all star gazers. Write to:
SKY PUBLISHING CORP.
49 BAY STREET RD.
CAMBRIDGE, MA 02138

Are We Alone?

Man has always been fascinated by the sky at night. With the recent discovery of planets circling around distant stars, one can't help but wonder whether life exists elsewhere in the universe. To find out more about our distant neighbors, send for the *skywatching series of booklets* dealing with our solar system and beyond. Send to:

Learning Something New

PUBLIC AFFAIRS OFFICE
HARVARD SMITHSONIAN CENTER FOR ASTROPHYSICS
60 GARDEN ST.
CAMBRIDGE, MA 02138

Quarter Horses

Whether you are presently an owner of horses or perhaps thinking of buying one - check out American Quarter Horses, the world's most popular breed of horse. Here's an interesting booklet you will want to have: *For An American Quarter Horse*. For a copy of this fascinating booklet (and a colorful bumper sticker too), drop a card to:
AMERICAN QUARTER HORSE ASSN.
AMARILLO, TX 79168

What's A Tennessee Walking Horse?

Here's one every equestrian will want to have. Send a card for the *Tennessee Walking Horse* plus a colorful postcard showing the three horses chosen by the breeder's association as the world's greatest pleasure and show horse. Write to:
TENNESSEE WALKING HORSE
BOX 286
LEWISBURG, TN 37081

Self Improvement

Would you like to take charge of your life — control your smoking, lose weight, attract more love or make more money? Maybe you should look through the

Love Tapes catalog. Based on sound psychological principles, these tapes will help you develop your full potential. Send a card to:
EFFECTIVE LEARNING SYSTEMS
5221 EDINA IND BLVD.
EDINA, MN 55434

Home Fire Detection

Learn how to protect your family and your home with smoke detectors—a must for all homes. Send a card to:
"HOME FIRE DETECTION,"
NATIONAL FIRE PROTECTION ASSOCIATION
BATTERYMARCH PARK
QUINCY, MA 02269

The Wright Brothers

With men on the moon and rockets to Jupiter it's hard to believe that manned flight began just 87 years ago with an historic 120 foot journey that lasted all of 12 seconds. All the fascinating details are found in this historical recap called, *Wright Brothers.* Send a card to:
WRIGHT BROTHERS NATIONAL MEMORIAL
ROUTE 1, BOX 676
MANTEO, NC 27954

Learning Something New

Facts About Oil

This nicely illustrated guide to petroleum tells all about the history of oil exploration and shows how the search for oil is conducted. Ask for the *"energy information series"* and you'll receive a great package of excellent booklets dealing with many forms of energy including wind, nuclear, geothermal, coal, oil and more. Send a card to:

AMERICAN PETROLEUM INSTITUTE
PUBLICATIONS SECTION
1220 L ST. N.W.
WASHINGTON, DC 20005

Truth About Nuclear Energy

Is nuclear energy the answer to our energy needs or are the risks of nuclear disaster just too great? To help you answer this question, here is an excellent package of books that is free for the asking. Topics covered include nuclear power plants, the structure of the atom, magnetic fusion, the story of nuclear energy and a whole lot more. They will also include information about wind energy and conservation. Ask for the *Nuclear Energy information package.* It's very informative and it's free from:

U.S. DEPARTMENT OF ENERGY
PO BOX 62
OAK RIDGE, TN 37830

Managing Your Money

Everyone spends money, but not everyone knows how to do it right. Spending money wisely takes skill, time and experience. To help you learn how

to shop smart, the FTC and the National Association of Attorneys General have put together a fun activity booklet called *The Real Deal*. To get your free copy, write to:
YOUR STATE ATTORNEY GENERAL
OFFICE OF CONSUMER PROTECTION
YOUR STATE CAPITAL
OR TO: THE FEDERAL TRADE COMMISSION
6TH & PENNSYLVANIA AVE., NW, ROOM 103
WASHINGTON, DC 20580
Or visit their web site: **www.ftc.gov**

How To Be A Better Writer

The National Council of Teachers of English have compiled some handy tips to help make your children better writers. If they start with good writing skills as early as possible, they will have no problem with the written word later on. Ask for *How to Help Your Child Become A Better Writer*. Specify English or Spanish edition. Send a SASE to:
NATIONAL COUNCIL OF TEACHERS OF ENGLISH
DEPT. C, 1111 KENYON RD.
URBANA, IL 61801

Fun With Mazes

If you like puzzles and mazes, you will love this freebie. You will receive a complimentary 11"x 17" maze valued at $2.95. Send $1.00 for postage and handling and ask for it from:
PDK ENTERPRISES
PO BOX 1776
BOYES HOT SPRINGS, CA 95416

Learning Something New

All About Mining

America has been blessed with enormous amounts of natural resources that enrich our lives all thanks to the people in our mining industry. Teachers will love, *What Mining Means to Americans* which is a fascinating look at this important industry. Write to:
NATIONAL MINING ASSOCIATION
1130 17TH ST. N.W.
WASHINGTON, DC 20036-4677

Who Wants An Aluminum Car?

Today, through greater use of aluminum parts our cars are getting far better miles per gallon. This is just one of the many uses of aluminum. If you would like a better understanding of the history of aluminum, the ways it is made and how it's used, ask for the free *Story of Aluminum* and *Alcoa* from:
ALCOA
150 ALCOA BUILDING.
PITTSBURGH, PA 15219

What Exactly Is The Chamber Of Commerce?

Do you have any idea what the Chamber of Commerce is? Who runs it? What does it do? For a concise booklet answering your questions, write to:
CHAMBER OF COMMERCE OF THE U.S.
1615 H ST. N.W.
WASHINGTON, DC 20062

Learning Something New

Pitch This One!

If you have ever thought about taking up horse shoe pitching, now's the time. (Did you know that former President George Bush used to pitch horseshoes?) To find out more about this fun sport and to learn all the rules and tips for throwing the perfect horseshoe pitch. Send for your free copy of the *Official Rules For Horseshoe Pitching*. Send a SASE to:
NHPA, RR2
Box 178
LaMonte, MD 65337

Cleaning Up The Environment

Bethlehem Steel would like you to know what they are doing to clean up the air and water. For example, at one plant they have spent over 100 million dollars for air and water quality controls. For a free copy of *"Steelmaking & The Environment,"* send a card to:
Bethlehem Steel Corp.
Public Affairs Dept., Room 476MT
Bethlehem, PA 18016

Free Sample Science Project Plan

If you enjoy doing science experiments, this one's for you. You'll receive 9 sample science project Instruction Plans including: Volcano model, microwave effects on seeds, testing biodegradables, synthetic cola plus five more. They list materials needed and gives instruction about how to do the project. Includes a full listing of 265 others avail-

able at nominal cost. Great for science students and teachers. Send a name & address label and $2.00 postage and handling to:
SCIENCESOUTH
PO BOX 50182
KNOXVILLE, TN 37950

Learning to Be More Romantic

Since the beginning of time, women have accused men of not being romantic. Finally there's help and it's called *The RoMANtic*. Each 12 page newsletter gives dozens of practical, creative and inspiring ideas and stories on dating, gift-giving, anniversary celebrating and more. To learn how to rekindle the romantic spark and have more fun in your relationships, send 3 first class stamps to:
THE ROMANTIC SAMPLE ISSUE OFFER
714 COLLINGTON DR.
CARY, NC 27511
OR CHECK OUT SAMPLE ISSUES AT THEIR WEB site:
www.theromantic.com

Raising Children Drug Free

One of the most important concerns every parent has is how to raise their children free of drugs and the abusive use of alcohol. Developing strong loving relationships with our children is essential as is teaching proper standards of right and wrong and setting and enforcing rules. Equally important is teaching children the facts about alcohol and drugs. If you are a parent, you will absolutely want

Learning Something New

to get a free copy of *Growing Up Drug Free....A Parent's Guide To Prevention*. In this excellent guide you will find very specific activities and lessons, full color photos and descriptions of drugs and drug paraphernalia. It comes to you from the Department of Education. Call them toll-free at: **1-800-624-0100**

Learn About Coal

If you're a teacher or a student interested in finding out more about coal and how it is found, extracted, transported and used, be sure to get the informative booklets and poster available free from the American Coal Foundation. When you write, be sure to indicate your organization or school, grade level, and phone number so they can provide appropriate materials for you. A few of the items available include:

Coal Poster - A large colorful poster with important coal information

Coal: Ancient Gift Serving Modern Man

Let's Learn About Coal - includes puzzles and word games explain how coal is formed.

What Everyone Should Know About Coal - Describes the different types of coal, how it is used and how it effects the envirnment.

Coal Science Fair Ideas - to help spark interest in coal plus tips to help you get started with a project. Write to:

AMERICAN COAL FOUNDATION
1130 17TH ST NW, SUITE 220
WASHINGTON, DC 20036-4604

Free Money For College

If you're a parent with children in college or about to go off to college, you have discovered just how expensive it is. The good news is that there are all kinds of financial assistance programs available for virtually everyone. All that is necessary is to go through a series of steps in your search for the money you will need.

Here we've listed a number of important and easy to use resources to help you effectively direct your search for college money. One of the most efficient ways of locating financial assistance that applies to you is to use the Internet. Naturally this means having access to a computer. If you do not yet own a computer, you can check with your local library or ask a friend who has a computer to allow you to use theirs. Also most schools today have computers your child can use.

Free College Aid

It's a little known fact but there are literally billions of dollars in financial aid available to help students pay for their college education. This money is available from thousands of public and private sources. Much of this money is available as outright

Free Money For College

grants that never has to be repaid. Still more money for college is available through low-cost loans and work-study programs. The first place to check is with the financial aid office of the college of your choice. Counselors will help you locate all the sources of money including scholarships, grant-in-aid, work study programs and low interest government-backed student loans. Next, you will definitely want to use the Internet as a tool to search for financial assistance. In the listings that follow, you'll find the most important sources.

Free Computer Search To Locate College Scholarships And Grants

Are you looking for money for college? The Internet is the very best way to search for the financial aid that is waiting for you. Start your search with this computerized web site which was developed by the nation's financial aid administrators. At this web site you will find a number of great scholarship searches that are entirely free.

What you will do is fill out a detailed questionnaire on your computer screen while you are online. The information you list about yourself and your background on this questionnaire will be compared to the information in huge databases and you will be notified of the grants, scholarships and loans you qualify for. To begin your search go to the web site: **www.finaid.org/finaid**

Once you are at the finaid.org web site you will find several other sites (listed below) where you will find the questionnaires that will begin your search. They will ask you to answer several pages of specific questions about your background and financial situation. Based on the answers to your these questions it will set up a personalized profile that will match your specific skills, needs and interests. It will begin the search through its massive database for all of the money that is available for you. Once the search is completed, it will report to you exactly what assistance you qualify for and exactly how to get it.

And despite the enormous value of this search and the fact that other organizations have charged up to $300 for this service, there is no charge to you for these extensive searches!

• **FastWEB:** A database of more than 300,000 private-sector scholarships, grants, fellowships and loans is the Internet's largest free scholarship search site. Also, FastWEB Classifieds offers a tailored search of employment opportunities across the U.S. that is available to students absolutely free.
Internet address: **www.fastweb.com**

• **SRN Express:** A version of the Scholarship Resource Network (SRN) database with information from several hundred thousand financial aid sources with a special focus on scholarship information. They also have information on student loan forgiveness programs for college graduates who need alternatives for loan repayment.
Internet address: **www.srnexpress.com**

Low Cost Loans To Pay for College

Sallie Mae is the leading source of money for col-

Free Money For College

lege loans. They will be delighted to help you find the money you will need to pay for college.

The College Answer Service. First, they have a toll free hotline where you can speak to a financial aid expert who will answer your questions dealing with paying for college, loans, aid packages, advice on financial aid applications, deadlines, and lots more. You will also learn how to save hundreds of dollars with the lowest cost student loans available. Due to the low interest rates they offer, loans with Sallie Mae can cost a lot less to pay back. Call them Monday through Friday between the hours of 9am to 9pm EST at: **1-800-891-4599.**

Sallie Mae also has a number of helpful booklets including *Paying For College* and *Borrowing For College.*

Paying For College is a comprehensive guidebook which provides thorough advice on planning for a college education. The book addresses key financial aid terms, formulas for calculating the 'Expected Family Contribution', an overview of the federal student loan program and a summary of loan repayment programs …many of which reward students for on-time payment.

Borrowing For College helps students and their parents choose low-cost student loan lenders in their area. To get free copies call: **1-800-806-3681**

www.sallie.mae.com One visit to this web site and you will see just how valuable it is. You'll be able to do a free online search for scholarship money available from over 300,000 sources. Plus you can e-mail your financial aid questions & get fast advice from experts.

Free Money For College

Student Loans & Grants

If you're a college student or plan to be one and are short of money to continue your education, be sure to get a free copy of *Funding Your Education* and *The Student Guide*. They are the most comprehensive resources of student financial aid from the U.S. Department of Education. It covers major aid programs including Pell Grants, Stafford Loans and PLUS loans. Contact:

THE U.S. DEPARTMENT OF EDUCATION
400 MARYLAND AVE. S.W. ROOM 2097
WASHINGTON. D.C. 20202
OR CALL THEIR INFORMATION HOTLINE: **1-800-4-FED-AID**

Also, for information on Federal student aid backed by the U.S. Government, be sure to visit the Department of Education's web site at:
www.ed.gov

Paying For College

With the costs of going to college spiraling out of sight many students are not able to attend college without financial assistance. This guide will help you with all the many questions you have about paying for your college education. Ask for *Meeting College Costs*, free from:

THE COLLEGE BOARD
45 COLUMBUS AVE.
NEW YORK, NY 10023-6992

Free Money For College

Free Help Choosing The Right College

Selecting the right college or university can be a challenging and time-consuming task but one that will bring immeasurable rewards for the rest of your life. To help you make the right choice, State Farm Insurance has a fantastic guide from U.S. News and World Report. In its close to 300 pages you will find valuable information about tuition, room and board, financial aid, entrance requirements and lots more on over 1,400 universities and colleges. To get your free copy of this important guide, call State Farm toll-free at:
1-888-733-8368

College Planning

T. Rowe Price's College Planning Guide helps parents project what a college education may cost for their young children so you can plan ahead and start saving now. It's free. Call: **1-800-225-5132.**

$1,500 To Pay For College

Paying for college can be a huge burden, but now there's hope. In fact it's called the 'Hope Scholarship' and actually it's even better than a scholarship because it's an income-tax credit aimed at middle income people. There are no applications to fill out. All you do is when you file your tax return, you subtract the amount of the credit right from the amount you owe. In effect, the government gives you up to $1,500 back per student. Here's how it works:

- The income tax credit equals 100% of the first $1,000 paid in college tuition and fees plus 50% of the next $1,000, for a total of $1,500.
- The credit is for you, your spouse or your dependent children in their first and second academic year as long as they're enrolled at least half time in a 2 year or 4 year college or in a trade school.
- You can claim as many credits as you have qualified students. So for example, if you have two children in their first or second year of college, you get $3,000.
- To qualify for the full credit your adjusted gross income must be under $40,000 if you are single (between $40,000 and $50,000 you still get a partial credit) or $80,000 if you are married (between $80,000 and $100,000 you still get a partial credit.)
- Tuition must be paid in the same year you claim the credit. For example, you must have paid the tuition in 1999 to claim a credit on your 1999 tax return.
- In addition to the Hope Scholarship, there is also

the Lifetime Learning credit of $1,000 which can be taken for any student of any age, for any number of years and even for a single adult education course, for example. Right now this credit is worth up to $1,000 (20% of the first $5,000 paid in tuition and fees) and you can take just one credit per tax return no matter how many students you may have in school. While you can't take both credits at once for the same student, you can take the Hope credit for one and the Lifetime Learning credit for another.

If you qualify, these tax credits can be an important source of additional money for college. For more information, ask the IRS or your accountant.

Money Matters

A Share Of America

Getting Help When You Invest and *Understanding Stocks and Bonds* and two fascinating guides that tells all about how the stock market works and the important role it plays in our nation's economy. The New York Stock Exchange also has an excellent series of educational aids, huge wall posters, ticker tape, teacher guides and more. Write to:
NY STOCK EXCHANGE
EDUCATIONAL SERVICES
11 WALL ST.
NEW YORK, NY 10005

Do You Need A Financial Planner?

Are you are always having difficulty making ends meet? Maybe you would like to have more money to enjoy your retirement. You might need the help of a financial planner. *When and How to Choose a Financial Planner* is a free booklet available from the National Endowment for Financial Education, that will help you choose a planner. This 12 page guide gives basic information on when you should seek advice, as well as how to go about choosing a finan-

cial planner. To get your free copy, write to:
NATIONAL ENDOWMENT FOR FINANCIAL EDUCATION
DEPARTMENT 1778
5299 DTC BLVD. SUITE 1300
ENGLEWOOD, CO 80111-3321

Finding The Right Financial Adviser

Everybody with assets to protect, regardless of their age, should have a financial advisor. Just remember, you worked hard for your money and now it's time to make your money work harder for you. Oppenheimer Funds has published a guide, *Finding A Financial Adviser Who's Right For You*. It will take you through the process step-by-step of selecting names, conducting interviews, making the final decision, and maintaining a relationship that will be profitable. This is a must for anyone looking for help in making intelligent financial planning decisions. To order your free copy call:
1-800 525-7048.

How To Make Educated Investments

American Century Investments is offering free investor education materials you might find useful. Here are some of the more popular ones:

IRA CHOICES AND CHALLENGES, a 16 page booklet that compares the different types of IRAs created by the 1997 Tax Relief Act

INVESTING WITH A PURPOSE, a 26 page booklet that

explains the concepts of diversification and asset allocation, offers four sample portfolios based on your stage in life, and includes a do-it-yourself investor profile questionnaire

College Planner, a slide-rule calculator for determining college costs

Post-Retirement Calculator, a slide-rule calculator for determining how long your savings will last, depending on how much you spend

Fast TaxFacts, a laminated card with tax rates and general information on IRA rules and IRA Rollovers and much more.

For your free copy of any or all of these booklets or calculators, call American Century Investments toll-free at:
1-800-345-2021

Tax Saving Investments

If would like to lower your income taxes maybe you should be looking at investments that are completely or partially free of federal, state or local income tax. Lebenthal, one of the nation's leading municipal bond dealers has the *Lebenthal Municipal Bond Information Kit* that will show you the advantages of investing in tax-exempt bonds. For your kit, call them toll-free at:
1-888-425-6116

Before You Buy A Franchise

Did you ever think of starting your own business maybe by buying one of the thousands of franchises

Money Matters

that are available? Before you decide to make your mark as an franchise entrepreneur, you owe it to yourself to learn more about franchising. Some valuable sources to contact are:

The *ACCESS Franchise Directory*, the most comprehensive database of franchise information on the Internet. This site lists more than 2500 franchises at their web address:
www.entremkt.com

The Federal Trade Commission, which has an excellent 12 page pamphlet called *A Consumer Guide to Buying a Franchise*. You can download it from the FTC's Web site:
www.ftc.gov

Free Help Starting A Business

Service Corps of Retired Executives (SCORE) can give you free advice on starting a small business. This is a group of working and retired executives and business owners who donate their time and expertise to provide individual confidential business counseling and business workshops for aspiring entrepreneurs and small business owners. To find the SCORE office nearest you, call them toll-free at:
1-800-634-0245

Money To Start A Business

If you've always wanted to start a business but never had the money to do it, now's your chance. The U.S. Small Business Administration (SBA) is a great re-

source you can use for starting that business. They have a variety of programs to help the new entrepreneur including a loan guarantee program you might want to use. The SBA has offices throughout the U.S. But to find out more, first call the SBA Answer Desk at:
1-800-827-5722
Or visit the U.S. Small Business Administration web site:
www.SBAonline.SBA.Gov

Searching The Web For The Best Mortgage Deal

Before you shop for a new mortgage online, check to find out what rates are being charged in your area. Even a slightly lower interest rate can often save you many thousands of dollars over the repayment period of your loan. Once you've become an informed consumer you can shop intelligently for the best mortgage loan whether it's on the Internet or at your local financial institution. Here are three online sites where you can find up-to-date rate information and lots more. They don't offer mortgages directly but will provide you with all kinds of highly useful information you can use:

FANNIE MAE
www.fanniemae.com/index.html
Provides all kinds of mortgage and home refinancing information. They also list the co-op, condos and houses that they own due to foreclosures throughout the nation. A great place to shop for a terrifc buy on your next home.

MORTGAGE MARKET INFORMATION SERVICE, INC.
www.interest.com/rates.html
Employs an easy-to-use click-on map to find up-to-date information about mortgage rates and lenders in specific areas around the country.

MICRO SURF
www.microsurf.com
This site is the largest independent source of mortgage information on the Internet. While they are not lenders or brokers, they do allow you to compare the rates offered by 1,300 lenders nationwide who update their rates daily.

Choosing The Mortgage That's Right For You

Are you ready to shop for a mortgage? This easy to read 40 page guide can help. It walks you through the mortgage shopping process in three easy steps. Discover how big a mortgage loan you can afford, how to choose the mortgage that's right for you, and how to compare terms commonly used among lenders. This guide is free from:
FANNIE MAE
PO BOX 27463
RICHMOND, VA 23286-8999.
OR CALL 1-800 688-HOME

Money Matters

Save Thousands of Dollars – Shop For Your Mortgage Online

Your home mortgage is the most important financial transaction your family is likely to ever make. But if you have ever shopped for a mortgage you know how long, tedious... and expensive the process can be. Now there may be a better way...online mortgages.

With the application filed out on your home computer and sent electronically, online mortgage applications offers you a combination of speed, convenience and cost savings. Financial experts agree that getting your mortgage online will almost definitely save you money. In fact, sometimes the savings can total tens of thousands of dollars over the term of the mortgage! The reason is that the online mortgage companies deal with lenders throughout the country and they are constantly searching for the very best rates to offer you. Mortgage approval can often be a matter of minutes instead of weeks or even months that it takes the traditional way.

In addition, several of the online mortgage companies offer you a variety of additional services that include help in finding a home, tips on negotiating and inspecting the home you plan to buy and lots more. Here are three of the leading online mortgage companies you can contact directly through their Internet sites:

Intuit Inc.: www.quickenmortgage.com

E-Loan: www.eloan.com

HomeShark: www.homeshark.com

Money Matters

Free Money...Do You Have Unclaimed Funds Waiting For You?

Did you know that there are actually $300 billion dollars in unclaimed funds waiting for their rightful owner to come along? What often happens is that people move and forget to notify everyone of their new address. You may have a bank account from years ago with money that was never withdrawn. Also, there are 3 million stock brokerage accounts with securities that belong to shareholders who are currently lost. If you think there's even a remote possibility that you have funds or securities you have forgotten about, be sure to check at these web sites and see what you have and how you can claim your funds. It's like winning the lottery!

The first Internet website is for a lost funds search company called The CapitaLink. Their web address is:
www.ifast.com

And, 25 states with web sites have a combined site where you can search by name for unclaimed property they hold. Check out this web site at:
www.unclaimed.org

Download Coupon Savings

One of the traditional ways of saving money is to clip coupons and use them in your shopping. The trouble is that it takes a lot of time to scour the newspapers to find the coupons you will use. Now there's an easier way of getting those same savings without the hassle...dowloading them from the Internet.

One of the leading companies helping you get these coupons online is called *CoolSavings*. Their electronic method of couponing has met with great success and their web site has quickly become one of the most visited Internet sites. The way it works is that you go to their web site and fill out a brief online questionnaire, select the coupons you want, download them into your computer and print them out. You'll find a vast array of companies at their web site including everything from local pizza delivery stores to national chains like J.C. Penney, Toys 'R Us and McDonalds. To check out their free web site go to:
www.coolsavings.com

IRA - Roth IRA – What's The Difference?

You probably know that Individual Retirement Accounts commonly known at 'IRA's' are allowed to help you save tax sheltered money for retirement. But do you know what the difference is between an IRA and a ROTH IRA? To help taxpayers learn more about all kinds of IRA's and so you can determine which is right for you, the IRS has updated its 'Publication 590' that focuses on these types of accounts. Call them at:
1-800-829-3676

OR VISIT THEIR WEBSITE AT: **WWW.IRS.USTREAS.GOV**

Money Matters

Planning For Retirement

Whether you are just starting to invest or already have a plan, Charles Schwab has a free source book that will help you with those important financial decisions. *The Essential Investor* will help you plan for a more secure financial future. It includes a checklist of investing essentials to get you started as well as sample portfolios and even a quick retirement planner. Ask for *The Essential Investor* when you call:
1-800-924-0868

The Best Online Broker

The financial newspaper, Barrons, rates Morgan Stanley Dean Witter Online as the #1 overall online broker. If you buy or sell securities over the Internet and would like to get important financial information about MSDW's online brokerage services, call toll-free:
1-800-58-INVEST
Or visit their web site:
www.msdw.com

Understanding Mutual Funds

A Guide to Understanding Mutual Funds is available free from the Investment Company Institute, the mutual fund industry's principal trade group. This guide describes the various types of funds and explains the risks involved, discusses how funds are structured, and how to set up an investment plan. They also discuss important tax considerations and

give you a guide to finding and analyzing information on funds yourself. To get your free copy, call:
202-326-5800

Mutual Fund Report Card

Are you holding the right mutual funds? Charles Schwab has a series of report cards for different mutual funds that give you their ratings, performance and growth records. You can request up to three reports for any mutual funds even if they're not available through Schwab. There's no cost or obligation. Call them toll-free at:
1-800-540-8117
Or visit their web site at: **www.schwab.com**

Women and Money

The *Money Minded* web site is designed specifically for women. It addresses questions about saving, family goals, and investing mostly from a woman's perspective. On the site you'll find featured entrepreneurs and financial risk-takers who offer their great advice and important information for women and their money. Their web address is:
www/.moneyminded.com/index.htm

Mutual Fund Info

Waterhouse Securities, Inc. will send you the *Top Performing Mutual Funds Guide* and the *Mutual Funds Information and Comparison Guide*. If you

Money Matters

invest in mutual funds or are thinking of investing, you'll definitely want these free guides. Call toll-free:
1-800-708-9283
Or visit them at their web site:
www.waterhouse.com

Getting Your Budget In Shape

To help you keep your budget in shape, the Internet has a number of helpful sites that will help you:

SMART CALC:
You'll find a number of very useful calculators at this web site that will help you budget your spending, determine how much your mortgage payments will be... and lots more.
www.smartcalc.com

HEALTHY CASH
Are you an overspender? Are there things you can do to avoid the devastating effects of this habit? To discover your 'Spending Personality,' take a self-test online at *Healthy Cash* which is at the Health World Online Web site at:
**www.healthy.net/library/articles/cash/
assessment/assessment.htm**

THE MONEY WISE HOME GUIDE:
**www.mpicture.com/homeguide/financial/
debt.htm**

Money Matters

Tips To Get Financially Fit

- Pay off your credit card debt to reduce interest expenses. Start with the credit cards that have the highest finance charge. If possible pay off your balance every month.
- Switch to using credit cards with no annual fees.
- Be a smart shopper and always shop around before you buy something especially big ticket items.
- If you do find it necessary to carry balances on your credit card, be certain you are not using a card that charges a high percentage rate on unpaid balances. Remember, you can get the interest rate lowered with most credit cards just by asking for a lower rate. Tell them you are thinking of dropping their card and using another one that charges a lower interest rate. You'll be amazed at how often they will offer you a substantially lower rate rather than lose you as a customer.
- Join a credit union if you're eligible. Credit unions generally charge lower fees than banks especially if you maintain only small balances in your checking and savings accounts.

Money Facts

The Federal Reserve Bank of Atlanta has a free fascinating booklet that describes how currency is designed, printed, circulated and eventually destroyed. There's even a section on how to redeem bills that might have been damaged in a fire or chewed up by the family dog. Ask for *Fundamental Facts About*

U.S. Money. Write to:
FEDERAL RESERVE BANK OF ATLANTA
PUBLIC AFFAIRS DEPT.
ATLANTA, GA 30303

Fast Banking

The American Bankers Association's free booklet on *A Dozen Ways to Save Time and Money at the Bank* offers a variety of tips on money management. It will help you take charge of your finances. For a free copy, write to:
ATTENTION: *"A DOZEN TIPS'*
THE AMERICAN BANKERS ASSOCIATION
1120 CONNECTICUT AVE. N.W.
WASHINGTON, D.C. 20036

Free Help Choosing The Right Mortgage

Are you ready to shop for a mortgage? This easy to read 40 page guide can help. It walks you through the mortgage shopping process in three easy steps. Discover how big a mortgage loan you can afford, how to choose the mortgage that's right for you, and how to compare terms commonly used among lenders. This guide is free from:
FANNIE MAE
PO BOX 27463
RICHMOND, VA 23286-8999
OR CALL TOLL-FREE: **1-800 688-HOME**

Important Tax Infomation For Mutual Fund Investors

This helpful 20 page booklet, *Tax Do's & Don'ts For Mutual Fund Investors*, lists 13 points to consider about the tax aspects of mutual fund investing. For example, it warns you *not* to assume that all fund distributions are the same, that you owe no taxes on reinvested dividends or that you owe no tax if you exchange shares from one fund for shares of another in mutual fund 'families.' For a copy of the free booklet, write to:
ICI
1401 H St. N.W., Suite 1200
Washington, D.C. 2005

Finding The Right Tax Professional

When tax time comes around it's always an excellent idea to have a tax pro help you. To help you through the difficult process of choosing the right tax pro, you might want to start by getting the names of professionals in your area and interviewing a number of them. For the names of tax experts in your area, call the National Association of Enrolled Agents toll-free at:
1-800 424-4339.

Before You Go Into Business

If you've ever thought of going into business and

starting a new corporation, here's a booklet you will definitely want to get. *Starting Your Own Corporation* will answer many of the questions you may have regarding setting up the right kind of corporation. For your free copy, call the 'Corporation Company' at: **1-800-542-2677**

Personal Finance Helplines

If you are not sure where to turn for good advice regarding your personal finances, here are several toll-free hotlines you can turn to for help. They will either provide you with the information you need or they will tell you where you can go for further assistance.

Financial Planning

THE INSTITUTE OF CERTIFIED FINANCIAL PLANNERS - FOR BROCHURES & REFERRALS, CALL: **1-800-282-7526**.

THE AMERICAN INSTITUTE OF CERTIFIED PUBLIC ACCOUNTANTS' PERSONAL FINANCIAL PLANNING DIVISION CALL: **1-800-862- 4272**.

THE INTERNATIONAL ASSOCIATION FOR FINANCIAL PLANNING CALL: **1-404-395-1605**.

THE NATIONAL ASSOCIATION OF PERSONAL FINANCIAL ADVISERS. CALL: **1-800 366-2732**.

THE AMERICAN SOCIETY OF CLU AND CHFC. CALL: **1-800-392-6900**.

Money Matters

Investing For Retirement

IRA Transfers is a free brochure that explains tax-sheltered retirement investing. It can help you get the most from your investments. It is published by the AARP Investment Program from Scudder, Stevens & Clark - a group of no-load mutual funds designed for members of the AARP, but open to investors of any age. (No-load means there is no sales commission.) For free a copy, call: **1-800-322 2282, Ext. 8271.**

The State Tax Laws: A Guide for Investors Aged 50 and Over is another free publication from AARP. Scudder prepared this 112 page guide in conjunction with the National Conference of State Legislatures. For a copy call them toll-free:
1-800-322-2282, EXT 8254

Should You Buy U.S. Government Securities?

Americans have been buying Series E Savings bonds for many years. But few people know they can also buy Treasury Bonds and Bills that pay even higher interest. For more information on how you can get in on this no-risk, high-yield investment, write for *U.S. Securities Available to Investors*. From:
PUBLIC DEBT INFORMATION
U.S. DEPARTMENT OF THE TREASURY
WASHINGTON, D.C. 20226

Money Matters

Choosing The Right Stock Broker

The best way to find a good stockbroker is to ask for referrals from friends, professional acquaintances or from your family. If you have any questions and would like to check on a particular broker's background, call The National Association of Securities Dealers at:
1-800-289-9999

How Much Interest Are You Getting On Your Savings Bonds?

Did you know that all Series E Savings Bond issued since 1941 are still earning interest? If you own any bonds tucked away in a safety deposit box and would like to know exactly how much they're worth today, write for *Tables of Redemption Values For Savings Bonds* from:
BUREAU OF PUBLIC DEBT-SAVING BOND OPERATIONS
200 THIRD AVE.
PARKERSBURG, WV 26101-1328
Or visit their Web site: **www.savingbonds.gov**

Get Your Money Back

Did your dog chew up some money you left on the table? Did it get partially destroyed in a fire? Well the U.S. Department of Treasury can help get that money back for you. Drop them a line with a plausible detailed explanation. Once the claim is processsed and verified, the actual payment is made by federal check. For more information write:

Money Matters

U.S. DEPARTMENT OF THE TREASURY
OFFICE OF CURRENCY STANDARDS
15TH STREET & PENNSYLVANIA AVE., N.W.
WASHINGTON, D.C. 20220
OR CALL: **1-202-622-2000**

Getting A New Mortgage

If you are looking for a new mortgage either to buy a new house or to take advantage of lower mortagage rates, it is important that you learn how to evaluate the type of mortgage that is best for you. As a first step you might call First Financial Equity on their toll-free number for more information and for answers to your mortgage questions. Call them toll-free:
1-800-454-0505

How To Evaluate Your Investments

Before you make any significant investment, learn what to look for to find the one that's best for you. Also discover how to evaluate your investment and determine how well it meets your objectives. The first step is to ask for *Evaluating Investment Performance,* when you contact:
NEUBERGER & BERMAN
INDIVIDUAL ASSET MANAGEMENT GROUP
605 THIRD AVE.
NEW YORK, NY 10158
OR CALL: **800-234-9840**

Money Matters

Global Utilities Fund

Basic utilities such as water and electricity are always in demand and telecommunications is growing in all countries. That's why the Franklin Global Utilities Fund might be a growth fund for you. They will manage a portfolio especially designed for you. If this sounds like something you would consider, call today for a free brochure and prospectus:
1-800 342-5236 OR WRITE:
FRANKLIN FUNDS
777 MARINERS ISLAND BOULEVARD
SAN MATEO, CA 94404-1585

Savings Just Because You're Over 50

Now that an ever growing part of the population is over 50 years old, there are lots of bargains and discounts available just for the asking. Remember if you don't ask you'll never know. In any store you shop in always check to see if there are certain days or certain times when seniors are offered discounts or specials. Many hotels offer discounts on their rooms as well as discounts if you eat in their restaurants. You can also apply for a travel club card if you are a member of AARP…The American Association of Retired Persons. Their toll-free phone number is:
1-800-424-3410

Learning About Mutual Funds

If you would like to learn all about mutual funds and find out which are the best ones for you, check

out the Strong Equity Performers from Dreyfus. Call them toll-free at:
1-800 THE LION EXT 4043
Or visit a Dreyfus Financial Center via the Internet at:
www.dreyfus.com/funds

The Lowest Cost Life Insurance - Guaranteed!

If you are looking for the maximum life insurance coverage at the lowest cost...this one's for you. A company called Quotesmith actually guarantees they will find the lowest term life rates in America or they'll send you $500.00! That's quite a claim but it's worth checking them out.

What they do when you request a quote by calling their toll-free number is scan the 350 insurance companies in their database and give you the lowest price quotes that that search comes up with. There is no charge for their service so you may want to give them a try. It could save you a bundle. You can call them toll-free at:
1-800-431-1147

Tax-Free Income Fund

If you are in a high tax bracket and would like to lower your tax bite, did you know you can start earning tax-free income with as little as $1,000 with instant liquidity and no sales or redemption fee? For more information on tax-free investing, call:
1-800-638-5660

Money Matters

Free Fund Raising Kit

If your school or organization needs money, this *free fund-raising kit* will teach you how. This kit will help show your group how to collect member's recipes and publish them into a great cookbook. Write for your free kit to:
FUNDCRAFT
410 HIGHWAY 72 WEST
BOX 340
COLLIERVILLE, TN 38017

Lower Your Insurance Premiums

Did you know that if you're in the market for Medicare and Medigap policies for health insurance for yourself or a parent, your premiums will be lowest if you enroll between three months before, to four months after your 65th birthday? After that the premiums may grow by 10 percent each year you wait. For more information, ask for The Social Security Administration's free *Guide to Health Insurance for People with Medicare*. Contact:
THE HEALTH INSURANCE ASSOCIATION OF AMERICA
PUBLICATION OFFICE
555 13TH ST. NW SUITE 600-E
WASHINGTON, D.C. 20004
OR CALL TOLL-FREE: 1-800-772-1213

Mutual Funds For Investors Over 50

You've worked hard to save money for your retirement and to help it grow, now you must be sure you do everything you can to preserve and protect that

important investment. *Understanding Mutual Funds: A Guide for Investors Aged 50 and Over*, defines the basics to help older individuals choose funds appropriate for their needs. It's your free! Contact:
AARP Investment Program
Scudder Processing Center
Box 5014, Janesville, WI 53547
Or call: **800-322-2282, ext 4884**

Check Out Money Market Funds

If you want higher interest than you will get in a bank but still want instant access to your money, be sure to check out the money market funds. To find out more about money market funds, contact one or more of these large funds and ask for their *prospectus and information package:*

DREYFUS SERVICE CORP., 600 MADISON AVE., NEW YORK, NY 10022
OR CALL: 1-800-645-6561

FIDELITY CASH RESERVES, P.O. BOX 832, BOSTON, MA 02103. CALL: 1-800-544-6666.

IRS Or H&R Block?

Few people realize that the IRS is committed to giving taxpayers every legitimate deduction they're entitled to. The IRS has toll-free numbers throughout the country you can call for assistance and/or forms. As a start, for answers to your income tax

Money Matters

questions, call The Internal Revenue Service's tax hotline toll-free:
1-800-829-1040

The IRS also has a series of helpful publications such as *Federal Income Tax* available free of charge. Call the toll-free number for this publication or a list of the others available.

The IRS also has a toll-free number to assist deaf/hearing-impaired taxpayers who have access to TV-Phone/Teletypewriter equipment (800-428-4732).

"Congratulations! You've Just Won...."

It's a simple fact of life...there are people out there who wouldn't give a second thought to conning you out of your life savings. One of the most common scams is calling elderly people with an exciting announcement such as... *"Congratulations, Mr. Jones, you're name has been selected as the winner of an exciting cruise. Isn't that great? All you need to do to claim your prize is to put up a good faith deposit by sending us a check for $$$$$$."*

Hang up the phone right there. One rule you must always follow is:

Never...EVER buy anything or pay money to claim your *'free prize.'* No reputable company will ever ask you to send them money to get a 'free' prize.

For more information on these scams and what you can do to keep from falling prey to one, get your free copy of *Telemarketing Travel Fraud*. It's your

free from:
**Public Reference
Federal Trade Commission
Room 130
Washington, DC 20580**
Or Call them at: **202-326-2222**

Be Your Own Broker

If you have a computer and like to make your own investment decisions without the help of a stockbroker, this one may be for you. Charles Schwab has free computer software you can use to buy and sell securities over the Internet for just $29.95 for up to 1,000 shares. The software also allows you to do your own research using various Internet databases, track the stocks you are interested in and lots more. For more information call:
1-800-E-Schwab

For a listing of online brokers that allow you to trade for a small fraction of what it would cost you from a full service broker, see the listings at the end of this section.

Money Matters

Save Hundreds of Dollars On Every Stock Trade By Trading Online

12 ONLINE BROKERS CHARGING $20 PER TRADE OR LESS

If you are an active trader or investor in stocks and make all of your own buying and selling decisions without the advice of a broker, you can save a lot of money on your trades by using an online broker.

Here are stock brokerage firms that charge $20.00 per transaction or less for online trades. Some, like Ameritrade, even charge less than $10 for trades that would cost several hundred dollars at a full-service firm! The services they offer, speed of execution and investor financial requirements vary from one firm to the next. Most firms also let you trade using their toll-free phone number but they generally charge somewhat more for these trades than those you make online. To find out more, check out their Internet sites at the web addresses listed here or call their toll-free phone numbers.

Money Matters

BROKER	INTERNET ADDRESS	TOLL-FREE
Ameritrade	www.ameritrade.com	800-669-3900
Brown & Co.	www.brownco.com	800-965-1191
Bull & Bear Securities	www.bullbear.com	800-847-4200
Morgan Stanley Dean Witter	www.msdw.com	800-688-6896
CSFB Direct	www.csfbdirect.com	800-825-5723
E*trade	www.etrade.com	800-786-2575
JB Oxford & Co.	www.jboxford.com	800-656-1776
Quick & Reilly	www.quick-reilly.com	800-368-0446
Scottrade, Inc.	www.discountbroker.com	800-619-7283
Sunlogic Securities	www.sunlogic.com	800-556-4600
Wall Street Electronica	www.wallstreete.com	888-925-5783
TD Waterhouse	www.tdwaterhouse.com	800-934-4479

Computers & The Best Internet Sites

They'll be a time in the not too distant future that having a computer will be as common as having a telephone...and just as essential. One of the main reasons for having a computer is to gain access to the Internet (sometimes called the World Wide Web or just the 'Web'). What this means is that just by typing in an address of a web site, your computer is instantly transported to a place that could very well be on the other side of the world...all for the price of a local phone call!

If you don't have a computer yet but would like to see just what the Internet is all about, here are a number of ways of getting started.

First, virtually all libraries across the nation have computers you can use free of charge with access to the Internet. It's very easy to use and the librarian will be happy to show you how to get started.

Next, if your budget will allow it, you might want to get your own computer and 'modem' (a little box that hooks you up via your phone line to the Internet.) The most affordable way to get started is with a used computer which you can buy for as little as $100-$200 at stores like Computer Renaissance which sells only used computers. (Incidentally, to use the Internet it isn't necessary to have the newest or fastest computer. However it is good idea to get a fast modem (cost: $50-$120) which will speed your access to the Internet.

Finally, if your budget will allow, there is now a computer called the Apple iMac (under $1,000) which is already set up as it comes out of the box with everything including a built-in modem to get you online in a matter of ten minutes.

Free Computer Services

One of the big advantages of owning a computer is that it puts the world right at your finger tips. At a touch of a key you have instant access to people and sources of information that may be on the other side of the globe. In an instant you can surf the Internet with thousands of fascinating web sites. To get started with free software and in many cases with free online trials, call these toll-free numbers: **America Online** general info: **1-800-827-6364.** To get up to 500 free hours to get started on **America OnLine, call: 1-888-265-8002.**
Compuserve: 1-800-848-8199
AT&T Worldnet: 1-800-640-4488
Microsoft Network: 1-800-386-5550
Prodigy: 1-800-776-3449
Earthlink: 1-800-876-3151

KEEP IN MIND: If you don't have a computer or Internet access at home, most libraries have computers you can use and librarians who are happy to show you how to use them.

Free Computers Stuff & The Internet

Free Clip Art

If you use pre-drawn clip art in your computer graphics programs for newsletters or ads, you will want to check out the vast array of high quality clip art at this web site. In addition to the thousands of pieces of beautifully drawn clip art at this site, you'll also find links to other sites where you'll find even more clip art...all of it free. Visit their web site at: **www.clipart.com**

Free Computer Supplies

Right now there's intense competition going on between several nationwide computer retailers. Just to get you into their store, each of them offers free computer supplies with a full rebate. For example, in the last several weeks the authors have received several hundred computer diskettes, surge protectors, laser paper, a keyboard, a computer mouse, and other computer related items all of which came with a 100% rebate. Hundreds of dollars in supplies absolutely free! Check your local newspapers for full page ads and inserts for CompUSA, Circuit City and other chain stores.

Best Deals on PC's & Macs

If you are looking for the best deals around in computers, software and accessories, some of the best prices you will find are from mail order companies. Even if you decide to buy from a local store, calling mail order companies will allow you to comparison shop to get the lowest price. Each of the companies listed here have been in business for a number of years and have an excellent reputation for customer satisfaction. When you call, ask for their latest catalog which will be full of important information to help you make an intelligent buying decision. Most companies have a 24-hour customer service line and your orders arrive promptly, often the very next day

PC Connection: 1-800-800-1111
Mac Connection: 1-800-800-0002
PC & MacWarehouse: 1-800 255-6227
DataCOM: 1-800-328-2261
DirectWare: 1-800 490-9273
MacZONE: 1-800-248-0800
PC ZONE: 1-800-258-2088
Tiger: 1-800-888-4437
MacMALL: 1-800-222-2808
MEI: 1-800-634-3478

Free Help With Your Macintosh

If you own a Macintosh or are thinking of buying one and have questions you need answered, there's a toll-free number you can call for help. Apple Help line: **1-800-SOS-APPL.** Or visit their web site: **www.apple.com**

Free Computer Business Information

Computer Business Services will send you free cassettes and color literature on one of today's quick-

est growing industries. We all know the computer industry has taken off like a rocket, and now it's possible for you to be a part of it. To receive free cassettes and color literature on their business opportunities, write to:
COMPUTER BUSINESS SERVICES
CBSI PLAYA, STE. 1180
SHERIDAN, IN 46069

Free Computer Supply Catalog

If you or your company owns a computer, you will want to get a copy of the *Global Computer Supplies Catalog*. This full color catalog lists thousands of computer-related products of all types. Drop a postcard to:
GLOBAL COMPUTER SUPPLIES
11 HARBOR PARK DRIVE
PORT WASHINGTON, NY 11050 OR CALL:
1-800-8-GLOBAL (THAT'S 1-800-845-6225)

Free On The Internet

Thousands of pieces of software are available absolutely free on the Internet. If you have a computer and a modem, accessing the Internet is a simple and easy way to open up a whole new world. Among other things, you will find 'freeware', 'shareware' and free computer application upgrades waiting for you to download into your computer. You will also find full text of hundreds of useful government booklets and reports on a host of fascinating subjects all of which you can download free.

Free Computers Stuff & The Internet

Exploring the Internet...

Web Sites Just For Seniors

If you are a senior citizen, here are Internet addresses of sites that are of special interest to you. Be sure that when you type in the address that you are careful to type it in correctly. Even a very small mistake like the adding or leaving out a space or a period will mean you will not be able to access the site

American Association of Retired Persons:
www.aarp.org

A.A.R.P. Guide to Internet Resources Related to Aging: www.aarp.org/cyber/guide1.htm

Achoo: www.achoo.com

National Library of Medicine's MEDLINE:
www.nim.nih.gov/databases/freemedl.html

National Council on the Aging: www.ncoa.org

New Lifestyles: www.newlifestyles.com

Bigtime Savings With Online Auctions

If you love shopping for bargains, you're in for the time of your life with these Internet auction sites. You can bid on everything from cameras to computers and golf clubs... anytime day or night, 24 hours a day, all without ever leaving the comfort of your home. But just remember that as with a traditional auction you must be careful not to get caught in a bidding frenzy and bid too much just to get something you could have bought for less in a store.

A couple of tips: Find out whether the item is new, used or refurbished. New products should come with a manufacturer's warranty. Check the warranty and return policies.

When buying from someone online, be wary of sellers with e-mail accounts which could be used to mask the seller's identity. Wherever possible, pay for your purchase with your credit card since that will offer you the best protection in case there's a problem. In some instances you are b uying from a private individual but in others (like egghead.com) you are buying directly from a large company which adds an additional layer of protection.

Here are several of the most popular Internet auction sites:

www.ebay.com
This is the largest Internet auction site with everything imaginable from antiques to Beanie Babies. To find the items you are interested in you can enter key words and they will do the work of finding a match for the item you are interested in.

www.surplusauction.com
This site is operated by egghead.com. You'll find all kind of computer equipment and other electronics. Also at **www.egghead.com** you'll find a continuous auction on every kind of item imagineable such as Yamaha keyboards and cordless phones. In addition, at egghead.com you'll find an online liquidation center called surplus direct which is a great place to shop for super bargains of all kinds.

www.auctionwarehouse.com
This site focuses strictly on computer-related equipment.

www.onsale.com
Here you'll find an ongoing auction featuring a wide range of items from tech stuff to vacuum cleaners.

www.ubid.com
At this auction site you'll find not only computer products but all kinds of consumer electronics as well.

www.webauction.com
This auction site is operated by one of the largest computer mail order companies, MacWarehouse.

www.auctionx.com
A good site for computers and other tech equipment.

Free Things, Great Bargains & More On The Internet

Although only a few years old, the most revolutionary change of this century in the way we live, shop, and exchange information has been the advent of the Internet. The Internet has placed the entire world just a mouse click away from you. You can now shop for amazing bargains anywhere in the world. You can empty your attic of old treasures you no longer need (and pick up some extra cash) by selling them at an online auction site. But best of all for all lovers of free things, you can now stuff your mailbox with hundreds of terrific samples and trial offers...all absolutely free and all without ever leaving the comfort of your home.

The day is rapidly approaching when access to the Internet will be as common and as necessary as having a phone. But today although over 80 million people have access to the Internet, what can you do if you don't have a computer yet? Does this mean you have to miss out on all the wonders you'll find on the Internet? Fortunately the answer is "no". You have several options.

The simplest option is to use the computer you'll find at your local library. Virtually all libraries now have computers you can use and a librarian who is happy to show you how to log on to the 'net'. Next, since the prices of computers and Internet access has come way down (and will likely continue to drop), now might be the time to consider taking the plunge and getting a home computer. In fact if you shop around, you'll find numerous offers that allow you to get a computer for free or nearly free just by signing up for Internet access. In any event, no matter what direction you choose, be sure to get some form of Internet access...*soon*.

Now let's take a look at the best the Internet offers for lovers of free things and for bargain shoppers. First lets look at the best sites for those who love getting something for nothing.

www.totallyfreestuff.com
At this site they are trying to build the most comprehensive list of 'free stuff' on the Internet. Just checking through their 29 categories, you'll find just about everything from pet food to CD's, audio tapes, stickers and posters of all types, and product samples like popcorn, milk substitute, Alka Seltzer, nasal strips, Papers, skin care products, pedicure kit...to mention just a few. A great place to visit for all lovers of free things.

www.4free.net
Free health products, free games, free pet stuff and free samples are just a few of the 47 different categories of free things that you'll find at this web site. You can even sign up for news and special offers geared to your interests with hundreds of subjects to choose from.

Free Computers Stuff & The Internet

www.weeklyfreebie.com

Each week you'll find an updated list of free things in categories list pets, food, travel, catalogs, computers and coupons. This site features links to other Internet sites that give away free things. For example, if you click on 'coupons' you are then given a wide choice of categories such as clothing, health & beauty and food. Let's say you then click on 'food', you'll discover links to web sites for Mrs. Fields cookies, I Can't Believe It's Not Butter and Ragu to mention just a few. At each site you'll find information on getting free coupons for various products.

www.freeshop.com

You'll find a hundreds of free and trial offers here at the freeshop.com site. There are dozens of categories to choose from. Start by clicking on the areas of greatest interest to you and you will be presented with an array of products and offers to pick from. Just as an example, there are over 500 magazine offers, over 300 offers for kids & family and more than 100 software offers to choose from...and that's just the beginning. Note that many of the offers are trial offers where you may receive a free issue of a magazine. If you don't want to continue your subscription after you have looked over the free issue, you simply cancel, keep the issue and you owe nothing.

www.freemania.com

Check at the freemania.com web site for the five new free things they add each day plus the hottest and most valuable freebies of the week. Select from listings for apparel, health freebies, cosmetics, food samples and games to mention a few. You'll also find links to over 300 free catalogs so your mailbox will always be filled to overflowing.

www.nojunkfree.com
At this site they believe in bringing you the best freebies on the web. They promise to always filter out all of the stuff they consider to be junk. They offer you a free bi-weekly newsletter filled with free stuff. The web master at this site not only describes the free things you'll receive but also ranks the listing based on the quality of the items received.

www.ncbuy.com
It's called 'The Club' and at this site the free things you'll find change from one week to another. As an example of the kinds of freebies you may find, a recent visit to this site revealed freebies that included a 'Puppy Love Scrapbook' from Purina, a Rainbow Kids Baby Hat, and a personalized Auto e-mail newsletter with driving tips and information on auto recalls and repairs. You'll also find 'SellStuff' which is online classifieds where you can buy or sell used all kinds of things.

IMPORTANT NOTE:
Many of the offers you'll find at the various free things sites are what are called 'trial offers'. With a trial offer you have a certain amount of time to preview the product or publication. After that time, you can keep the product and pay for it or cancel your order and owe nothing. For example, at www.smartbiz.com/cd you will receive a free issue of

Catholic Digest filled with spiritually uplifting and inspirational articles plus wholesome activities for the entire family. That issue is yours to keep with no obligation to continue with a paid subscription. But if you do decide to continue with a subscription to Catholic Digest you'll also receive a free book, *All About Angels*. That's a trial offer.

Just be wary if you are asked to submit your credit card number. With this type of offer your credit card will be charged automatically if you don't cancel within the time allowed (usually 30 days). Unless you are sure you will contact them if you decide not to continue, our advice would be to avoid any offer where you are asked to submit your credit card number to get your freebie.

Free Musical Greeting Card

BlueMountain.com is one of the coolest sites on the Internet today. Here you can e-mail anyone you choose an animated electronic greeting card personalized with your name and message. There are dozens of delightful cards for all occasions to choose from...birthdays, sympathy, weddings and anniversaries plus lots more. Once you've selected the card and personalized it with your message, you then e-mail to the person you are sending it to. Instantly it pops into their e-mail waiting for them to open. When they do open it, they will find a beautifully drawn card with figures that do a little dance to music. You're sure to love this site...and so will the people you send the cards to.
BlueMountain.com

Free Computers Stuff & The Internet

Saving Money With 'Online' Coupons

If you enjoy saving money using coupons, you gonna love this suzicoupon.com site. In fact you'll think you've died and gone to coupon heaven because you'll find virtually every type of coupon imaginable. Here are just a few examples of the dozens of categories available. Let's say you're planning to get married. At Suzi Coupon's "Weddings" link you'll find coupons for discounts on formal wear rental, flowers, photographer and even important detailed information on planning a wedding. Another example is getting a free starter supply of Similac baby formula plus money-saving coupons through the "Clickable Coupon" link. You'll also find coupons for oil change & tires, hotels and plane fare, pet food, infant care and even computer hardware & software. Check it out.
www.suzicoupon.com

Instant Coupon Savings

How would you like to join the more than 3 million smart shoppers who have enrolled in coolsavings.com? Once you fill out a short form online you will be given a free enrollment that will entitle you to receive coupons of your choice downloaded right into your computer and printed out on your own printer. You can start saving money immediately rather than have to wait for your coupons to arrive by mail.
www.coolsavings.com

Catalog Shopping At Home

In addition to using retail stores and the Internet to shop, many people enjoy shopping from mail order catalogs. If that describes you, check out the following Internet sites where you find hundreds of free catalogs waiting for you.

www.shopathome.com
Here you'll find more than 300 catalogs to choose from featuring everything from tasty steaks to tasteful apparel. Simply click on the catalogs you would like to receive and they'll be sent to you.

http://catalog.savvy.com
This site is almost overwhelming in scope. While the individual catalogs are not listed, at any one time up to 10,000 catalogs are available. The way it works is that you select from a list of over 400 topics. Once you click on a topic and fill in your name & address, you will receive any number of catalogs that feature products that you've indicated an interest in.

http://catalog.netcart.com
Although at this site you again select only categories of products you're interested in and not individual catalogs, you will see what free catalogs you're ordering. Choose from a long list of categories including automotive, toys, audio, video, books, fashion and crafts to mention a few.

Free Computers Stuff & The Internet

Get Rid Of Spam

When you sign up for all kinds of free things online, in addition to receiving your free gifts from the company you request them from, you may also receive 'junk mail' or junk e-mail (known as 'spam') once your name has been sold to other companies. You may find the mountain of mail interesting but in case you don't, you can request that your name be removed from these lists. This service is free when you contact Popular Demand at:
www.populardemand.com/popd_unlistme/index.popd

Get The Lowest Interest Rate On Loans

If you have to borrow money for any purpose... mortgage, debt consolidation, credit card repayment, car loan...you know how expensive the interest can be especially if you have to finance a large amount payable over several years. Until recently you were at the mercy of your local bank or lending institution and the rates they charged. Now with the Internet no matter where you live you can actually shop the entire nation for the lowest interest rate at lendingtree.com

LendingTree is the only online loan marketplace where lenders compete for your business. And since they are competing for your business, you will find great rates and terms. You then choose the loan that's best for you. You're likely to find this the easiest way to get a loan you've ever experienced. They

also have loan calculators that will help you determine the amount to borrow and estimate your monthly payments. Check them out at:
www.lendingtree.com

Cheap Threads on the WEB

Bargain hunters who don't want to run all over the place to check out the outlet malls can now check these bargains out on the web:
www.bluefly.com:
Discounts up to 75% Shoes, clothes, accessories, housewares. You type in your size and favorite designer and it will show you items that match.

www.outletmall.com
Men's and women's shoes, clothes and beauty products. The longer the merchandise is on the site the lower the price drops.

www.cyberShop.com
Housewares, electronics, luggage, jewelry, toys, and apparel at discount prices.

Air Fare Bargains

www.priceline.com
Priceline has come up with a novel way of saving you money on your next trip. The way it works is that Priceline gets listings of unsold airline seats and unbooked hotel rooms. Using the Internet you then can name the price you want to pay for the airline ticket or the hotel room. If your price is acceptable you are then booked and if not they will suggest a price that should get you the space you're looking for. The reason it works so well is that airlines and hotels would rather accept a lower price than have their space go unused and get nothing. At this site you will also find attractive rates on home mortgages and automobiles.

www.aa.com
At American Airlines the Internet specials can be viewed online at their web site. If you see a low fare that you want, act quickly because most are quickly snapped up.

my.netscape.com
MyNetscape offers free Web pages which include an airfare tracking service. Once you enter your favorite destinations, the prices are automatically updated when you return to your page.

www.smarterliving.com
At the Smarter Living Web site users can sign up for a free weekly e-mail that summarizes special offers from 20 airlines.

Travelocity.com
Travelocity can help you find the lowest airfares. To make it easy for you, Travelocity generates a color calendar with highlighted dates to indicate the days on which the fare is valid.

Save On Drugs & Vitamins

www.drugstore.com
Here's a great way to shop for all your health needs, as well as beauty products and information. It's a great way to shop for your next prescription without having to wait on line at the pharmacy. They focus on helping you make your life easier by shopping online.

www.planetrx.com
Planet Rx offers prescription drugs as well as OTC medicines, vitamins, herbs, medical supplies and even personal care products such as hair care and eye care products. Planet Rx is not only a place to shop but you also can get unbiased health information that is personalized for you or your family.

Free Computers Stuff & The Internet

Should You Buy or Lease Your Next Car?

How can you get the lowest price on your next car? Should you buy your car or lease it? If you aren't sure about the advantages and disadvantages, next time you look for a car, or you are looking for the best deals there are several sites to check out.

To find the Kelly Blue Book, where you can get information on how much the dealer pays for a car:
www.kbb.com

For financing rates:
www.carwizard.com

For terrific lease deals:
www.intellichoice.com

For the lowest prices on your next car :
www.autobytel.com

If you're interested in getting a good deal on a used car, try:
www.autoconnect.com

To get new car reviews, check prices and compare financing and insurance quotes, go to:
www.carprices.com

Free Computers Stuff & The Internet

Bargain Shopping with Online Auctions

Online auctions are the hottest rage on the Internet today. If you love the challenge and excitement of competing for a super bargain, you must check out the online auction sites. You can do a search through their enormous databases which at any one time may have several million different items being auctioned by individuals throughout the country. You will find everything under the sun from outboard motors to jewelry to furbys and antiques. One thing you should keep in mind as you start placing your bids for items you want is to be careful not to get so caught up in the process that you wind up bidding more for an item than it is worth just so you will 'win' the bidding.

eBay is one of the world's largest online auction sites. It was the first to initiate the person-to-person auction format. The site is easy to use because the seller gets plenty of space to display and describe the item they are auctioning. To make it more comfortable for customers to trade online, eBay offers free insurance through Lloyds of London. Visit them at:
www.ebay.com

Another attractive auction site to check out is ubid. Where eBay focuses mainly on individuals who want to sell items they no longer want, ubid focuses on businesses that want to dispose of surplus inventory, refurbished products and small lots. Check it out, you could come across a great deal:
www.ubid.com

At CNET Auctions you can buy or sell any type of electronic equipment including computers, monitors, printers, digital cameras. You can check them out at:
www.auctions.com

At Yahoo! Auction you you'll find just about everything you can imagine listed within the hundreds of categories of items you can bid on. They will even keep track of all of the open auctions you are currently bidding on. Visit their site at:
http://auction.yahoo.com

Online Computer Auctions
If you are looking for a great buy on computer equipment, try checking out the computer auction sites. These auctions are operated by large computer retailers like Egghead and MicroWarehouse so you can place your bids with confidence. At these sites you will find all kinds of hardware, computers and peripherals with bids often starting as low as $1.00.
www.surplusauction.com
www.auctionwarehouse.com
www.webauction.com

Free Computers Stuff & The Internet

Win Up To $10 Million At This Site

An Internet company called iWon has come up with a unique way of attracting people to its web site...they have a sweepstakes where they give away $10,000 each day, $1 million each month and $10 million once a year. The way it works is that when you go to their site, you have a variety of things you can do...read the news, buy anything from autos to mortgages or search the Internet for other sites you may be interested in. But each time you use iWon to go to a site you earn points. The more sites you visit, the more entries you earn. These entries then automatically enter you in a lottery where you have a chance at winning big cash prizes. All this is free just for using their site. To learn more and to earn entry into their lottery, visit their web site at:
www.iwon.com

Religion

Free King James Bible

If you would like a 764 page copy of the King James version of the Bible, it's yours free from The Church of Jesus Christ of Latter Day Saints...The Mormons. They may ask if you would like to speak with a church member but that is your option and is not required to receive the free bible. They also have a beautifully produced video called *Lamb of God* that is yours for asking. For a free copy of the *King James Bible* or the *Lamb of God* video (both of which will be sent by mail), call toll-free:
1-800-535-1118

Free Devotional Reading For Each Day

Our Daily Bread provides inspirational readings from the scriptures for each day of the month. You'll get a new book each month. Ask them to add your name to their mailing list for this devotional guide plus discovery series booklets as well as a campus journal for young people. All free from:
RADIO BIBLE CLASS
P.O. BOX 2222
GRAND RAPIDS, MI 49555

Religion

Free Catholic Information

The Knights of Columbus has dozens of booklets available on all aspects of the Catholic religion. The only cost is a nominal postage charge (generally 25¢ per booklet). They also have a 10 part home-study Catholic correspondence course that is free for the asking. The course is for both Catholics and non-Catholics who would like to learn more about Catholicism. It is sent in an unmarked envelope. For a complete listing of publications or to get your free correspondence course write to:

CATHOLIC INFORMATION SERVICE
KNIGHTS OF COLUMBUS
BOX 1971
NEW HAVEN, CT 06521

You Can Make A Difference In This World

News Notes are inspirational brochures published by the Christophers 10 times a year and are free for the asking. The Christophers exist for one purpose: to spread the message that one person can make a difference in this world. Write and ask for information on titles available in any of these categories, *News Notes*, books, videocassettes, they even have Spanish language material. Send a postcard to:

THE CHRISTOPHERS
12 EAST 48TH ST.
NEW YORK, NY 10017

Religion

Free Gospel Of Saint John Course

If you would like to learn more about the life of Christ, you can receive a free Gospel of John in English or Spanish (please specify) and a Gospel of John Correspondence Course. Drop a postcard to:
THE POCKET TESTAMENT LEAGUE
PO BOX 800
LITITZ, PA 17543

Beautiful Inspiration

Often in our daily lives events become too much to handle. The Salesian Missions have a beautiful series of booklets that are a pleasure to read and provide inspiration to help make our lives more fulfilling. Excellent! Send a postcard and ask for the *free inspirational booklets* from:
SALESIAN MISSIONS
2 LEFEVRES LANE
NEW ROCHELLE, NY 10801

Inspiration And Prayer

The Lutheran Laymen's League has several religious publications you might like to have. A few of the titles currently available are: *'Escape From Loneliness'*, *'I Am An Alcoholic,'* *'Stress - Problem or Opportunity?'* and *'The Truth About Angels.'* All of them are free from:
INTERNATIONAL LUTHERAN LAYMEN'S LEAGUE
2185 HAMPTON AVE.
ST. LOUIS, MO 63139

Religion

Free From The Worldwide Church Of God

The Worldwide Church of God has an excellent series of booklets available without charge (nor will they make any solicitations of any kind). Titles change frequently so drop a card for a current list of books available. Write to:

WORLDWIDE CHURCH OF GOD
PASADENA, CA 91123.
OR CALL TOLL-FREE: **1-800-423-4444**

Free Bible Reading Guides

For a new understanding of the Bible, you may want to receive the simplified Bible Reading Guides that are yours free from the Real Truth Ministries. To enroll in this bible course, call toll free:
1-800-863-5789

Free for Cars & Drivers

If Your Car's A Lemon...Call This Toll-Free Number

If you're having problems with your car and can't seem to get satisfaction from the dealer or manufacturer don't despair - help is on the way. The Auto Safety Hotline is anxious to hear about your complaint so they can get to work on it. They've even set up a toll-free hotline and an Internet site for you to contact them to report your problem. To report your problem, call toll-free:
1-800-424-9393. OR WRITE TO:
NATIONAL HIGHWAY AND TRAFFIC SAFETY ADMINISTRATION
400 7TH ST., S.W.
WASHINGTON, DC 20590
Or visit their Internet site at: **www.nhtsa.dot.gov**

If at this point you would just like to gather more information about recalls and auto defect reports, call this toll-free number operated by the Technical Information Services division of NHTSA:
1-800-445-0197

NHTSA does not get involved in individual cases of complaints between the conusmer and the dealer or manufacturer. If you have such a complaint, call the Federal Trade Commission for assistance at:
1-202-326-3128

Free For Cars & Drivers

Does Your Car Really Need A Tune-up?

Whether you have a new car or an older one, you want to be prepared for any trouble you may encounter. Most of us are very trusting souls when it comes to a car repair. We rely on the mechanic as the expert. When he tells us the car needs a tune-up or has any other problem, we have him check it out immediately. The Car Council wants us to be aware of *The Eight Most Common Signs Your Car Needs a Tune-up*. It's full of easy to understand advice on what to look for before it's too late. To get your free copy simply write to:

THE CAR COUNCIL
DEPT. T-M-S
1 GRANDE LAKE DR.
PORT CLINTON, OHIO 43452

Car Shopping On The Internet

Thinking of buying a car? Want to negotiate the best deal and save thousands of dollars? The Internet has scores of Web sites with auto information. The most useful ones reveal invoice cost, road-test performance and rebates and incentives. Try these:

For up-to-date information, analyses and columns from auto industry experts, check out the **Car Connection**'s web site at:
WWW.THECARCONNECTION.COM

For lease help, chat rooms and more, go to the **Auto Channel**, which has links to every automaker's Web site: **www.excite.com/autos**

Free For Cars & Drivers

Edmund's Vehicle Price Guide. Find out how much the car dealer pays for the car you are thinking of buying. Also discover how much the "holdback" allowance is. The holdback allowance is an additional profit the dealer gets from the manufacturer after the car is sold. It's usually about 3 percent of the suggested retail price. The site also has information on rebates and incentive plans. **www.edmunds.com**

The Kelly Blue Book web site can give you a good idea what your trade in is worth, or the real value of a used car you want to buy. **www.kbb.com**

Consumer Product Ratings site offers ratings of cars, hotels, restaurants volunteered by online users. (They are not affiliated with Consumer Reports magazine.) You can reach them on the Internet at: **www.consumeratings.com**

What Does Consumer Reports Think?

If you would like to see just what Consumer Reports thinks of the car you are thinking of buying, visit their Internet site. You will find evaluations of over 180 makes of new cars. Access to their site costs $2.95 a month but you can visit their *Best of the Best* page for free. **www.consumerreports.org**

Free For Cars & Drivers

Save Thousands On Your Next Car Purchase Or Lease

One of the very best ways of saving a lot of money on the purchase or lease of a vehicle is to use the online vehicle brokers. They have nationwide networks of thousands of dealers of every make of auto or truck.

CONSUMER CAR CLUB

In addition to offering you online auto insurance quotes, an auto comparison guide and a loan-versus-lease cost comparison, they also offer three ways to buy a car or truck. First, they will refer you to a dealer at no charge. They also offer a factory direct ordering service for $179 and a Personal Shopper service for $179. Visit their site at: **www.carclub.com**

NATIONWIDE AUTO BROKERS

They will sell you a car and even bring it right to your front door. How's that for convenience! Their advertised prices range from $50 to $125 over dealer invoice. They charge $11.95 for the first price quote on the car of your choice and $9.95 for each additional quote. Check out their Web site at: **www.carconnect.com**

CARS@COST

They offer many models of new cars at dealer invoice plus their fee. Their fees range from $249 to $499 depending upon the car you are buying. **www.carscost.com**

Free For Cars & Drivers

Dealer Referral Services

As a smart shopper it's essential to inform yourself fully before you go out to buy your next car. One of the best ways to gather the information you'll need to make an intelligent choice and get the very lowest price is by visiting these online Internet sites where you will not only learn lots of valuable information about cars, but also get referrals to auto dealers in your local area.

Microsoft CarPoint

This Online Car Buying web site previews various car models and offers "test drives" of selected cars. You'll find lots of reviews, photos and reports on safety, road tests, and more. You'll also find very useful features like side-by-side comparisons and even an affordability calculator. Check it out before you buy your next car. Their web address is: **www.carpoint.msn.com**

AUTOWEB.COM

At this site you'll find well organized information that will help you buy a new car, buy or sell a used car, check out insurance rates from State Farm on the car you are thinking of buying, check financing from Nations Bank and find a list of dealers in your area. Visit them on the Internet at: **www.autoweb.com**

AUTOBUYER

There's not too much detailed information but this is a great place to visit to get a dealer quote on the car of your choice without the pressure of a car salesman in the showroom. Their web address is: **www.autobuyer.com**

Free For Cars & Drivers

AUTO-BY-TEL
With several million customers, this is one of the largest and most useful web sites around. They have links to six car pricing sites, over 2,700 dealers in their referral network and a great reputation to boot. You'll find a lease-buy comparision calculator and even an online finance application. Visit their web site at: **www.autobuytel.com**

CARSMART
A great consumer buying guide with loads of very useful information on topics like financing, best time to buy a new car, air bags, anti-lock brakes and much more. You can even get insurance and financing quotes, links to dealer and manufacturers' sites and vehicle pricing reports ($4.90 each report). **www.carsmart.com**

For AAA Members

If you're a member of AAA, you should know that they offer an excellent tour service. Contact your local AAA office and tell them the destination you would like to drive to and they'll give you detailed road maps with your route outlined in pencil. Many local offices also offer members a car buying service that can save you thousands of dollars on your next auto purchase or lease.

Free For Cars & Drivers

10 Ways To Slash Auto Insurance Costs

1. **MAINTAIN A GOOD DRIVING RECORD.** Accidents and speeding tickets are a fast way to drive up your premiums. Drive carefully and defensively. Consider walking or taking other means of transportation or car pooling to reduce your risk of accidents.

2. **RAISE YOUR DEDUCTIBLES.** This is the amount you must pay for any loss before your insurance kicks in. If your current deductible is $250 or less, raising it to $500 can save you 15%-30%.

3. **PROTECT AGAINST THEFT.** Security devices like care alarms and even having your serial number etched on the window saves you 15% on your comprehensive auto insurance.

4. **ASK ABOUT DISCOUNTS.** Insurance companies offer special deals and discounts if you are retired, belong to a business association, have been insured with a company for a number of years, insure all your cars or have your home and car with the same firm.

5. **TAKE A DRIVER IMPROVEMENT COURSES** to get a discount. For example, AAA has a Driver Improvement Program for people 55 and older that leads to car insurance discounts.

6. **REDUCE YOUR COVERAGE OR ELIMINATE COVERAGE YOU DON'T NEED.** For example, many new cars now come with towing or road service included. If that's the case you can eliminate that coverage from your auto insurance.

Free For Cars & Drivers

7. **MANY INSURERS GIVE DISCOUNTS TO DRIVERS OVER 50 OR THOSE WITH LOW ANNUAL MILEAGE.** Others give students with good grades a 5% discount. If your child maintains a B average or better in school or has taken driver's education you may be eligible for discounts. If you child is away at college as long as the car stays home and college is 100 miles or more away depending on the insurance company, you may also be eligible for discounts.

   Rates are also much lower when the teenage driver is considered only an occasional driver of the parent's cars.

8. **CHECK INSURANCE RATES *BEFORE* YOU BUY A CAR.** The cost of insuring a Porsche is much higher than the cost of insuring an inexpensive family car.

9. **SHOP AROUND.** Talk to friends and neighbors about their insurance coverage and rates. Get quotes from several companies, compare rates and coverage.

10. **GET A CAR WITH ANTI-LOCK BRAKES AND AIR BAGS AND SAVE AN ADDITIONAL 5%.**

Free For Cars & Drivers

Be A Good Neighbor... Be A Good Friend

State Farm wants to help give you, your college, civic group or professional organization free *designated driver presentation items*. They're a colorful way to remind your friends and associates of the importance of safe driving. They will send your group a free designated driver kit. It has a presentation guide, video and sample speeches. Write to:

STATE FARM INSURANCE COMPANIES
ACTION NETWORK-PUBLIC AFFAIRS
DESIGNATED DRIVER PROGRAM
ONE STATE FARM PLAZA
BLOOMINGTON, IL 61710

Should You Buy That Car Or Lease It?

If you can't decide whether to buy or lease a vehicle you need to have this guide...*A Consumer Education Guide to Leasing vs. Buying* free from the National Vehicle Leasing Association. Simply write your name and address on a 3 x 5 card and send it with $1.00 postage & handling to:

HEGGEN & ASSOCIATES INC.
PO BOX 5025
EVANSTON, IL 60204-5025

Free For Cars & Drivers

How Safe Are Your Tires?

Did you know that when you keep your tires properly inflated that the air provides a cushion of protection when you hit a pothole? If the tire is under inflated you could damage the wheel. If it is over inlated the tire will be damaged. For the best information around for caring and protecting your tires, send for a free copy of *The Motorist Tire Care and Safety Guide*. Send a long SASE to:
TIRE INDUSTRY SAFETY COUNCIL
PO BOX 3147
MEDINA, OHIO, 44258

A Safer Car

Before you go shopping for your next car, be sure to get a copy of *Injury, Collision and Theft Losses - Shopping For A Safer Car*. This informative booklet will help you make an intelligent choice about which is the safest vehicle for you. It provides you with an excellent safety and loss comparisons for hundreds of passenger cars, vans, pick ups and utility vehicle models. Write to:
HIGHWAY LOSS DATA INSTITUTE
DEPT R 92-2
1005 N. GLEBE RD., SUITE 800
ARLINGTON, VA 22201

Free For Cars & Drivers

Automobile Hotline Numbers

If you thinking of buying or leasing a car in the near future, be sure you get all the information you need to make an intelligent decision before you go to the dealer showroom. Your first step should be to call the toll-free hotline phone number for the cars you are interested in. The manufacturers will send you beautiful color product information booklets and even video tapes featuring their cars.

ACURA	1-800-TO-ACURA
BMW	1-800-334-4BMW
BUICK	1-800-4-RIVIERA
CADILLAC	1-800-333-4CAD
CHEVY MONTE CARLO & GEO	1-800-950-2438
CHEVY TAHOE (SPANISH)	1-800-950-TAHOE
CHRYSLER	1-800-4-A-CHRYSLER
DODGE	1-800-4-A-DODGE
FORD	1-800-392-3673
GMC SIERRA	1-800-GMC-TRUCK
HONDA	1-800-33-HONDA EXT 435
HYUNDAI	1-800-826-CARS
ISUZU	1-800-726-2700
JAGUAR	1-800-4-JAGUAR
JEEP	1-800-925-JEEP
LAND ROVER	1-800-FINE-4WD
LEXUS	1-800-USA-LEXUS
LINCOLN	1-800-521-4140
MERCEDES	1-800-FOR-MERCEDES

Free For Cars & Drivers

MITSUBISHI	1-800-55-MITSU
NISSAN	1-800-NISSAN-3
OLDMOBILE	1-800-442-6537
PONTIAC	1-800-2-PONTIAC
PORSCHE	1-800-PORSCHE
SAAB	1-800-582-SAAB EXT 201
SUBARU	1-800-WANT-AWD
TOYOTA	1-800-GO-TOYOTA
VOLKSWAGEN	1-800-DRIVE-VW
VOLVO	1-800-960-9988

Free For Sports Fans

99 Tips For Family Fitness

One of the best ways to stay in shape is by involving the whole family in a fitness progam. In *99 Tips* you'll find a slew of fun fitness activities for kids and parents alike. You'll also find advice from notable athletes like Troy Aikman. Just send a postcard to:

99 Tips For Family Fitness
MET-Rx Foundation For Health Enhancement
2112 Business Center Drive
Irvine, CA 92715

Free Hockey Cards

If you are a hockey fan, you'll definitely want to send for this freebie. When you request it you will receive 10 free hockey cards. To get your cards, just send a long SASE and 50¢ to:
DANORS Department H
5721 Funston Street Bay 14
Hollywood, FL 33023

Free For Sports Fans

Pitch This One!

Did you know that former President George Bush used to pitch horseshoes? If you think you might find this sport interesting, and would like to find out more about it, now's the time. To discover more about this fun sport and to learn all the rules and tips for throwing the perfect horseshoe pitch, send for your free copy of the *Official Rules For Horseshoe Pitching*. Send a SASE to:

NHPA
RR2 Box 178
LaMonte, MD 65337

Senior Sports

Healthy eating and exercise are the keys to keeping fit, feeling great and living longer. Whatever your favorite sport Go out and *DO IT!* If you are unable to participate in a fitness program, WALK.

Did you know that there is a Seniors Softball World Championship and a Seniors Softball World Series each year?

For more information on Senior Athletic Competition like Senior Softball, write to:

U.S. National Senior Sports Organization
14323 S. Outer Forty Rd.
St. Louis, MO 63017

And also to:

Senior Sports International
5726 Wilshire Blvd.
Los Angeles, CA. 90036

Also contact your local senior center, city recreation dept, library or YMCA.

Free For Sports Fans

Women: Get Involved With Sports

This organization encourages women to get involved in sports. They will offer your group or school free films of women in sports to help encourage other women to be active and stay active. They also publish a guide listing scholarships to American colleges and universities for women who are into sports. It's a myth that only men get sports scholarships to college. Call them toll-free: **1-800-227-3988.** Or visit them at their web site: **www.lifetimeTV.com/wosport**

Outdoor Sports

L. L. Bean, the outdoor sporting specialists for 67 years, would like to send you a copy of their *catalog*. It features fine quality apparel and footwear for the outdoorsman or woman as well as equipment for camping, fishing, hiking and canoeing. Send a postcard to: **L.L. Bean
Freeport, ME 04033**

The Story Of The Olympic Games

The History of The Olympics gives you the complete story of the Olympics starting with the earliest recorded game in 776 B.C. and traces the game's history right up to through the present. For your free copy, write: **U.S. Olympic Committee
1750 East Boulder St.
Colorado Springs, CO 80909**

Free For Sports Fans

Free From Your Favorite Team

How would you like to receive photos of your favorite teams? Most sports clubs have all kinds of freebies for their loyal fans. These neat freebies often include team photos, souvenir brochures, stickers, fan club information, playing schedules, catalogs and lots more. All you have to do is write to your favorite sports teams at the addresses in this book. Tell them you're a loyal fan and ask them for a "fan package."

Even though it's not always necessary, it's always nice idea to send a long self-addressed-stamped envelope with your name and address written in so they can return your freebie right in your own envelope.

Sometimes it takes a while to get an answer since most teams are flooded with mail. Just be patient and you'll hear from them.

Free For Sports Fans

Hockey

National Hockey League
75 International Blvd. Suite 300
Rexdale, Ontario Canada M9W 6L9

Eastern Conference

Boston Bruins
1 Fleet Center, Suite 250
Boston, MA 02114

Buffalo Sabres
Memorial Auditorium
140 Main St
Buffalo, NY 14202

Carolina Hurricanes
5000 Aerial Center Ste 100
Morrisville, NC 27560

Florida Panthers
Miami Arena
100 NE Third Ave., 10th Fl
Ft. Lauderdale, FL 33301

Montreal Canadians
2313 St. Catherine St. W.
Montreal, Quebec,
Canada H3H 1N2

New Jersey Devils
Byrne Meadowlands Arena
PO Box 504
E. Rutherford, NJ 07073

New York Islanders
Nassau Colliseum
Uniondale, NY 11553

New York Rangers
Madison Square Garden
4 Penn Plaza
New York, NY 10001

Ottawa Senators
301 Moodie Dr., Suite 200
Nepean, Ontario,
Canada K2H 9C4

Philadelphia Flyers
The Spectrum
Pattison Place
Philadelphia, PA 19148

Pittsburgh Penguins
Civic Arena, Gate #9
Pittsburgh, PA 15219

Tampa Bay Lightning
501 E. Kennedy Blvd.,
Tampa, FL 33602

Washington Capitals
U.S. Air Arena
Landover, MD 20785

Free For Sports Fans

Western Conference

Anaheim Mighty Ducks
Arrowhead Pond of
Anaheim
2695 Katella Ave
Anaheim, CA 92806

Calgary Flames
Olympic Saddledome
PO Box 1540, Station M
Calgary, Alberta, Canada T2P 3B9

Chicago Blackhawks
1901 W. Madison
Chicago, IL 60612

Colorado Avalanche
1635 Clay St.
Denver, CO 80204

Columbus Blue Jackets
Nationwide Blvd.
Columbus, OH 43215

Dallas Stars
211 Cowboys Pkwy
Irving, TX 75063

Detroit Red Wings
Joe Louis Arena
600 Civic Center Dr.
Detroit, MI 48226

Edmonton Oilers
Northland Coliseum
7424-118 Ave
Edmonton, Alberta,
Canada T5B 4M9

Los Angeles Kings
PO Box 17013
Inglewood, CA 90308

Minnesota Wild
317 Washington St.
St. Paul, MN 55102

Phoenix Coyotes
2 North Central
Phoenix, AZ 85004

St. Louis Blues
PO Box 66792
St. Louis, MO 63166

San Jose Sharks
San Jose Arena
525 W. Santa Clara St.
San Jose, CA 95113

Toronto Maple Leafs
Maple Leaf Gardens
60 Carlton St
Toronto, Ontario,
Canada M5B 1L1

Vancouver Canucks
Pacific Coliseum
100 N. Renfrew St
Vancouver, B.C.,
Canada V5K 3N7

Free For Sports Fans

Basketball

National Basketball Association

Atlanta Hawks
1 CNN Center
South Tower, Suite 405
Atlanta, GA 30303

Boston Celtics
151 Merrimac St., 4th Fl.
Boston, MA 02114

Charlotte Hornets Fan Mail
100 Hive Dr.
Charlotte, NC 28217

Chicago Bulls
1901 West Madison
Chicago, IL 60612

Cleveland Cavaliers
1 Center Court
Cleveland, OH 44115

Dallas Mavericks
Reunion Arena
777 Sports St.
Dallas, TX 75207

Denver Nuggets
1635 Clay St.
Denver, CO 80204

Detroit Pistons
2 Championship Dr.
Auburn Hills, MI 48326

Golden State Warriors
Oakland Coliseum Arena
7000 Coliseum Way
Oakland, CA 94621

Houston Rockets
10 Greenway Plaza
Houston, TX 77046

Indiana Pacers
300 E. Market St.
Indianapolis, IN 46204

Los Angeles Clippers
L.A. Memorial Sports Arena
3939 S. Figueroa
Los Angeles, CA 90037

Los Angeles Lakers
Great Western Forum
P.O. Box 10
Inglewood, CA 90306

Miami Heat
1 Southeast Third Ave.
Miami, FL 33131

Milwaukee Bucks
1001 N. 4th St.
Milwaukee, WI 53203

Minnesota Timberwolves
600 1st Ave. North
Minneapolis, MN 55403

New Jersey Nets
405 Murray Hill Parkway
E. Rutherford, NJ 07073

New York Knicks
Madison Square Garden
2 Penn Plaza
New York, NY 10121

Free For Sports Fans

Orlando Magic
P.O. Box 76
Orlando, FL 32802

Philadelphia '76ers
Veteran Stadium
P.O. Box 25040
Philadelphia, PA 19147

Phoenix Suns
P.O. Box 1369
Phoenix, AZ 85001

Portland Trail Blazers
700 N.E. Multnomah St.
Ste 600
Portland, OR 97232

Sacramento Kings
1 Sports Parkway
Sacramento, CA 95834

San Antonio Spurs
100 Montana Street
San Antonio, TX 78203

Seattle Supersonics
P.O. Box C900911
Seattle, WA 98109-9711

Toronto Raptors
20 Bay Street Ste. 702
Toronto, Ontario
Canada M5J 2N8

Utah Jazz
301 W. South Temple
Salt Lake City, UT
84101

Vancouver Grizzlies
General Motors Place
800 Griffith Way
Vancouver, BC
Canada V6B 6G1

Washington Bullets
U.S. Air Arena
Landover, MD 20785

Free For Sports Fans

Football
National Football League
280 Park Ave.
New York, NY 10017
212-450-2500

American Conference Football Teams

Baltimore Ravens
11001 Owings Mills Blvd.
Owings Mills, MD 21117

Buffalo Bills
1 Bills Dr.
Orchard Park, NY 14127

Cincinnati Bengals
1 Bengals Drive
Cincinnati, OH 45204

Cleveland Browns
80 First Avenue
Cleveland, OH 44146

Denver Broncos
13655 Broncos Pkwy.
Englewood, CO 80112

Indianapolis Colts
7001 W. 56th St.
Indianapolis, IN 46254

Jacksonville Jaguars
One Stadium Place
Jacksonville, FL 32202

Kansas City Chiefs
1 Arrowhead Dr.
Kansas City, MO 64129

Miami Dolphins
Pro Player Stadium
2269 NW 199th St.
Miami, FL 33056

New England Patriots
Foxboro Stadium - Route 1
Foxboro, MA 02035

New York Jets
1000 Fulton Ave.
Hempstead, NY 11550

Oakland Raiders
1220 Harbor Bay Pkwy
Alameda, CA 94502

Pittsburgh Steelers
Three Rivers Stadium
300 Stadium Cir.
Pittsburgh, PA 15212

San Diego Chargers
Qualcomm Stadium
San Diego, CA 92160

Seattle Seahawks
11220 NE 53rd St.
Kirkland, WA 98033

Tennessee Oilers
Baptist Sports Park
7640 Highway 70 S.
Nashville, TN 37221

Free For Sports Fans

National Conference Football Teams

Arizona Cardinals
8701 S. Hardy Drive
Phoenix, AZ 85284

Atlanta Falcons
One Falcon Place
Suwanee, GA 30174

Carolina Panthers
800 South Mint Street
Charlotte, NC 28202

Chicago Bears
1000 Football Drive
Lake Forest, IL 60045

Dallas Cowboys
Cowboys Center
1 Cowboys Pkwy.
Irving, TX 75063

Detroit Lions
1200 Featherstone Rd.
Pontiac, MI 48342

Green Bay Packers
1265 Lombardi Ave.
Green Bay, WI 54307

Minnesota Vikings
9520 Viking Dr.
Eden Prairie, MN 55344

New Orleans Saints
5800 Airline Hwy
New Orleans, LA 70003

New York Giants
Giants Stadium
E. Rutherford, NJ 07073

Philadelphia Eagles
3501 South Broad St.
Philadelphia, PA 19148

San Francisco 49ers
4949 Centennial Blvd.
Santa Clara, CA 95054

St. Louis Rams
One Rams Way
St. Louis, MO 63045

Tampa Bay Buccaneers
1 Buccaneer Pl.
Tampa, FL 33607

Washington Redskins
PO Box 17247
Dallas International Airport
Washington, D.C. 20041

Free For Sports Fans

Baseball

Major League Baseball
350 Park Ave.
New York, NY 10022

American League Baseball Teams

Baltimore Orioles
333 W. Camden Street
Baltimore, MD 21201

Boston Red Sox
Fenway Park
Boston, MA 02115

California Angels
P.O. Box 2000
Anaheim, CA 92803

Chicago White Sox
333 W. 35th St.
Chicago, IL 60616

Cleveland Indians
Jacobs Field
2401 Ontario Street
Cleveland, OH 44115

Detroit Tigers
Public Relations
2121 Trumbull Ave.
Detroit, MI 48216

Kansas City Royals
P.O. Box 419969
Kansas City, MO 64141

Milwaukee Brewers
P.O. Box 3099
Milwaukee, WI 53201

Minnesota Twins
501 Chicago Ave. South
Minneapolis, MN 55415

New York Yankees
Yankee Stadium
Bronx, NY 10451

Oakland Athletics
Oakland Coliseum
Oakland, CA 94621

Seattle Mariners
P.O. Box 4100
Seattle, WA 98104

Texas Rangers
P.O. Box 90111
Arlington, TX 76004

Toronto Blue Jays
1 Blue Jay Way-Sky Dome
300 Bremmer Blvd., Ste 3200
Toronto, Ont., Canada
MSV 3B3

Free For Sports Fans

National League Baseball Teams

Atlanta Braves
P.O. Box 4064
Atlanta, GA 30302

Chicago Cubs
Wrigley Field
1060 West Addison St.
Chicago, IL 60613

Cincinnati Reds
100 Riverfront Stadium
Cincinnati, OH 45202

Colorado Rockies
1700 Broadway Ste 2100
Denver, CO 80205

Florida Marlins
Joe Robbie Stadium
2267 NW 199th St.
Miami, FL 33056

Houston Astros
P.O. Box 288
Houston, TX 77001

Los Angeles Dodgers
1000 Elysian Park Ave.
Los Angeles, CA 90012

Montreal Expos
PO Box 500, Station M
Montreal, Quebec, Canada H1V 3P2

New York Mets
Shea Stadium
Flushing, NY 11368

Philadelphia Phillies
Veteran Stadium
P.O. Box 7575
Philadelphia, PA 19101

Pittsburgh Pirates
Three Rivers Stadium
Pittsburgh, PA 15212

St. Louis Cardinals
250 Stadium Plaza
St. Louis, MO 63102

San Diego Padres
P.O. Box 2000
San Diego, CA 92112

San Francisco Giants
Candlestick Park
San Francisco, CA 94124

Traveling Free Or At Big Savings

The Four Best Ways To Get Free Travel

Most people don't know it but there are lots of ways you can get free or almost free travel. Here are a few of the best...

If you have a unique skill or hobby, many cruise lines will give you a free trip in exchange for giving a lecture about your specialty on one of their cruises. They often have theme cruises you might fit in with. For example, if you are a fitness specialist, they often look for people to teach aerobics on board. So if you have a unique skill...let's say you're an amateur magician or perhaps a financial advisor, the cruise line will often give you a free trip just for spending an hour a day instructing others while on the cruise. Check the travel section of your local newspaper or check the toll-free directory for the phone numbers of the cruise lines. If you have a computer, you can also reach the cruise lines via the Internet. See the Internet listings at the end of this section.

There are some courier services that will ask you to carry a package anywhere in the world they travel to. With that you get a free trip for carrying the parcel. Sometimes you can get to stay a few extra days

Travel

as long as you can catch their plane on the return flight. For more information, contact the International Association of Air Travel Couriers at: **561-582-8320** or on the Internet at: **www.courier.org**

A common practice of all airlines is to overbook their flights since they know from experience that a certain percentage of people do not show up for their flight and the airline wants to leave with a full plane. When too many passengers show up the the airlines will offer free tickets to anywhere they fly just for changing your flight. One great method of getting free airline tickets is as soon as you get to the airport for your next trip, volunteer to take the next flight out if they are overbooked in exchange for a free ticket on a future flight. (See the following report: *10 Tips On Getting Free Travel When Your Plane Is Overbooked*.)

Frequent flyer programs are still a good deal that costs you nothing. Many charge cards will give you frequent flyer miles just for using their cards. Check with your charge card company. Also, make sure you are a member of the airline's frequent flyer club if you plan on doing any airline travel. They usually don't put a time restriction on them.

When they travel, some families look for housesitters. In return for watching their home, you get a free place to live. If you like to travel, you can even trade apartments and homes with people in other parts of the country (or the world) through different real estate exchanges. Check the classified section of your local newspaper.

Travel

Lowest Air Fares

While planning your next trip, be sure you are getting the best fares to and from the cities you will be visiting. There are a number of companies that specialize in getting you the lowest fares available. They check constantly with the various airlines and track their prices to insure that when you contact them you will get the best fare. For example, recently Global Discount Travel Services had fares from New York to San Francisco of just $111 one way. While fares change constantly, similar savings are available to and from many other major cities both within the U.S. and on international flights. To check their fares, call them at: **1-888-777-2222** Or visit their web site at: **www.lowestfare.com**

Also check the following web site where you can actually 'name your own price' for hotels and airfare: **www.priceline.com** Or call them at: **1-800-PRICELINE.**

Adventure Tours For Seniors

A great number of seniors who are in fairly good physical condition want trips that involve challenges and cultural learning experiences. These seniors are looking for new adventures and also want to learn about local culture and nature in such places as Africa and South Africa. Elder Treks specializes in senior adventure tours to 30 different countries including Africa and South Africa. If you are looking for that adventurous tour call Elder Treks at: **1-800-741-7956** Or visit their web site: **www.eldertreks.com**

Travel

10 Tips On Getting Free Travel When Your Plane Is Overbooked

A lot of plane flights are overbooked. That means that the airline has sold more tickets than there are seats on the plane. The reason they overbook is that often people do not show up for their flights and the airline wants to fly with as full a passenger load as possible. When a flight is overbooked, the airline must offer inducements to passengers to voluntarily take a later flight. The inducement generally will be a voucher for free plane tickets on their airline. If the flight is very overbooked, you might be able to get an even better deal that might include vouchers for more than one flight, upgrade to first-class on their next flight, overnight hotel stay if there are no more flights until the next day and even cash. Here are ten useful tips:

1. Volunteer *before* airline representatives offer vouchers, if you think your flight may be oversold.

2. Make an informed decision. Ask how long it will be until the next flight leaves for your destination.

3. If there are no takers after a voucher is announced for a low amount and it's a popular flight don't raise your hand. The voucher value is likely to increase.

4. Use the voucher immediately. Most expire within a year and are not replaceable if lost or stolen.

5. Ask for a meal voucher.

Travel

6. When using a travel voucher, plan in advance. In some cases, limited seating may make it more difficult to redeem your free or discounted travel exactly when you want to.

7. If you have a travel agent, show him or her the front and back of your voucher to determine whether it qualifies for a particular flight.

8. Read the fine print. Some vouchers may not be used on certain days and holidays.

9. Many vouchers themselves are not transferable. But the recipient generally can buy a ticket for someone else,.

10. Be polite but don't be afraid to ask for more...for example, in addition to travel vouchers you might ask for an upgrade to first class on the next fight out. Remember, they *must* get people off the overbooked flight and will offer whatever it takes.

Travel

Travel Bargains For Older Citizens

One of the great benefits of becoming a senior are those discounts on just about everything from 'senior day' at your local retail store to movies, theater, restaurants and best of all...travel.

Next time you plan to venture out on any trip, be absolutely sure to ask about senior discounts.

There are a number of ways for seniors to get discount travel. For example, the airlines offer discount booklets you can purchase for substantial savings on your air fare.

Next, don't forget to become a member of AARP... The American Association of Retired Persons. (No, you don't have to be retired but you or your spouse must be 50 years of age or older.) For a membership fee of $10 per year, (including your spouse) you'll receive a magazine, *Modern Maturity*, newspaper updates and a membership card that gets you discounts on just about everything (hotels, insurance, drugs and more.) Once you're a member, to get your discounts you simply show your membership card or call their member services toll-free phone number: **1-800-424-3410** Or visit them on the Internet at: **www.aarp.org**

Most of the airlines offer special programs for seniors. Before you book your plane reservation, check with the airline you are planning to travel on to be sure they offer at least 10% discount for seniors 62 and older. They also have programs where you can purchase coupon booklets or passport programs that allow you to travel domestically and internationally at substantial discounts.

Travel

CONTINENTAL AIRLINES has a Freedom trip booklet and Senior passport program that allows you to enjoy discounted domestic and international travel. Call them from 6:30 am to 10 pm Central time.at:**1-800 441-1135** or **1-800-248-8996**

DELTA AIRLINES has a discount program for domestic and international for seniors 62 and older. Call: **1-800-221-1212**

For information on **AMERICAN AIRLINES SENIOR DISCOUNT** program, call them at: **1-800-237-7981**

TWA(which is now merged with American Airlines) has a senior coupon book you can purchase for domestic travel plus they will include a coupon for 20% off international travel. Anyone 62 or older can take advantage of these great money savings programs. Call them toll-free at: **1-800-221-2000**

Discount Airline Coupons For Seniors

If you are a senior citizen you're eligible to purchase *Senior Citizen Airline Coupons*. Prices are always subject to change but right now with Senior Citizen coupons you can fly anywhere an airline flies within the 48 states for no more than $298 round trip or even less on some airlines. Airlines that go to the U.S. Virgin Islands, Puerto Rico and the Bahamas, and several that fly to Canada even throw in those destinations for the same low price.

Travel

The coupons are usually sold in a book of four one-way flights. Prices will change but currently on American, United and Delta the books cost $596; On Continental or U.S. Airways: $579; On America West: $548; and on Northwest: $540. Continental also sells a book of eight coupons for $1079.

Each coupon is good for a one-way fare, and while some airlines require a 14 day advance reservation, you can also use them to fly standby. You don't have to travel round trip, so there's no minimum stay. *Senior Coupon* travel also earns you frequent flier miles. With most airlines a couple cannot share a coupon book.

TWA is the only airline that sells coupon books for companions of any age for $648. To use the coupons you must travel with a qualifying senior.

America West and US Air both allow a senior to share a coupon book with a child aged 2-11.

Also, don't forget to check with all the airlines for special seniors' clubs and senior discounts. For example, American, Delta and United run senior clubs that offer zoned fares ranging from $98-$298, round trip, for travel within the lower 48 states, depending on distance. In other words, you pay no more than the usual senior-coupon price for a long trip, and get an even better price on shorter trips. Those clubs also offer discounted international travel that isn't available with the regular coupons. Remember as a senior you get at least a 10% discount but check with the airline for an even bigger discount and the best travel deal.

Travel

50% Discount On Hotels

Want to save a lot of money the next time you book a hotel reservation in a large city? Try using a 'hotel broker'.

Just like airline-ticket consolidators, hotel brokers are outlets through which hotels rent some of their vacant rooms... *cheap*.

Hotel brokers are given blocks of discounted rooms by big city hotels. They in turn pass the bulk of the savings onto you. They concentrate mainly on big cities...Boston, Chicago, Los Angeles, New York, San Francisco, Washington, and more. A few even handle larger cities overseas, such as London, Sydney, Paris and Hong Kong. Where they operate, these consolidators can cut your hotel costs by as much as 50%. The brokers are classified into two groups.

BOOKING-AGENT BROKERS:

Some brokers make a reservation for you at the discounted rate. Once you have your confirmed discounted reservation you simply check in at the hotel as you ordinarily would and pay the discounted amount when you check out.

PREPAY BROKERS:

Other brokers are like tour operators. They sell hotel rooms at the same reduced rates they would in package tours. Here you must prepay for your entire stay in order to get the best rate, and the broker sends you a voucher, which you use to pay upon arriving at the hotel.

When comparing the two types of brokers just keep in mind that with the first method where you pay at the checkout, you don't have to worry if you

Travel

are forced to cancel or reschedule your trip.

The largest PREPAY-VOUCHER BROKER is Hotel Reservations Network, or HRN. Hotel Reservations Network: **1-800-964-6835.** Or visit their web site at: **www.180096hotel.com** (You'll also find a link to HRN on many other discount-travel Web sites.)

The largest BOOKING-AGENT BROKER is:
QUICKBOOK
You can call them toll-free at: **1-800-789-9887.** Or visit their Web site at: **www.quikbook.com**

Another BOOKING-AGENT BROKER is Express Reservations which specializes only in New York and Los Angeles hotel bookings:
EXPRESS RESERVATION:
Call them toll-free at: **1-800-356-1123.** Or visit them on the Internet at: **www.express-res.com**

If you plan to travel to Florida and would like to save money on hotels, be sure to check with the Florida Tourist Bureau, Inc. Despite the official sounding name they are not a state agency but rather a private travel company that specializes in saving you up to 50% on your hotel accomodations throughout Florida. They work on the prepaid voucher system where you book your room and pay in advance in exchange for a very substantial discount at the best hotels and motels. Call them toll-free at: **1-888-246-8728.**

Travel

Half-Price Hotels

Many people have found that membership in a discount club is an excellent way to save money on their travel. If you spend more than a few nights a year in hotels, the annual price of membership in a good hotel discount club can be a good investment.

Most clubs promise 50% discounts off rack rate, subject to availability and the occupancy level the hotel expects. Here are some of the largest discount programs:

Great American Traveler: 1-800-548-2812

Encore: 1-800-638-8976.

15% Senior Savings On Amtrak

For seniors who prefer to travel by train, Amtrak offers year-round discounts for anyone 62 and older. These discounts include 15% off regular fares, special one way fares, Explore America Fares and special group fares. They also have beautiful brochures describing their fun vacation packages. Call Amtrak toll-free at: **1-800-USA-RAIL** (that's 1-800-872-7245). Or visit the web site: **www.amtrak.com**

Jet Vacations

If you plan to travel to France and want to save money on everything... quality air travel, hotels, car rental, ski packages, sightseeing, call Jet Vacations This company specializes in trips to Paris, France and to the Riviera. Plan your trip early and save. Call them toll-free and learn how you can enjoy

France 3,435 different ways. Call *Jet Vacations* at: **1-800-538-0999.**

Before You Travel

Planning a trip? Before you go you'll want to get a copy of *Lightening The Travel Load Travel Tips*. This handy booklet is filled with "how-to" materials on selecting, packing, traveling and caring for luggage. Send a postcard to:

SAMSONITE TRAVELER ADVISORY SERVICE
11200 E. 45TH AVE.
DENVER, CO 80239

Importing A Car

Can you save money by buying a foreign car on your next trip abroad? What are the customs requirements? What should you know about emission standards on a car you import yourself? For answers, send a postcard asking for *Importing A Car* and also *U.S. Customs Pocket Hints*. It's yours free from:

U.S. CUSTOMS SERVICE
WASHINGTON, DC 20229

Free Travelodge Directory

There's a *free directory* of the more than 500 TraveLodge motels and motor hotels waiting for you. It lists location, room rates and a map for each TraveLodge. You'll also find information on their new group rates, family plan and bargain break

weekends. Contact:
TRAVELODGE INTERNATIONAL
250 TRAVELODGE DR.
EL CAJON, CA 92090
1-800-578-7878

Free Days Inn Directory

Quality accommodations for the American traveler at economical rates has been the motto of Days Inn since its founding in 1970. For a *free directory* of the 301 Inns and 229 Tasty World Restaurants with their rates, maps, toll free numbers and more, call:
1-800-325-2525

Free Holiday Inn Directory

For a complete listing of all Holiday Inns both in the U.S. and worldwide, request a free copy of their huge directory. In seconds you can locate any of the thousands of Holiday Inns with room rates, list of recreation activities, even a map for each hotel. Call toll free:
1-800-238-8000. OR WRITE:
HOLIDAY INN
3 RAVINIA DR. SUITE 2000
ATLANTA, GA 38195

Enjoy A Club Med Vacation

Club Med's unique vacation resorts have delighted thousands of people tired of 'the same old thing'. If you're interested in a fun vacation that really is

Travel

something different, send for the free color *travel booklet*. Club Med offers seniors 55 and older a $100 discount on stays of 7 nights or more. To get your free booklet or for more information on their clubs, contact them at: **Club Med, Inc., 3 E. 54th St., New York, NY 10019.** Or call: **1-800-CLUB-MED** (that's 1-800-258-2633). Or visit their web site at: **www.clubmed.com**

Barefoot Adventure Cruise

Are you ready for something different? For a vacation unlike any you've ever been on, consider sailing a tall ship to a small island in the Caribbean. The full color *Barefoot Adventure* will tell you all about 'Barefoot' shipboard adventures aboard schooners that once belonged to Onassis, Vanderbilt and the Duke of Westminster. Call toll free: **1-800-327-2600.** Or send a postcard to:
WINDJAMMER BAREFOOT CRUISES
BOX 120
MIAMI BEACH, FL 33119

Safety Guide

Did you ever wonder if you should be concerned about your health and safety when you travel to foreign destinations? Travel Medicine has a free *Travel Safety Guide* that offers practical quick tips on insect protection, medical kits, mosquito nets, protective clothing and water filters and more. Before you venture out on your next travel adventure, make sure you send for this free guide. Write to:

Travel

TRAVEL MEDICINE INC.
351 PLEASANT ST., SUITE 312
NORTHAMPTON, MA 01060

Foreign Exchange

If you plan to travel abroad, did you know that you can now buy francs, pounds or yen over the Internet? This service can be useful for travelers who want to have small amounts of currency upon arrival in a foreign country. At their web site, International Currency Exchange lists rates at which they sell foreign currency. If you decide to buy, you can pay by check or credit card and receive currency in 2-4 days via express mail. You can call them toll-free at: **1-877-630-8100**. Or visit their web site: **www.foreignmoney.com**

A Diet For Jet Lag?

Do you travel frequently and find that you suffer from jet lag? If so this free wallet size card should help. It summarizes the amounts and types of food you should eat and tells you the best times to eat to reduce the effects of jet lag. Ask for *The Anti-Jet Lag Diet*. To get a copy, send a long SASE to:
Argonne National Laboratory
Jet Lag Diet
9700 S. Cass Ave.
Argonne, IL 60439

Travel

Volunteer For A Free Vacation

Regardless of how young or old you are, one of the most fascinating ways to enjoy a wilderness experience in a national park is by being a volunteer.

A variety of government agencies including the U.S. Forest Service, The National Park Service, U.S. Army Corps of Engineers, plus individual state park systems welcome volunteers to serve as campground hosts in exchange for a free stay. Every year hundreds of thousands of people who love the outdoors volunteer their services for anywhere from one day to a full year.

In addition to acting as hosts, volunteers also help as caretakers, researchers, ranger assistants, trail repair crews, plumbers and carpenters. This reflects the growing interest in 'doing vacations' or educational travel. In exchange for their services, volunteers may receive free camping and other recreational privileges that often include cabins, house trailers or bunkroom accommodations at no cost. While some volunteers are given an expense allowance, most should expect to pay for food and transportation costs.

If this sounds like a vacation you might be interested in, you can contact the park, forest, refuge, fish hatchery or other facility that you are interested in or check with the following:

NATIONAL PARK SERVICE,

They are looking for 95,000 volunteers a year who are interested in a stay of up to one or three months in one of the nation's 369 parklands to help with trail projects, species control and campground hosts. To get a brochure listing all of the parks in the U.S.

Travel

along with an application, send a postcard to the address below. **National Park Service, *Volunteers in Parks* Coordinator, 1849 C St. N.W. Suite 7312, Washington, DC 20240.** Or visit their web site at: **www.nps.gov/volunteer**

U.S. FOREST SERVICE
Check in your local telephone operator or in the phone book blue pages for the phone number of the nearest U.S. Forest Service office. In their *Volunteers in the National Forests Program* they have up to 100,000 volunteers every year to serve in one of the nation's 155 national forests or 20 national grasslands.

The U.S. Forest Service also has a program called *Passports In Time.* This program welcomes families for one day to one week stays that focuses on archaeological digs and historical restorations. Call them toll-free at: **1-800-281-9176.**

Bureau of Land Management, Environmental Education and Volunteer Program, 1849 C St., N.W. LS-1275, Washington, DC 20240. 1-202-452-5078.

They need roughly 20,000 volunteers a year for their National Volunteer Program. Volunteers will be restoring watersheds, building trails, staffing visitor centers, patrolling cultural sites, writing brochures and conducting educational programs in federal lands, mostly in the West.

Travel

U.S. Fish and Wildlife Service, Division of Refuges, National Volunteer Coordinator Office, 4401 North Fairfax Dr., Room 22203, Arlington, VA 22203.
This service oversees hundreds of wildlife refuges and fish hatcheries throughout the nation. Volunteers are needed to help with raising fish, banding birds, restoring fragile habitats, and conducting tours of the habitats and fisheries.
To get a visitors guide and map with all of the national wildlife refuges, call: **1-800-344-9453**.

U.S. Army Corps of Engineers: 1-800-865-8337.
They manage 460 lakes throughout the country. Volunteers are needed to help with a variety of programs that include archaeological digs, pest control and campground hosts.

Alaska Division of Parks and Outdoor Recreation, Alaska State Parks Volunteer Coordinator, 3601 C Street, Suite 1200, Anchorage, AK 99503-5921. 1-907-269-8708.
Alaska has one of the most extensive summer volunteer programs to help out as archaeological assistants, back-country ranger assistants, researchers and trail crew members. They will pay transportation expenses from Anchorage plus a small expense allowance for commitments of two weeks to three months.

To volunteer closer to home, try checking your local phone directory for your state's Department of Parks and Recreation and ask about their parks volunteer programs.

Travel

Healthy Travel To Foreign Lands

If you are on medication and plan to travel abroad be sure to get this free booklet. Put out by the International Society of Travel Medicine, it lists over 500 medicine clinics in 44 countries (including the U.S.). You'll also find answers to questions you may have about health risks in the countries you are visiting, what shots are needed, which medicines to pack and how to get medical assistance while you are there. Ask for the *Travel Medicine Clinics booklet*. Free from: **ISTM Clinic Directory c/o Imodium A-D Drawer D, 1675 Broadway, 33rd Floor, New York, NY 10019.**

Before you travel, you may also want to check with the following organizations for updates on illnesses in the countries you will be visiting: **The World Health Organization, 1-202-974-3000.**

THE CENTERS FOR DISEASE CONTROL & PREVENTION
1-404-332-4559

INTERNATIONAL ASSOCIATION FOR MEDICAL ASSISTANCE TO TRAVELERS
Links travelers to doctors in 130 countries 1-716-754-4883.

Internet Sites For Travelers

Surfing the worldwide web is one of the easiest and most convenient ways to simplify your travel planning and to save money. If you are planning to travel and have access to the Internet either at home, at work or at your public library, here are a number of sites you will want to visit.

Travel

TRAVELOCITY
www.travelocity.com

If you would like to quickly check for the lowest plane fares from any major city to any other major city in the U.S., be sure to check out this site. Updated on a daily basis, you will find a listing of the lowest air fares at that time. You will also find several other features of interest including:

- **PRICESHOPPER** - great buys on vacation and cruise packages in the U.S. and abroad.
- **HOT DEALS** - for steals, deals and all round great travel bargains worldwide.
- **FLIGHT PAGING** - Keeps you informed of changes to your flight's departure or arrival times and gate assignments - all sent to your alphanumeric pager.
- **FARE WATCHER E-MAIL** - Sends low fare updates directly to your e-mail quickly and reliably.
- **SHOP SAFE GUARANTEE** - They protect every credit card transaction you make on Travelocity
- **REVIEWS** - for independent, non-biased reviews of vacation choices.
- **WEATHER FORECASTS** - Complete updated weather forecasts for cities around the world.

※ ※

www.weather.com

What's the weather like in the city you are about to fly to? Are there any flight delays due to bad weather? For answers, go to this web site, a service of the Weather Channel. Before your next trip check to see what weather's in store for you.

※ ※

Travel

www.biztravel.com
If you travel by plane a lot, you know how frequent flyer miles can add up quickly. To track just how many frequent flyer and frequent stay credits you have accumulated with various accounts, visit this site. Companies that participate in this program include United Mileage Plus, American AAdvantage, Delta SkyMiles, Continental OnePass, Northwest WorldPerks, Marriott Honored Guest Awards, Marriott Miles, Hilton Honors, and ITT Sheraton Club.

※※※※※※※※※※※※※※※※※※※※※

www.delta-air.com/womenexecs
As a result of a partnership between American Express and Delta Airlines, the woman executive can now enjoy The Executive Woman's Travel Network™. It will provide you with fight upgrades, companion fares of just $99 and savings of $30 to $100 on air fares. Plus you'll be kept informed of special offers and exclusive airfares.

※※※※※※※※※※※※※※※※※※※※※

www.thetrip.com
This site is designed to save the money for small business travelers. You can book airline tickets, hotel rooms and car rentals at lower rates. To help you save money 'thetrip' will automatically search for flights from alternate airports and for connecting flights. You will also find Frommer City Guides with restaurant and hotel reviews plus maps with point-to-point directions from anywhere in the U.S. to anywhere else.

Travel

※※※※※※※※※※※※※※※※※※※※

www.reservation.com
This is the web site for Preview Travel. It allows you to make airline and rental car reservation online.

※※※※※※※※※※※※※※※※※※※※

www.expedia.com
This is Microsoft's travel web site. While it is primarily geared toward leisure travelers, business travelers will find a number of useful features including city maps and restaurant listing. Another nice feature is expedia's low-fare tracker that will alert you to discount fares for cities you select.

※※※※※※※※※※※※※※※※※※※※

www.webflyer.com
The ultimate site for the frequent flyer. You will find all kinds of special bonus mileage offers and exclusive discount fares available only online. It's best feature is the fact that it tracks all airline, hotel and car rental discounts by city and saves you time by listing them all at one site.

※※※※※※※※※※※※※※※※※※※※

www.quikbook.com
This web site has been called one of the web's best sites for hotel discounts by *Consumer Reports Travel Letter*. At this site you will find out where you can get big hotel discounts of up to 60% in major cities like New York, Atlanta, Los Angeles, Boston to name a few.

Travel

✺✺✺✺✺✺✺✺✺✺✺✺✺✺✺✺✺✺✺✺

www.vicinity.com
Vicinity provides a variety of services for the business traveler including
- BUSINESS FINDER - find the nearest businesses, hotels, travel destinations or other points of interest in any city. Includes interactive maps and driving directions.
- MAPBLAST. With this free service you can generate interactive maps of residences of businesses that you can use or e-mail to associates.
- YELLOW PAGES - dynamic local listings of 16 million businesses nationwide.

✺✺✺✺✺✺✺✺✺✺✺✺✺✺✺✺✺✺✺✺

City.Net: www.city.net

Epicurious: www.epicurious.com (Gourmet Magazine & Conde Nast Web site)

The Travel Channel: www.travelchannel.com
Yahoo: www.yahoo.com/recreation/travel

✺✺✺✺✺✺✺✺✺✺✺✺✺✺✺✺✺✺✺✺

Travel

Cruise Lines Web Sites

If you are thinking of taking a cruise and aren't sure which cruise is right for you, before you book, be sure to check out the web sites of the cruise lines you are considering. Here's a selection of web sites of cruise lines:

American Hawaii Cruises:
www.cruisehawaii.com

The Big Red Boat: www.bigredboat.com

Carnival Cruise Lines: www.carnival.com/

Celebrity Cruises: www.celebrity-cruises.com/

Clipper Cruise Line: www.clippercruise.com/

Cunard Lines: www.cunardline.com

The Delta Queen Steamboat Co.:
www.deltaqueen.com

Holland America Line:
www.hollandamerica.com/intro.html

KD River Cruises of Europe:
www.rivercruises.com

Norwegian Cruise Lines: www.ncl.com/ncl

Premier Cruise Lines: www.asource.com/dolphin/

Radisson Seven Seas Cruises:
www.regalcruises.com/

Renaissance Cruises: www.rencruises.com/

Travel

Royal Caribbean International:
www.royalcaribbean.com

Royal Olympic Cruises: www.epirotiki.com

Silversea Cruises: www.asource.com/silversea/

Spice Island Cruises: www.indo.com/cruises/spice island/

Tall Ship Adventures: www.asource.com/tallship/

Windjammer Barefoot Cruises:
www.windjammer.com

Windstar Cruises: www.windstarcruises.com

World Explorer Cruises: www.wecruise.com/

Travel

5 Tips To Save Money On Plane Travel
www.travelocity.com

Finding the lowest fare isn't always easy. Discount fares typically have restrictions that can be difficult, sometimes frustrating, to interpret. If you're looking for the cheapest price, here are a few suggestions that will help.

1. Make your reservation early. Many discount fares require that you make a reservation 7, 14 or 21 days before your trip depending on the fare. The best international fares often require a reservation 30 days in advance. Making a reservation as soon as you know your travel dates increases your chances of finding a fare you can live with.

2. Flying on a weekday usually costs less. Flights on Tuesday, Wednesday and Thursday usually offer the lowest fares. Fares are sometimes (but not always) higher on Monday and Friday than on other weekdays. Saturday flights occasionally have discount fares, but as a rule it's more expensive to fly on a weekend than a weekday.

3. Stay over a Saturday night. Most low fares require that you stay over at least one Saturday night before your return flight. However, some fares may only require you to stay a minimum of 3 or 4 days.

Travel

4. One airline is better than two. It's almost always less expensive to use only one airline for the entire trip instead of two. In fact booking two airlines can, in some cases, cost hundreds of dollars more. Airlines sell only a limited number of seats at the lowest fares. When those seats sell out, the price goes up. If you don't at first succeed, try an earlier or later flight. To get the lowest roundtrip fare, that fare must be available on both the departing and return flights you select. If the fare is sold out on either of these, the price you end up with will be much higher.

5. Try an earlier or later flight if you can't find the fare you want or if possible, consider flying on another day.

Traveling The USA

Planning ahead can make all the difference in the world between having great fun and having a run-of-the mill trip.

One of the very best sources of information are the tourist offices for the states you plan to visit. These offices are set up to provide maps, brochures and other information about the tourist attractions, climate, restaurants and hotels for their states.

If you plan to tour any part of the U.S.A., call the tourist offices of each of the 50 states you intend to visit. When you call them, tell them which areas of the state you plan to visit and indicate any special sight-seeing interests you may have. Often they can provide you with additional materials on the areas that interest you most.

The following is a list of state tourism offices. Where a toll-free number or web site is available, it is given.

ALABAMA
Bureau of Tourism & Travel
P.O. Box 4927
Montgomery, AL 36103-4331
205-242-4169 or 1-800-ALABAMA

Travel

ALASKA
Alaska Division of Tourism
P.O. Box 110801
Juneau, AK 99811-0801
907-465 2010

ARIZONA
Arizona Office of Tourism
2702 N. 3rd Street
Suite 4015
Phoenix, AZ 85004
602-230-7733

ARKANSAS
Arkansas Department of Parks and Tourism
1 Capitol Mall
Little Rock, AR 72201
501 682-7777 or
1-800-NATURAL

CALIFORNIA
California Office of Tourism
Department of Commerce
PO Box 1499 Dept TIA
Sacramento, CA 95812
800-862-2543

COLORADO
Colorado Tourism Board
P.O. Box 3524
Englewood, CO 80150
303-592-5410
Ask for a vacation planning kit
call 1-800-433-2656

Travel

CONNECTICUT
Tourism Promotion Service
CT Dept. of Economic Development
865 Brook Street
Rocky Hill, CT 06067
203 258-4355 or 800-CT-BOUND (nationwide)

DELAWARE
Delaware Tourism Office
Delaware Development Office
99 Kings Highway
P.O. Box 1401
Dover, DE 19903
1-800-441-8846 (nationwide)

DISTRICT OF COLUMBIA
Washington Convention and Visitors Association
1212 New York Ave., NW 600
Washington, DC 20005
202-789 7000

FLORIDA
Department of Commerce Visitors Inquiry
126 Van Buren St
Tallahassee, FL 32399-2000
904 487-1462

GEORGIA
Tourist Division
P.O. Box 1776
Atlanta, GA 30301-1776
1-800 VISIT GA
(1 800 847-4842)

Travel

HAWAII
Hawaii Visitors Bureau
2270 Kalakaua Ave. Suite 801
Honolulu, HI 96815
808-923-1811

IDAHO
Department of Commerce
700 W. State St. 2nd Fl.
Boise, ID 83720
208-334-2470 or
1-800-635-7820

ILLINOIS
Illinois Department of Commerce & Community Affairs Tourist Information
100 W. Randolph St Ste 3-400
Chicago, IL 60601
312-814-7179

INDIANA
Indiana Dept. of Commerce
Tourism & Film Development Division
One North Capitol Suite 700
Indianapolis, IN 46204-2288
317-232 8860 or 289-6646

IOWA
Iowa Department of Economic Development
Division of Tourism
200 East Grand Avenue
Des Moines, IA 50309
515-242-4705
1-800 345-IOWA

KANSAS
Travel & Tourism Development Division
Department of Commerce
700 SW Harrison
Topeka, KS 66603-3712
913-296-2009
1-800-2-KANSAS

KENTUCKY
Department of Travel Development Dept. MR
PO. Box 2011
Frankfort, KY 40602
1-800-225-TRIP

LOUISIANA
Office of Tourism
PO. Box 94291
Baton Rouge, LA 70804
504-342-8119 or
1-800-33-GUMBO

MAINE
Maine Publicity Bureau
P.O. Box 2300
Hallowell, ME 04347
207-582-9300

MARYLAND
Office of Tourism Development
217 E. Redwood St.
Baltimore, MD 21202
1-800-543-1036

Travel

MASSACHUSETTS
Executive Office of Economic Affairs
Office of Travel and Tourism
100 Cambridge St., 13th Fl
Boston, MA 02202
617-727-3201

MICHIGAN
Travel Bureau
Department of Commerce
P.O. Box 30226
Lansing, MI 48909
1-800-5432-YES

MINNESOTA
Minnesota Office of Tourism
121 7th Place East Suite 100
Metro-Square Bldg.
St. Paul, MN 55101
612-296 5029 or
1-800-657-3700

MISSISSIPPI
Mississippi Division of Tourism
P.O. Box 1705
Ocean Springs, MS 39566
601-359-3297 or
1-800-927-6378

MISSOURI
Missouri Division of Tourism
Truman State Office Bldg.
301 W. High St.
PO. Box 1055
Jefferson City, MO 65102
314-751-4133

Travel

MONTANA
Department of Commerce
Travel Montana
1424 9th Avenue
Helena, MT 59620
406-444-2654 or
1-800-541-1447

NEBRASKA
Dept of Economic Development
Division of Travel and Tourism
301 Centennial Mall S.
P.O. Box 94666
Lincoln, NE 68509
402-471-3796 or
1-800-228-4307

NEVADA
Commission on Tourism
Capitol Complex
Carson City, NV 89710
1 800-NEVADA 8

NEW HAMPSHIRE
Office of Vacation Travel
P.O. Box 856
Concord, NH 03302
603-271-2666 or for recorded weekly events, ski conditions, foliage reports 1-800-258-3608

NEW JERSEY
Division of Travel and Tourism
20 West State Street
Trenton, NJ 08625
1-800-JERSEY-7

Travel

NEW MEXICO
New Mexico Department
of Tourism
Lamy Bldg.
491 Old Santa Fe Trail
Santa Fe, NM 87503
505-827-7400 or
1-800 545-2040

NEW YORK
NYS Tourism
Box 992,
Latham, NY 12110
or call 1-800-CALL NYS

NORTH CAROLINA
Travel and Tourism Division
Department of Economic & Community
Development
430 North Salisbury St.
Raleigh, NC 27611
919-733-4171 or
1-800-VISIT NC

NORTH DAKOTA
North Dakota Tourism Promotion
Liberty Memorial Building
Capitol Grounds
604 E. Boulevard
Bismarck, ND 58505
701-224 2525 or
1-800-435-5663

OHIO
Ohio Division of Travel and Tourism
Vern Riffe Center
77 S. High Street
Columbus, OH 43215
1-800 BUCKEYE

OKLAHOMA
Oklahoma Tourism and Recreation Dept.
Literature Distribution Center
2401 N. Lincoln Suite 500
Oklahoma City, OK 73105
1-800-652-6552

OREGON
Tourism Division
Oregon Economic Development Dept.
775 Summer St. NE
Salem, OR 97310
1-800-547-7842

PENNSYLVANIA
Bureau of Travel Marketing
453 Forum Building
Harrisburg, PA 17120
1-800-VISIT PA, ext. 257

RHODE ISLAND
Rhode Island Tourism Division
One West Exchange St.
Providence, RI 02903
1-800-556-2484

Travel

SOUTH CAROLINA
South Carolina Division of Tourism
Parks and Recreation
P.O. Box 71
Columbia, SC 29202
1-800-872-3505

SOUTH DAKOTA
Department of Tourism
711 E. Wells Ave.
Pierre, South Dakota 57501

TENNESSEE
Department of Tourist Development
P.O. Box 23170
Nashville, TN 37202
615-741-2158

TEXAS
Travel Information Services
Texas Department of Transportation
P.O. Box 5064
Austin, TX 78763 5064
512-483-3705

UTAH
Utah Travel Council
Council Hall, Capitol Hill
Salt Lake City, UT 84114
801-538 1030

VERMONT
Agency of Development and Community Affairs
Travel Division
134 State St.
Montpelier, VT 05602
802 828-3236

Travel

VIRGINIA
Virginia Department of Economic Development
Tourism Development Group
River Front Plaza West 19th Fl.
Richmond, VA 23219
1-800-VISIT-VA

WASHINGTON
Washington State Dept. of Trade and Economic Development
101 General Administration Bldg.
P.O. Box 42500
Olympia, WA 98504
206-753-5630

WASHINGTON, D.C.
See District of Columbia

WEST VIRGINIA
Division of Tourism and Parks
State Capitol Complex
Bldg. #6 Room #564
1900 Kanawha Blvd. East
Charleston, WV 25305-0317
1-800 CALL-WVA

WISCONSIN
Travel Information
Division of Tourism
123 W. Washington Ave.
P.O. Box 7606
Madison, WI 53707
1-800-432-TRIP

Travel

WYOMING
Wyoming Division of Tourism
I-25 at College Drive
Cheyenne, WY 82002
1-800-225-5996

National Parks

Enjoy the great outdoors. Get back to nature. Visit our beautiful national parks. There's a series of interesting guides to the 7 most popular national parks free for the asking. Send for any (or all) guides you'd like:

"Rocky Mountain National Park, Colorado"
"Mt. McKinley National Park, Alaska"
"Mesa Verde National Park Colorado"
'Hot Springs National Park, Arkansas"
"Hawaii National Park"
"Yellowstone National Park"
"Carlsbad Caverns, New Mexico"..

You might also want the *free map* of the National Park System. Request by name the guides you would like. Write to: **Dept. of the Interior, National Park Service, Washington, DC 20240**

Chocolate Town USA

If you are looking for a really fun time, why not try a special theme weekend at the fun Hershey Park in Hershey, Pennsylvania. For more detailed information, call: **1-800-HERSHEY**

Foreign Travel

Before you travel abroad be sure to contact the tourist office for the countries you plan to visit. They are delighted to send you a beautiful package of travel brochures, places to visit and a whole lot more.

ANTIGUA & BARBUDA
Antigua & Barbuda Dept of Tourism, 610 Fifth Avenue, Suite 311, New York, NY 10020

ARGENTINA
For maps and color brochures describing Argentina drop a card to: **Argentina Embassy, 1600 New Hampshire Ave., Washington, DC 20009**

ARUBA
Go sailing, scuba diving in the turquoise Caribbean, casinos, discos and lots more. Ask for "Sun Worshippers" with hotel rates and tourist information. Write: **Aruba Tourist Office, 1000 Harbor Boulevard, Weehawken, NJ 07087**

AUSTRIA
Write for the "*Austrian Information package*" and you'll receive a beautiful assortment of travel guides and student education opportunities. Drop a card to: **Austrian National Tourist Office; 500 Fifth Ave., New York. NY 10110**

BAHAMAS
Bahamas Tourist Office: call toll-free 1-800-422-4262

BARBADOS
Discover the many sides of Barbados that make it a luscious vacation spot. A nice tow *package* including several huge wall posters are yours for the asking. Write: **Barbados Board of Tourism, 800 Second Ave., New York, NY 10017**

BELIZE
Belize Tourist Board, 83 North Front Street, PO Box 325, Belize City Belize, Central America

Brazil
Brazil Reservations, 1050 Edison St. Suite C2, Santa Yorez, CA 93460. Or call: 1-800-544-5503

BRITISH VIRGIN ISLANDS
British Tourist Board, 370 Lexington Avenue, New York, NY 10017

BRITAIN
There's always something new to discover in England, Wales, Scotland & Ireland. Drop a card requesting the *Britain Information package* and you'll receive a beautiful color magazine, photos, maps, tours, etc. Send to: **British Tourist Authority, 551 Fifth Ave., New York, NY. Or call: 1-800-462-2748**

BRITAIN BY RAIL
Tour scenic Britain by rail. BritRail offers unlimited travel on most rail, bus & ferry routes. For a free guide travel hints as well as bargain ticket rates write to: **BritRail. Travel International, 1500 Broadway, New York, NY 10017**

BERMUDA
Thinking of traveling to Bermuda? Don't go without

Travel

this information package.. It includes travel tips, a map, hotel rates, and more. Write to: **Bermuda Dept. of Tourism. PO Box 77050, Woodside, NY 11377**

CANADA
"Touring Canada" is a big guide to 54 exciting tours of Canada. You'll learn where to go, what to see, what clothes to bring and much more. You'll find there's more to do in 'our neighbor to the north' than you had ever imagined. Write to: **Canadian Government Office of Tourism Ottawa, Canada KIA OH6**

CANCUN & COZUMEL
Cancun & Cozumel Tourist Office, 405 Park Avenue, Suite 1401 New York, NY 10022

CARIBBEAN SUN FUN
Discover the fun and excitement each of the Caribbean islands has to offer. Ask for the *travel package* free from: **Caribbean Tourism Assn., 20 E. 46th St., New York, NY 10017**

CAYMAN ISLANDS
Cayman Islands Tourism, 420 Lexington Avenue, #2733, New York, NY 10170

China - Taiwan
Taiwan Visitors Association, One World Trade Center, New York, NY

CURACAO
Curacao Tourist Board, 475 Park Ave. South Suite 2000, New York, NY 10016

Travel

EGYPT
Travel back in time to the cradle of civilization. Explore the pyramids and discover the old and new wonders of Egypt. Ask for the *Egypt Information package.* Write to: **Egyptian Government Travel Office, 630 Fifth Ave., New York, NY 10111**

FRANCE
The *France Information package* is a mini-tour of France with a large full color tour book plus Paris on a budget, a tour of Paris, hotels and motels in France off-season packages, and more. Contact: **French Government Tourist Office, 444 Madison Ave., New York, NY 10022. Or call: 1-212-838-7800**

GERMANY
"Welcome To Germany" is a beautiful guide full of color photos that are absolutely breathtaking. This is just part of the Germany Tour package free from: **Lufthansa German Airlines, 1640 Hempstead Turnpike, East Meadow, NY 11554**

GERMANY TRAIN TRAVEL
If you're planning a trip to Germany one of the best ways to tour the country is by train. With German Rail you will have unlimited travel plus discounts on many bus and boat routes. For free information write: **GermanRail, 747 Third Ave., New York, NY 10017**

Travel

GREECE
To help you make your trip to Greece more enjoyable, here's a large packet of brochures, maps and booklets on the beautiful Greek Islands. Request the *Greece Tour package* from: **Greek National Tourist Organization, Olympic Tower, 645 Fifth Ave., New York, NY 10022**

GRENADA
Grenada Board of Tourism, 820 Second Avenue, Suite 900 D New York, NY 10017

GUYANA
Guyana Tourism, c/o Caribbean Tourism Organization 80 East Broad Street Suite 3200, New York, NY 10004

HUNGARY
Like beautiful picture post cards, the color illustrations in this package will take you for a tour of the sights and attractions of Hungary. Ask for the *Hungary Travel package* which includes a map of the country. Send a card to: **Consulate General of Hungary, 223 East 52nd St., New York, NY 10022 Or call: 212-752-0661**

INDIA
Dozens of scenic color photos of India are included in the *India Tour Kit* yours free from: **Information Service of India, Embassy of India, Washington, DC 20008**

INDONESIA
For facts on the Indonesia archipelago including their history, geography, culture, maps, and more drop a card requesting their *information package.* Write to: **Consulate General of Indonesia, Information Section, 5 E. 68th St., New York, NY 10022**

Travel

IRELAND
Call: **1-800-SHAMROCK** or write to: **Irish Tourist Board, 345 Park Ave., New York, NY 10154**

ISRAEL
If you enjoyed the book you'll love the country. For a nice collection of *guide books and maps* of Israel and the Holy Land write to: **Israel Government Tourist Office, 350 Fifth Ave., New York, NY 10118**

ITALY
A beautiful arm chair tour of Italy is in store for you. Write for *"A Trip To Italy tour package"* with road maps and marvelous full color guide books. It's yours free from: **Italian Government Travel Office, 630 Fifth Ave., New York, NY 10111.**

IVORY COAST
Learn about the rites of Panther Men and the fascinating culture of the Agri Kingdom. All this and much more in the travel kit from: **Ivory Coast Embassy, 2424 Massachusetts Ave. N.W., Washington, DC 20008**

JAMAICA
Soft beaches, jungle waterfalls, hot discos and sailing in the sunshine—it's all in a beautiful full color book that features 56 great vacations. Ask for the free *"Jamaica Vacation Book"* from: **Jamaica Tourist Board, 8237 NW 66th St, Miami, FL 33160**

JAPAN
The *Japan Tour package is* an impressive collection of travel booklets in full color with marvelous illustrations. You'll receive a mini tour of Japan chuck full of facts about Japan's history with travel tips and many fascinating tid bits. For all this write to: **Japan Travel Bureau, 810 Seventh Ave. 34th Floor, New York NY 10019. Or call: 212-698-4900**

Travel

MARTINIQUE
Martinique Dept. of Tourism, 610 Fifth Avenue New York, NY 10020

MEXICO
For a set of over a dozen color brochures showing the sights and tourist attractions of Mexico, drop a post card to: **Mexican National Tourist Council, 405 Park Ave., New York, NY 10022**

MONTSERRAT
Montserrat Tourism Information, 485 Fifth Avenue New York, NY 10017

MOROCCO
Exotic Morocco has some of the most magnificent scenery in the world. For a kit of *travel information and tour packages* to this ancient kingdom drop a card to: **Royal Air Maroc, 55 East 59th St., New York, NY**

PORTUGAL
Discover all the beauty of Portugal— its beaches, entertainment and hotels — all in this package of full color brochures. Call: **TAP Air at 1-800-221-7370.**

RUSSIA
Write to: **Embassy of The Russian Federation, 1125 16th St. N.W., Washington, D.C. 20036**

St. Maarten
For beautiful travel brochures of the island of St. Maarten call: **1-800-ST-MAARTEN**

Scotland
For colorful brochures on Scotland, call toll-free: **1-800-343-SCOT**

Travel

SINGAPORE
Singapore's the place where all Asia comes together. Here's a beautiful color package of things to do and see plus a map and even a recipe booklet with delightful meals of Singapore. Write to: **Embassy of Republic of Singapore, 1824 'R' St. N.W., Washington, D.C. 20009**

SOUTH AFRICA
Write to: **Embassy of South Africa, 3501 Massachusetts Ave. N.W., Washington, D.C. 20008**

SPAIN
Write to: **Spain Office of Tourism, 666 Fifth Ave, New York, NY 10103**

SWITZERLAND
For a mini-tour of the Alps send a postcard for the *Swiss Tour package*. You'll receive beautifully illustrated booklets, maps, travel tips, recipes and more. All of this comes to you free from: **Swiss National Tourist Office, 608 Fifth Ave., New York, NY 10020**

THAILAND
Come to Thailand and enjoy its dazzling scenery, incredible shopping bargains and the special joy of sharing the Thai people have. Drop a postcard to: **Tourism Authority of Thailand, 3440 Wilshire Blvd., Suite 1101, Los Angeles, CA 90010.** Or: **Tourism Authority of Thailand, 5 World Trade Center, Suite 2449, New York, NY 10048**

ZAMBIAN SAFARI
Zambia has a big package of travel & tourist information waiting for you. The beautiful color brochures are a mini-safari through the African bush. Write to: **Zambia National Tourist Board, 800 Second Ave., New York, NY 10017. Or call: 212-949-0133**

Travel

PERU and NATURE
Here are colorful maps, charts and pictures of native birds, flowers and animals. You'll also find a listing of national parks and reserves, as well as interesting archaeological and historical highlights. Write to: **Explorations, Inc., 27655 Kent Rd., Bonita Springs, FL 33923**

Hong Kong Tourist Information
If you are over 60 years old and are thinking of going on a shopping trip to Hong Kong, there's a free discount booklet that will save you money on your shopping. Write to: **Hong Kong Tourist Information, 590 Fifth Ave., New York, NY 10036**

NOVA SCOTIA, Canada
"Nova Scotia Holiday" is a beautiful color book that tells all about things to see, history, legends, customs crafts and more. Call toll-free: **800-341-6096** or write to: **Nova Scotia Information. P.O. Box 130 Halifax. Nova Scotia, Canada B3J 2M7**

Free From The Government

The U.S. Government Toll-Free Helpline

Have you ever tried to find an answer to a simple question about the Federal Government and ended up on a merry-go-round of referrals. Or you may have had a question about the Federal Government that was so difficult you had no idea where to begin. Well relax! Now there's one toll-free number you can call for assistance. It's called the *Federal Information Center* and it's a clearinghouse of all government agencies. It is designed to help the average person find the information they need quickly and effortlessly.

They will also refer you to the government agency that deals with the type of problem or question they may have. Their Information Specialists are extraordinary when it comes to finding the exact place you should contact for help. Some of the things they can help you with are... who you can contact for help with your social security benefits, sales & auctions of siezed properties, consumer complaints, veteran's benefits, offices of the aging and virtually all other branches of the government. Their hours of operation are 9 a.m. to 5 p.m EST.

Call them toll-free at: **1-800-688-9889.**

(Disabled individuals using text phones [TDD/TTY] may call toll-free anywhere in the U.S. by dialing 1-800-326-2996).

If you have access to the Internet you can also find help on all government related questions by going to: **www.info.gov**

Do You Know How Much Social Security You Will Get?

If you've ever wondered exactly how much money your Social Security benefits will be once you retire, there's an easy way to find out...get your Personal Earnings and Benefit Estimate Statement. For an estimate of what your retirement benefits might be call the toll-free phone number and ask for an *'earnings estimate request'* to fill out and return.

The Social Security Administration will then do a free search of their records and send you a detailed printout of how much has been contributed each year and how much your benefits will if you retire at different ages. Find out what disability benefits you qualify for... and how the value of your benefits compares with the amount of Social Security taxes you have paid over the years. This statement is yours free from the Social Security Administration.

At the same toll-free number they are also happy to answer any other questions you may have relating to your Social Security. Call: **1-800-772-1213.** You can also access them on the Internet at: **www.ssa.gov**

Do You Need Extra Money From Social Security?

Many low income seniors never realize it but even if they don't qualify for regular Social Security benefits, they may still qualify for thousands of dollars in extra income.

If you are over 65 and find that you have difficulty meeting your normal living expenses, or if you are blind or disabled at any age, you may qualify for a program called *Supplemental Security Income* (SSI).

This program was established to help seniors over the age of 65 who have too little income to pay for their basic needs and to help those who are not able to work because they are disabled regardless of their age.

To qualify you must meet a maximum asset and monthly income qualification but studies have shown that as many as half of the seniors who do qualify never receive SSI benefits because they don't realize that they are eligible for this extra income. However, once you do qualify for SSI, you will also automatically qualify for both Medicaid and Food Stamps.

To find out if you qualify, either contact your local Social Security office or call their toll-free helpline: **1-800-772-1213.**

Free From The Government

Free Food For Seniors

When you live on a limited budget you learn to cut corners wherever you can. But one of the areas you should never cut corners on is in eating properly. If you are living on a limited budget even if you are living with someone else, you may qualify for food stamps that will save you thousands of dollars. And as a senior, if you are not able to travel to the social services agency to apply for the food stamps, they may visit your home or take the application right over the phone. Check the blue pages of you local phone book for a social services agency in your area. You can also get the address and phone number by calling the OFFICE OF THE AGING in your area.

Locating A Missing Person

If you have a problem of trying to locate a missing relative or friend, a letter to the Social Security Administration may help. When you write be sure to include as much information as you can about the missing person including their last address and date of birth. Write to:

PUBLIC INQUIRIES
SOCIAL SECURITY ADMINISTRATION
6501 SECURITY BLVD.
BALTIMORE, MD 20235

Free From The Government

Free Books & Magazines

Did you know that the National Library Service has a large collection of books, magazines, journals, music materials in Braille, large type and recorded format for those who have temporary or permanent vision loss or physical limitations? Special playback equipment is available on a loan basis from the Library of Congress, and cassettes and CD's are available from over 155 participating libraries. And if you are unable to hold a book or have a serious visual handicap, you can borrow these materials postage-free. They will even pay the postage in sending the materials back to them. Contact them at the address and phone number below or ask your local library to find out what's available to you.

HANDICAPPED READERS REFERENCE SECTION
NATIONAL LIBRARY SERVICE FOR THE BLIND AND
PHYSICALLY HANDICAPPED
LIBRARY OF CONGRESS
WASHINGTON, DC 20542
800-424-9100. OR ACCESS THEM ON THE WEB:
www.loc.gov/nls

A Car For $200.00?

Yes you can really own a boat, luxury car, fancy gems even a house with all its treasures for just a tiny fraction of its true value. All these treasures are confiscated from drug raids or other illegal activities. The government has no use for these goods and can't store them all so they have contracted with private companies to auction off these goods.

At these auctions you have an excellent chance

Free From The Government

of getting goods for practically nothing. You can get a free copy of the *National Sellers List* which lists the local sellers of the Marshall Services goods. To get that list you must reach them either by fax or at their Internet site or from the Consumer Information Catalog: Their **fax** number is: **202-307-5020.** The Internet address is:
www.usdoj.gov/marshals/assets/assets.html

The IRS also has auctions throughout the country of property of every kind ...everything from houses to cars, jewelry and lots more...all seized for non-payment of taxes. For a list of sales and auctions for properties siezed by the IRS, request the list from:
TREASURY SALES & AUCTIONS
EG&G SERVICES, INC
37 PENDER DRIVE
FAIRFAX, VA 22030. OR CALL THEM AT:
703-273-7373

Striking It Rich

Did you know that the U.S. Government will let you prospect on public lands? If you would like to find out how to strike it rich on government lands, send a card to the Forest Service. Ask for *A Guide To Your National Forests*. Write to:
MINERALS AND GEOLOGY STAFF
FOREST SERVICE
DOA, BOX 2417
WASHINGTON, DC 20013

Free From The Government

Free Firewood

Did you know that in most of the 154 National Forests, firewood for your own personal use is free. To find out how you can get free firewood and also how to select, purchase and use firewood ask for the *Firewood Information package*. Free from:

FIREWOOD #559
FOREST SERVICE
BOX 2417
WASHINGTON, DC 20013

Buying U.S. Government Surplus...Cheap!!

Every year the federal government buys billions of dollars of every kind of merchandise imagineable. Much of this is never used and eventually the U.S. Government must sell all this surplus property on a regular basis. To find out how to buy everything from binoculars to autos at super low bargain prices, write to:

SURPLUS SALES CENTER
WASHINGTON NAVY YARD
WASHINGTON, DC 20408

You're Paying Too Much Income Tax

Wouldn't that be a welcome notice to receive from the IRS? Believe it or not many seniors really *are* paying a lot more income tax than they should be. The reason is that they just aren't aware of all the

deductions and exemptions they are entitled to. To be sure you're not paying more taxes than you should, ask for a free copy of *Protecting Older Americans Against Overpayment of Income Taxes..*
Contact:
SPECIAL COMMITTEE ON AGING
U.S. SENATE
WASHINGTON, D.C. 20410
202-224-5364

Lower Your Real Estate Tax

Throughout the nation, states and local governments are recognizing that seniors deserve a break when it comes to the real estate taxes they pay on their home. After all by the time they are 65 years old most seniors no longer have children in public school. And yet they're still paying school taxes on their real estate.

For example, New York State recently instituted what it calls the 'STAR' program. Under this program, seniors aged 65 or older who own a home are entitled to a whopping 40% reduction in the school taxes they pay as part of their real estate tax. This reduction is not based upon low income or financial need. It is available to *all* seniors in NYS who ask for it. But they will not get the reduction unless they ask. What that means is that you must check with your local town or county tax assessor's office to see if they offer a senior citizen tax reduction. Until you apply you could be paying thousands of dollars too much in real estate tax.

Free From The Government

Do You Know What Else The Secret Service Does?

You know that the Secret Service protects the President but did you know that the Secret Service has another important job? It was originally created to stamp out counterfeiting - a job they still perform. To learn more, ask for *"Counterfeiting and Forgery"* which shows how to detect a counterfeit bill. Write to:

U.S. Secret Service
1800 'G' St. N.W., Room 941
Washington, DC 20223

Just How Secure Is Your Home?

The F.B.I. would like every family to feel more secure. Learn how to better protect your family against crime. *A Way to Protect Your Family Against Crime* offers tips you and your family can safely use to take a bite out of crime. Ask for the free *Crime Resistance booklet*. You might also want a copy of the *Abridged History of the F.B.I.* All free from:

F.B.I. Public Affairs Dept.
10th & Pennsylvania Ave.
Washington, DC 20535

Pension & Retirement Hotline

If you have tax questions dealing with your pension or retirement plans, now you can ask the tax attorneys at the IRS for help. These attorneys specialize in tax law dealing specifically with pension and retirement plans. Now you can get expert tax advice right from the source...for free! Call them between 1:30 pm and 3:30 pm EST, Monday through Thursday. Call: **1-202-622-6074.**

"You're Too Old...You're Fired!!"

No you aren't likely to hear these exact words but that doesn't mean you won't be discriminated against because of your age. Just remember that if you are over 40 years old, the law is clear. It is against the law to discriminate against anyone because of their age when it comes to hiring, firing, pay, promotions and other conditions of employment. And to insure that an employer will not discriminate against you on the basis of your age, sex, race, or disability and get away with it, the government has set up The Equal Employment Opportunity Commission. If you feel that you have been a victim of discrimination by an employer (or potential employer), be sure to contact:

THE EQUAL EMPLOYMENT OPPORTUNITY COMMISSION
1801 L STREET NW
WASHINGTON, DC 20507
And to be connected to the EEOC office nearest you just dial:
1-800-669-4000

Golden Passport To Fun

Did you know that any senior citizen can buy a lifetime entrance to national parks, monuments, historic sites, recreation areas and national refuges for a one time fee of just $10.00! This also entitles you to a whopping 50% discount on fees for things like camping, swimming, parking, boat launching and cave tours. It's called the *Federal Golden Age Passport* and it could be worth its weight in gold. And for the blind and disabled there's the Federal Golden Access Passport which is completely free. To get your passport, call the National Park Service at: **202-208-4747**

$10,000 To Fix Up Your Home

Is your home in bad need of repair but you just can't afford the money to fix it up? Well now there's help in the form of grants of anywhere from $1,000 to as much as $10,000 with money coming from the U.S.D.A. Rural Housing Service.

Right now there are more than 2.5 million substandard homes across the nation. The federal government is helping remedy this situation by giving money to local non-profit groups who must use this money to make low-interest loans and outright grants that never have to be repaid. This money is for low-income homeowners aged 62 and older who otherwise would have to live in homes that are a safety or health risk.

To apply for a loan or grant, check the blue pages of your phone book under 'federal government' for your local *'U.S. Department of Agriculture – Rural Development'* office. If you can't find it in your local

Free From The Government

phone book, you can contact:
**U.S.D.A. RURAL HOUSING SERVICE
STOP 0700 1400 INDEPENDENCE AVE S.W.
WASHINGTON, DC 20250-0780
202-720-8732**
You can also check on the Internet at:
http://rdinit.usda.gov

Free Legal Services

If you've ever needed the services of an attorney you already know just how expensive legal help can be. But did you know that you can get legal help worth thousands of dollars - all paid for with money from the federal government or from legal services donated by attorneys who volunteer for "pro bono" (free) service to help those who can not afford legal representation.

See the back of this book for the *Free Legal Services Directory* which lists hundreds of legal service and pro bono attorney offices across the country. Find the office nearest you and call them the next time you need the services of an attorney.

Free Programs & Services From The U.S. Government

The U.S. Government offers thousands of special programs and services that your tax dollars have already paid for. But to benefit from them you must know they are there.

To keep you informed about these programs and to help you with a wide range of problems you may have, the government has hundreds of highly informative booklets that are yours free or practically free. These booklets are distributed through an agency called...**Consumer Information** which is located in Pueblo, Colorado.

All of the publications listed here are either free or are available for a very nominal charge. You can order up to 25 free publications by simply enclosing $2.00 as a processing fee. (See more complete ordering details at the end of this section.)

FEDERAL PROGRAMS

Americans With Disabilities Act: Questions and Answers.
Explains how the civil rights of persons with disabilities are protected at work and in public places. 32 pp. **513H. Free.**

Are There Any Public Lands for Sale?
Describes the federal program to sell excess undeveloped public land and why there is no more available for homesteading. 12 pp. **111H. $1.00.**

A Guide to Disability Rights Laws.
Covers the rights of persons with disabilities regarding fair housing, public accommodations, education, employment, and more. 14 pp. **514H. Free.**

Guide to Federal Government Sales.
Explains how to buy homes, cars, and other property from 17 federal sales programs. 19 pp. **112H. $2.00.**

How You Can Buy Used Federal Personal Property.
Describes used equipment and industrial items sold by the government, how they are sold, and where to call for more information. 5 pp. **318H. 50¢.**

National Sellers List.
The government sells real estate and personal property that has been forfeited to federal law enforcement agencies. Here's a list of addresses and phone numbers for dealers who sell these items. 8 pp. **319H. 50¢.**

Social Security: Your Number and Card.
Explains why we have social security numbers, when and how to get one, and how to protect its privacy. 2 pp. **515H. Free.**

U.S. Real Property Sales List.
Lists government real estate properties that are sold by auction or sealed bid. Tells how to get more

information on specific properties. 5 pp. **516H. Free.**

Your Right to Federal Records.
Use the Freedom of Information Act (FOIA) and the Privacy Act to obtain records from the federal government. Includes a sample request letter. 26 pp. **320H. 50¢.**

Benefits

Choosing a Doctor: A Guide for People With Medicare.
Useful information to find the right doctor, with worksheets to help decide what you want in a doctor, questions to ask, and more. 31 pp. **517H. Free.**

Choosing a Hospital: A Guide for People With Medicare.
Here are tips on choosing the best possible facility when you or a family member need hospital care. 19 pp. **518H. Free.**

Choosing Treatments: A Guide for People With Medicare.
Provides advice and worksheets to help you work

with your doctor to develop the best treatment plan for any health problem. 31 pp. **519H. Free.**

The Future of Social Security.
Find out more about today's Social Security system so you can help shape the system of tomorrow. 8 pp. **520H. Free.**

Medicare and Home Health Care.
This guide outlines what aspects of home health care are covered under Medicare, questions to ask when choosing home health care, and more. 21 pp. **521H. Free.**

Medicare and Other Health Benefits: Your Guide to Who Pays First.
Use this guide to help you determine whether Medicare or your other insurance pays first when you receive health care. 37 pp. **522H. Free.**

Medicare and Your Mental Health Benefits.
Your mental health is an important part of your overall well-being. Use this guide to learn what is covered under Medicare. 9 pp. **523H. Free.**

Medicare Hospice Benefits.
Hospice care is a special type of care for terminally ill patients. Tips on how to find a hospice program and where to get more information. 12 pp. **524H. Free.**

Medicare Preventive Services...To Help Keep You Healthy.
Use this guide to lower your risk of cancer, flu, pneumonia, diabetes, and other illnesses. 4 pp. **525H. Free.**

Free From The Government

Medicare Worksheet for Comparing Medicare Health Plans.
Health care coverage decisions aren't always easy. Check off these easy-to-follow points and get the best plan for your needs. 9 pp. **526H. Free.**

Pay it Right! Protecting Medicare from Fraud.
Each year, fraudulent claims increase Medicare expenses and premiums. Learn how to spot warning signs of fraud and how to report errors and concerns. 7 pp. **527H. Free.**

Request for Earnings and Benefit Estimate Statement.
A form to complete and return to Social Security to get your earnings history and an estimate of future benefits. 3 pp. **528H. Free.**

Social Security: Basic Facts.
Describes the different kinds of Social Security benefits, who receives them, and how they're financed. 17 pp. **529H. Free.**

Social Security: Understanding the Benefits.
Explains retirement, disability, survivor's benefits, Medicare coverage, Supplemental Security Income, and more. 41 pp. **530H. Free.**

Social Security: What Every Woman Should Know.
Discusses how a woman's benefits may be affected by disability, divorce, widowhood, retirement, or other special situations. 19 pp. **531H. Free.**

Free From The Government

Your Medicare Benefits.
It's important to be familiar with what your health care plan covers. Learn about both hospital and medical insurance with this booklet. 13 pp. **532H. Free.**

Retirement Planning

Your Guaranteed Pension.
Answers 18 frequently asked questions about the security of private pension plans, including benefits and plan termination. 11 pp. **588H. Free.**

401(k) Plans.
Covers what these retirement plans are and how they differ from other investment options. Learn what happens when you change employers, what to do if you need the money before retirement, and investing tips for your 401(k) plan. 14 pp. **583H. Free.**

Annuities.
An important tool in planning your retirement may be annuities. Use this guide's helpful quiz to see if annuities are right for you. 11 pp. **584H. Free.**

Finding a Lost Pension.
Thousands of retired workers in the U.S are entitled to pensions that they have not claimed. Here's how to find out if you have a lost pension, where to search, documents you'll need, and what to do when you find your pension fund. 36 pp. **133H. $2.00.**

Savings Fitness: A Guide to Your Money and Your Financial Future.
Get in shape financially. Create your personal savings plan and prepare for retirement with this step-by-step guide. 20 pp. **585H. Free.**

Top 10 Ways to Beat the Clock and Prepare for Retirement.
Gives practical tips to build your retirement savings and lists resources for more information. 2 pp. **586H. Free.**

Women and Pensions.
Provides a checklist of questions to ask about retirement benefits, including plan type, eligibility, penalties, spousal benefits, and more. 6 pp. **587H. Free.**

MONEY

Cold Calling.
When can sellers legally call? How can you stop them, what are the signs of a scam or fraud, and who can you contact for help? 15 pp. **339H. 50¢.**

Establishing a Trust Fund.
Trust funds can be a handy financial tool for many people. Learn what trusts can and can't do, their benefits, the role of a trustee, and more. 10 pp. **574H. Free.**

Making a Will.
Explains why a will is important, how to prepare one, what to include, and how to keep it current. 12 pp. **575H. Free.**

What You Should Know About Buying Life Insurance.
Describes various types with tips on choosing a company, an agent, and a policy that meets your needs. 23 pp. **576H. Free.**

Credit

Consumer Handbook to Credit Protection Laws.
Explains how consumer credit laws can help you apply for credit, keep up a good credit standing, and complain about an unfair deal. 44 pp. **340H. 50¢.**

Credit Matters.
Learn how to qualify for credit, keep a good credit history, get the best deal on a credit card, protect your credit once you have it, and how to deal with credit errors. 5 pp. **341H. 50¢.**

Fair Credit Reporting.
Learn what's in your credit report, how you can get a copy, and more. 2 pp. **342H. 50¢.**

Fair Debt Collection.
Describes what debt collectors may and may not do if you owe money. How and where to complain if you are harassed, threatened, or abused. 2 pp. **343H. 50¢.**

How to Dispute Credit Report Errors.
Gives tips on correcting errors, registering a dispute, and adding information to your file. 2 pp. **344H. 50¢.**

ID Theft: When Bad Things Happen to Your Good Name.
Protect your banking and credit info with this helpful guide. Includes resources to contact, and a sample letter to follow to officially report a dispute. 21 pp. **345H. 50¢.**

Managing Your Debts: How to Regain Financial Health.
Learn where to begin—what you can do for yourself, how credit counseling can help, facts about bankruptcy, and more. 2 pp. **346H. 50¢.**

Investing & Saving

66 Ways to Save Money.
Practical ways to cut everyday costs on transportation, insurance, banking, credit, housing, utilities, food, and more. 4 pp. **347H. 50¢.**

The Consumer's Almanac.
Organize your daily expenses, save and invest for the future, and manage your credit with monthly calendars and worksheets. 32 pp. **348H. 50¢.**

Get the Facts on Saving and Investing.
Use this guide's helpful tips and worksheets for calculating net worth, income, and expenses. 18 pp. **349H. 50¢.**

I Bonds Investor's Guide.
Follow this easy-to-read Q&A format to find out if I Bonds are a good way for you to save and invest money. 6 pp. **350H. 50¢.**

Introduction to Mutual Funds.
What are they, how to compare them, what to consider before investing, and how to avoid common pitfalls. 15 pp. **351H. 50¢.**

Investment Swindles: How They Work and How to Avoid Them.
Protect yourself against illegal, yet legitimate-sounding, telemarketing and direct mail offers. 22 pp. **577H. Free.**

Investors' Bill of Rights.
Here are some tips on what you should know about investments and what information you are entitled to before investing. 7 pp. **578H. Free.**

Planning Financial Security.
Here's a helpful step-by-step guide to improving your financial future. It features a worksheet to help track your spending, tips on creating a spending plan, and an investor's checklist. 12 pp. **579H. Free.**

Ten Questions to Ask When Choosing a Financial Planner.
Covers credentials, costs, services, an interview checklist, and resources to contact for more information. 12 pp. **580H. Free.**

U.S. Savings Bonds Investor Information.
Detailed information on bond purchase, interest, maturity, replacement, redemption, exchange, and taxes. 14 pp. **352H. 50¢.**

What You Should Know About Financial Planning.
Are you planning to buy a house or retire in the near future? This useful guide discusses the benefits of financial planning for these and other life-changing events. 13 pp. **581H. Free.**

Your Insured Deposit.
Explains what is protected and what isn't if your bank should fail, how much of your money is insured, what types of accounts are covered, and more. 21 pp. **582H. Free.**

SMALL BUSINESS

Avoiding Office Supply Scams.
Learn the most common office scams and tips to avoid receiving overpriced or unordered merchandise. 5 pp. **353H. 50¢.**

Copyright Basics.
Covers what can be copyrighted, who can apply, registration procedures, filing fees, what forms to use, and more. 12 pp. **354H. 50¢.**

SBA Programs & Services.
Find out how SBA can help you start or expand a business. Describes SBA's financial assistance programs, business development programs, and more. 36 pp. **589H. Free.**

Free From The Government

CARS

Buying a New Car.
Here's a step-by-step guide that can help you along the way. Use the guide's new car worksheet as a tool for bargaining with dealers. 2 pp. **301H. 50¢.**

Buying a Used Car.
Discusses your limited rights when buying from a dealer or private owner. 16 pp. **302H. 50¢.**

Glove Box Tips.
Five booklets to help you get your car ready for summer and winter driving, choose the right repair shop, and get the best work from your mechanic. 10 pp. **303H. 50¢.**

How to Find Your Way Under the Hood & Around the Car.
Instructions for 14 preventive maintenance services you can perform on your car. 2 pp. **304H. 50¢.**

How to Get a Great Deal on a New Car.
Step-by-step instructions for a proven negotiation technique to save money on your next car. 4 pp. **305H. 50¢.**

Keys to Vehicle Leasing.
Learn the difference between leasing and buying a car. Explains required information on a lease agreement, as well as your rights and responsibilities. 6 pp. **306H. 50¢.**

Nine Ways to Lower Your Auto Insurance Costs.
Tips on what to do to lower your expenses. Includes a chart to compare discounts. 6 pp. **307H. 50¢.**

CHILDREN

Learning Activities

Catch the Spirit: A Student's Guide to Community Service.
Ideas and information on how young people can help make their community a better place. 15 pp. **501H. Free.**

Helping Your Child Learn Geography.
Teach 5-10 year old children geography in ways that are challenging and fun. 33 pp. **308H. 50¢.**

Learning Activities for the Growth Season.
A 7-week schedule listing daily, fun learning activities for elementary age children. Poster. **309H. 50¢.**

Learning Partners.
Activities to help your preschool or elementary aged child learn reading, math, science, history, writing, and much more. 30 pp. **310H. 50¢.**

Timeless Classics.
Lists nearly 400 books published before 1960 for children of all ages. Divided into K-12 grade groups. 2 pp. **311H. 50¢.**

Parenting

Danger in the Home.
Use this handy checklist to detect potential hazards to children and how to make your home a safer place. 4 pp. **502H. Free.**

Fun Play, Safe Play.
Use this guide to discover the importance of play in your child's learning and development and how to buy safe toys. 24 pp. **503H. Free.**

Growing Up Drug Free.
Outlines what parents should know and can do to prevent or stop drug abuse, including alcohol and tobacco, at each age level. 46 pp. **504H. Free.**

Handbook on Child Support Enforcement.
A "how to" guide for getting the payments owed to you and your children. Lists state and federal offices for more information. 61 pp. **505H. Free.**

Help Yourself to a Healthy Home: Protect Your Children's Health.
Find out about potentially harmful products in your home and follow the easy action steps to keep your house healthy, especially if your family has allergies. 24 pp. **506H. Free.**

Learning Disabilities.
Explains the differences between learning problems and disabilities. Chart shows language and reasoning skills to watch for at different ages and more. 40 pp. **313H. 50¢.**

Parents' Guide to the Internet.
Information on equipment and software, costs, surfing the Internet, getting e-mail, and protecting your privacy. Lists interesting and fun online resources for parents and children. 16 pp. **314H. 50¢.**

Planning For Your Special Needs Child.
Learn about setting up a legal guardian and plan-

ning for your child's financial, medical and educational needs. 14 pp. **507H. Free.**

Protecting Your Child.
It's a parent's worst nightmare—a child lost or missing. Use this guide to teach your children about avoiding potential harm in person and in cyberspace. 12 pp. **508H. Free.**

EDUCATION

GED Diploma.
Explains what the General Educational Development Diploma tests cover, how to prepare, and where to get more information. 16 pp. **509H. Free.**

Nontraditional Education: Alternative Ways to Earn Your Credentials.
Get high school or college credit through the GED program, the National External Diploma program, correspondence and distance study, and standardized tests. 13 pp. **101H. $2.00.**

Planning for College.
Strategies to help you plan for tuition and fees along with helpful charts for estimating future costs. 10 pp. **510H. Free.**

Think College? Me? Now? A Handbook for Students in Middle School and Junior High.
Did you know students should start preparing for college in the seventh and eighth grades? Sound too early? Learn about the benefits of planning ahead for college. 24 pp. **102H. $1.25.**

EMPLOYMENT

Changing Your Job.
Use this guide to learn how to assess if your current job is right for you, what to do when you decide to look for a new job, and what happens to your benefits when you change jobs. 12 pp. **511H. Free.**

Employment Interviewing.
Follow these preparation tips, including important questions to prepare for and to ask your potential employer. Use the advice on references, job fairs and follow-up letters to get the job. 9 pp. **103H. $1.50.**

Health Benefits Under COBRA (Consolidated Omnibus Budget Reconciliation Act).
How to keep or buy coverage for yourself and family after a job loss, reduced work hours, divorce, or death. 24 pp. **315H. 50¢.**

Help Wanted—Finding A Job.
Describes both private companies and government agencies that offer help in finding a job. Lists precautions to take when contacting an employment service firm. 8 pp. **316H. 50¢.**

Here Today, Jobs of Tomorrow: Opportunities in Information Technology.
This booklet discusses the high demand for information technology workers and if this field is right for you. 13 pp. **104H. $2.00.**

High Earning Workers Who Don't Have a Bachelor's Degree.
Identifies 50 occupations requiring less than a bachelor's degree. 9 pp. **105H. $2.50.**

Matching Yourself With the World of Work.
Don't fall into a job that might not be a perfect fit for you. Find out what to look for in your ideal job with this guide. 19 pp. **107H. $2.25.**

OSHA: Employee Workplace Rights.
What to do if you question the safety of, or hazards in your workplace. Lists addresses and phone numbers for more information. 28 pp. **512H. Free.**

Resumes, Applications, and Cover Letters.
Use this guide's samples to format a winning cover letter and resume, and learn how new technology can help. 15 pp. **108H. $1.50.**

Tips for Finding the Right Job.
How to assess your skills and interests, create a resume, write cover letters, and prepare for a job interview. 27 pp. **109H. $2.00.**

Tomorrow's Jobs.
Discusses changes and trends in the economy, labor force, occupational growth, and more. 18 pp. **110H. $2.50.**

What You Should Know About Your Pension Rights.
This informative booklet details the rights, benefits, and protections you have under your pension plan. 48 pp. **317H. 50¢.**

Free From The Government

HEALTH

Action Guide for Healthy Eating.
This guide gives helpful hints to help you include more low fat, high-fiber foods in your diet. 17 pp. **533H. Free.**

Bulking Up Fiber's Healthful Reputation.
Explains how a high fiber diet is associated with a reduced risk of certain cancers, digestive disorders, and other ailments. 5 pp. **534H. Free.**

A Consumer's Guide to Fats.
Learn about the different kinds and what effect they have on your cholesterol level. 6 pp. **535H. Free.**

Eating for Life.
Tips on how to make healthful, appetizing food choices at home and when eating out. 23 pp. **117H. $1.25.**

Food Guide Pyramid.
This easy-to-read guide can help you select the nutrients you need and reduce the fat, cholesterol, and sodium in your diet. 29 pp. **118H. $1.00.**

Fruits & Vegetables: Eating Your Way to 5 A Day.
Eating fruits and vegetables can reduce the risk of heart disease and cancer. Gives ideas to help you meet the 5 A Day goal. 6 pp. **536H. Free.**

Growing Older, Eating Better.
Good nutrition can lessen the effects of aging and disease and improve the quality of life. Discusses the various causes of poor nutrition and how it can

be improved. 5 pp. **537H. Free.**

Listeriosis and Food Safety Tips.
Eating foods with the listeria bacteria can seriously affect pregnant women, newborns, and older adults. Learn about this illness, its symptoms, and how you can prevent it. 8 pp. **538H. Free.**

Preventing Food-Borne Illness.
Describes the bacteria that causes food-borne illness and how to handle food safely. Use the storage guidelines chart to know when to throw away those leftovers. 8 pp. **539H. Free.**

Sugar Substitutes: Americans Opt for Sweetness and Lite.
A sweet tooth can sabotage your effort to cut calories. Use this guide to find out about the low-calorie sugar substitutes available and how they fit into your diet. 5 pp. **540H. Free.**

Use a Food Thermometer.
Don't judge meat by its color—it can make you sick. Get the right thermometer and use the handy temperature chart for safe, delicious food. 3 pp. **541H. Free.**

Using the Dietary Guidelines for Americans.
How to choose a diet that will taste good, be nutritious, and reduce chronic disease risks. 2 pp. **321H. 50¢.**

Cosmetic Laser Surgery: A High-Tech Weapon in the Fight Against Aging Skin.
Lasers can help remove facial wrinkles and lines. This guide explains the procedure, its risks, how to

tell if it's right for you, and what to look for in a surgeon. 4 pp. **542H. Free.**

Getting Information From FDA.
Learn more about the Food and Drug Administration (FDA), what it does, and what information it can give you. 3 pp. **543H. Free.**

How to Find Medical Information.
This book will guide you through a variety of resources—from your local library, to the federal government, to the Internet—to help you get info on an illness or disorder. 24 pp. **544H. Free.**

Questions to Ask Your Doctor Before You Have Surgery.
Use this booklet to become a better informed and prepared patient. 13 pp. **120H. $1.00.**

Staying Healthy at 50+.
Covers everything from cholesterol levels, various cancers, weight control, and checkups, with helpful charts to keep track of your medications, shots, and screening test results. 64 pp. **121H. $2.50.**

Sun, UV, and You.
Explains what the UV (ultraviolet radiation) index is and how you can use it to avoid skin cancer, premature aging of the skin, and more. 12 pp. **545H. Free.**

Understanding Breast Changes: A Health Guide for All Women.
Describes the various types of breast changes that

women experience. Also discusses breast cancer screening, diagnosis, treatment, and prevention. 52 pp. **546H. Free.**

Understanding Prostate Changes: A Health Guide for All Men.
Learn about prostate enlargement and prostate cancer, including screening and treatment. 38 pp. **547H. Free.**

Water on Tap: A Consumer's Guide to the Nation's Drinking Water.
Explains where it comes from and how it's treated, what contaminants are, and what to do in case of a problem with either your public or private water supply. 22 pp. **548H. Free.**

Your Guide to Choosing a Nursing Home.
Discusses what to look for in a nursing home and alternatives to nursing homes. Includes an evaluation checklist and a list of helpful resources. 37 pp. **549H. Free.**

Drugs & Health Aids

An Aspirin a Day...Just Another Cliché?
You may reach for aspirin when you have a headache, but can aspirin really help reduce the risk of heart attack and stroke? Read about the benefits of aspirin in preventing cardiovascular disease and if taking it is right for you. 4 pp. **550H. Free.**

Basik Lasik.
Learn the details about Lasik eye surgery, who is a good candidate, how to find a surgeon, possible risks

and complications, and alternatives to Lasik. 5 pp. **322H. 50¢.**

Buying Drugs Online.
A new advantage of the Internet is being able to buy your prescription drugs online. Explains how online sales work, how to check for professional certification, and warning signs that a web site may be fraudulent. 6 pp. **551H. Free.**

It's Quittin' Time.
Describes the benefits and side effects of five stop-smoking aids: the anti-smoking pill, nasal spray, inhaler, nicotine patch and gum. Gives suggestions on creating a plan to stop smoking and more. 5 pp. **552H. Free.**

Keeping an Eye on Contact Lenses.
Describes the different types of contact lenses available, proper care, safety concerns, and potential problems. 5 pp. **553H. Free.**

Medications and Older Adults.
Suggestions on how to prevent dangerous drug combinations, how to make taking medications easier, how to remember medication, and how to cut their cost. 4 pp. **554H. Free.**

New Drug Label Spells It Out Simply.
Do you find it hard to read what's on the labels of over-the-counter medicines? That's about to change. Read the sample new label and see the difference. 4 pp. **555H. Free.**

Exercise & Diet

Do You Know the Health Risks of Being Overweight?
Being overweight increases your chances of developing serious health problems, like heart disease, diabetes, or cancer. This guide can help you lose weight safely and develop a healthier lifestyle. 10 pp. **323H. 50¢.**

Walking for Exercise and Pleasure.
Includes illustrated warm-up exercises and advice on how far, how fast, and how often to walk for best results. 14 pp. **122H. $1.00.**

Weight Loss for Life.
This guide will help you learn how to lose weight safely and stay healthy. 20 pp. **324H. 50¢.**

Weight Loss: Finding a Weight Loss Program That Works For You.
Fill in the personal health profile, follow the checklist to compare different weight loss programs, and use the Body Mass Index (BMI) Calculator to determine your BMI and set your weight goal. 11 pp. **325H. 50¢.**

Medical Problems

Anxiety—Fact Sheet.
Describes different types of anxiety disorders and what you can do if you recognize these symptoms in yourself or a loved one. 4 pp. **556H. Free.**

Arthritis: Timely Treatments for an Ageless Disease.
This guide explains the types of arthritis, new treatments available, unproven remedies to guard against, and more. 6 pp. **557H. Free.**

Atopic Dermatitis.
Individuals with atopic dermatitis, or eczema, suffer from a chronic disease that causes extremely itchy, inflamed skin. Find out more about this disease, its symptoms, and treatments. 37 pp. **558H. Free.**

Attention Deficit Hyperactivity Disorder.
Discusses symptoms, causes, diagnosis, and treatments of this disorder which affects many children and young people. 42 pp. **326H. 50¢.**

Bone Marrow Transplants Come of Age.
Bone marrow transplants save patients from diseases that once had no cure. Learn about the types of transplants, the transplant process, post transplant recovery, and donating bone marrow. 6 pp. **559H. Free.**

Breast Cancer: Better Treatments Save More Lives.
Every three minutes in the U.S., a woman learns she has breast cancer. Find out about improved diagnostic techniques, the stages of breast cancer, and new treatments and drugs that are available. 5 pp. **560H. Free.**

Cataract in Adults.
Cataract is a normal part of aging, but if it makes

performing routine tasks too difficult, you may need surgery. Learn more about symptoms and treatments. 13 pp. **123H. $1.00.**

Do I Have Arthritis?
Arthritis affects your health, your family, even your financial life. Read about common signs of arthritis and how medications and exercise can help. 28 pp. **561H. Free.**

Fever Blisters & Canker Sores.
Explains causes, treatments, and research on these mouth infections. 12 pp. **327H. 50¢.**

Getting Treatment for Panic Disorder.
More than 3 million American adults have episodes of intense, disabling fear. Learn when you need help and what treatment options are available. 5 pp. **562H. Free.**

Lupus.
Lupus is a disease in which the immune system attacks the body's healthy cells and tissues. Consult this guide's information charts for warning signs and available treatments. 33 pp. **563H. Free.**

New Hope For People With Sickle Cell Anemia.
Sickle cell anemia is a painful disease. But there may be a new hope for treating this disease—a new drug called Hydroxyurea. Find out more about this new drug and how its used. 5 pp. **564H. Free.**

Noninsulin-Dependent Diabetes.
About 90% to 95% of diabetics in the U.S. have noninsulin-dependent diabetes. Use this guide to learn more about this type of diabetes, who is at

risk, and how it is treated. 35 pp. **328H. 50¢.**

Osteoarthritis.
The most common type of arthritis is osteoarthritis, especially among older individuals. This guide discusses its symptoms (pain, swelling, and loss of motion) and treatments, and also illustrates helpful exercises. 36 pp. **565H. Free.**

Preventing Stroke.
Stroke is the third leading killer in the U.S. and the most common cause of adult-disability. Find out more with this booklet and estimate your risk with its informative stroke-risk chart. 8 pp. **329H. 50¢.**

Rheumatoid Arthritis.
This disease affects the everyday activities of 2.1 million people in the U.S. This publication discusses diagnosis and treatment and also has a medication chart for drug benefits and side effects. 33 pp. **566H. Free.**

So You Have High Blood Cholesterol.
High blood cholesterol can increase your risk of heart disease. Here are the facts about high cholesterol and how to lower yours. 36 pp. **124H. $1.75.**

Taking Charge of Menopause.
Learn about menopause, its symptoms, and health risks associated with it. 5 pp. **567H. Free.**

Understanding Treatment Choices for Prostate Cancer.
Newly diagnosed prostate cancer patients and their families face many treatment choices. Here's information on how prostate cancer is diagnosed, avail-

able treatment options, and follow-up care. 44 pp. **568H. Free.**

Urinary Tract Infections in Adults.
Urinary tract infections are a common but serious health problem. Find out more about the causes, symptoms, and treatments available. 8 pp. **330H. 50¢.**

Varicose Vein Treatments.
Explains treatments, risks, side effects, what to ask your doctor, and more. 2 pp. **331H. 50¢.**

HOUSING

Financing & Sales

100 Questions and Answers About Buying A New Home.
This great guide focuses on finances—from how much home you can afford to various loan programs, insurance, taxes, and more. 40 pp. **569H. Free.**

Buying Your Home: Settlement Costs and Helpful Information.
Describes the home buying, financing, and settlement (closing) process. Also gives tips on shopping for a loan. 35 pp. **125H. $1.75.**

Guide to Single-Family Home Mortgage Insurance.
Explains FHA mortgage insurance programs—including types available, how to qualify, how to ap-

ply, restrictions, and more. 14 pp. **332H. 50¢.**

How to Buy a Home With a Low Down Payment.
Describes how to qualify for a low down payment mortgage, determine what you can afford, and how mortgage insurance works. 9 pp. **570H. Free.**

How to Buy a Manufactured (Mobile) Home.
Tips on selection and placement, warranties, site preparation, transportation, installation, and more. 22 pp. **333H. 50¢.**

HUD Home Buying Guide.
Here are step-by-step instructions for finding and financing a HUD home. Includes charts to help you estimate mortgage payments. 11 pp. **571H. Free.**

Looking for the Best Mortgage — Shop, Compare, Negotiate.
Using these 3 steps can save you thousands of dollars on a home loan or mortgage. Find many useful tips in this booklet. 7 pp. **334H. 50¢.**

Twelve Ways to Lower Your Homeowners Insurance Costs.
Practical tips to help reduce your expenses. Lists phone numbers of state insurance departments for more information. 4 pp. **335H. 50¢.**

Home Maintenance

Am I Covered?
Answers 15 common questions regarding homeowners insurance and explains what is covered in a standard policy. 9 pp. **336H. 50¢.**

Cooling Your Home Naturally.
Ways to save electricity and keep your home cool with landscaping, roof treatments, and more. 8 pp. **126H. $1.00.**

Elements of an Energy-Efficient House.
Learn the benefits of having these elements—a well-built thermal envelope, controlled ventilation, high-efficiency heating and cooling systems, and energy-efficient doors, windows, and appliances. 8 pp. **127H. $1.00.**

Energy Savers: Tips on Saving Energy & Money at Home.
A practical guide on reducing your home energy use, with tips on insulation, weatherization, heating, and more. 36 pp. **337H. 50¢.**

Healthy Lawn, Healthy Environment.
Tips on soil preparation, grasses, watering, mowing, pesticides, choosing a lawn care service, and more. 19 pp. **338H. 50¢.**

Homeowner's Glossary of Building Terms.
Taking on a home improvement project can open a whole new world of terms you may not know. Here's a quick reference to help you keep up with the language of the trade. 12 pp. **128H. $1.75.**

How to Prune Trees.
Illustrated guide shows what to do, what not to do, tools to use and when for healthy, strong trees. 30 pp. **129H. $1.50.**

Making Your Home Safe from Fire and Carbon Monoxide.
Tips on preventing fires, creating an emergency exit plan, what types of safety equipment you need, and more. 6 pp. **572H. Free.**

Power$mart: Easy Tips to Save Money and the Planet.
Learn how to make energy-efficient choices that are good for your family, your finances, and the environment without sacrificing comfort. 24 pp. **573H. Free.**

Selecting a New Water Heater.
Describes how different types of water heaters work and important features to consider when buying. 6 pp. **130H. $1.00.**

Should You Have Your Air Ducts in Your Home Cleaned?
Tips on deciding if your ducts need cleaning, choosing a cleaning service, evaluating health claims, and keeping ducts clean. 20 pp. **131H. $2.00.**

TRAVEL

Fly Smart.
Lists more than 30 steps you can take to help make your flight a safe one. Includes a passenger checklist. 2 pp. **590H. Free.**

Fly-Rights.
Helpful advice for travelers on getting the best fares, what to do with lost tickets and baggage, can-

celed flights, and more. 58 pp. **134H. $1.75.**

Lesser Known Areas of the National Park System.
Listing by state of more than 170 national parks, their accommodations, locations, and historical significance. 49 pp. **135H. $3.00.**

National Park System Map and Guide.
Full color map lists activities at more than 300 parks, monuments, and historic sites. **136H. $1.25.**

National Trails System Map and Guide.
Full color map describes eight national scenic trails and nine national historic trails. **137H. $1.25.**

National Wildlife Refuges: A Visitor's Guide.
Use this full color map to plan a visit and learn about hundreds of endangered species and their habitats. **138H. $1.50.**

Passports: Applying for Them the Easy Way.
How, when, and where to apply for U.S. passports. Includes information on fees. 2 pp. **355H. 50¢.**

Travel Smart.
Tips on getting info on countries around the world—from health and safety warnings to passport and visa requirements. Also covers what records to copy and where to keep them. 6 pp. **356H. 50¢.**

Washington: The Nation's Capital.
This historic city houses the U.S. government and has many important landmarks. Use this guide to learn more about our country's heritage by exploring Washington D.C. **139H. $1.25.**

Free From The Government

Your Trip Abroad.
Traveling abroad can be exciting and educational. This booklet can help you prepare so you get the most from your vacation. 48 pp. **140H. $1.50.**

AND MORE...

Civil War at a Glance.
This full color map illustrates and briefly describes major Civil War battle campaigns. **141H. $1.25.**

Conserving the Nature of America.
Beautiful photos show how the U.S. Fish and Wildlife Service protects the fish, wildlife, and plants in more than 500 National Wildlife Refuges. Also provides info on volunteer and recreational opportunities. 24 pp. **591H. Free.**

Consumer Action Handbook.
No consumer should be without this helpful guide. It provides assistance with consumer problems and complaints, including a sample complaint letter. Lists consumer contacts at hundreds of companies and trade associations, state and federal government agencies, local and national consumer organizations, and much more. 148 pp. **592H. Free.**

Fishing Is Fun for Everyone.
You'll fall for fishing hook, line, and sinker. Find out what equipment you'll need, what kind of bait to use, how to cast and tie knots, and where to fish for more information. 11 pp. **593H. Free.**

Free From The Government

For the Birds.
How to attract different species of birds, feed them, and build or buy suitable homes. 50 pp. **357H. 50¢.**

Funerals: A Consumer Guide.
Learn about your rights as a consumer and what to keep in mind when making funeral arrangements. 4 pp. **358H. 50¢.**

Internet Auctions: A Guide for Buyers and Sellers.
Internet auctions offer a great way to buy or sell all kinds of products. Find out how auctions work, payment options, and how to protect yourself. 18 pp. **359H. 50¢.**

My History Is America's History.
Detailed poster has easy ideas for discovering and preserving your family's history, with useful tips on recording family stories. 2 pp. **360H. 50¢.**

Our Flag.
You may have grown up saluting the flag each morning at school. But are you familiar with its history and customs? Here is everything you want to know about the flag. 52 pp. **143H. $2.50.**

Shop Safely Online.
Is it really safe? Here are the facts about buying over the Internet and how to protect yourself. 2 pp. **361H. 50¢.**

Site-Seeing on the Internet.
This guide can help you navigate the Internet, learn the local customs and lingo, and know what to avoid during your travels. 11 pp. **362H. 50¢.**

Free From The Government

Smart Consumer's Guide to Telephone Service.
Handy tips on shopping for telephone service and discusses what help is available for low-income consumers. 4 pp. **594H. Free.**

U.S. and the Metric System.
Explains how to use metric in everyday life. Includes metric conversion charts and more. 10 pp. **363H. 50¢.**

Where to Write for Vital Records.
This useful guide offers listings for each state on how to obtain birth, death, marriage, and divorce certificates. 32 pp. **144H. $2.50.**

Your Family Disaster Supplies Kit.
Lists kinds of food, first aid supplies, tools, and other items you should stock for an emergency. 4 pp. **364H. 50¢.**

Ordering Free Booklets

While there is no charge for individual free publications, there is a $2.00 service fee for any order containing free booklets (whether by mail, phone, web or fax) to help defray program costs. Supplies may be limited, so order today!

Send check or money order payable to "Superintendent of Documents" or use your VISA, MasterCard, Discover/Novus Card, or prepaid GPO deposit account. Credit card orders must include the expiration date and your signature.

Allow 4 weeks for delivery.

Phone: To order by phone, call toll-free **1 (888)-8-PUEBLO**, that's **1 (888) 878-3256**, to place your credit card or GPO deposit account order M-F, 9am to 8pm ET. Priority handling is available on telephone orders; ask your operator for details. For faster service, have booklet item numbers, titles, and payment information ready.

Fax: Fax your credit card or GPO deposit account order to **719-948-9724**. Just fill in the mailing label, order form, and payment information. Sorry, no COD orders or correspondence can be accepted.

Ordering Information

IF YOU ORDER ONLY FREE BOOKLETS, MAIL YOUR ORDER TO:
S. James
CIC - 01A
P.O. Box 100
Pueblo, CO 81002

FOR ALL OTHER ORDERS, USE:
R. Woods
CIC - 01A
P.O. Box 100
Pueblo, CO 81002

You can also get these booklets online, along with other consumer news, updates, and information. Use your modem or Internet connection to access this information electronically. Internet address: **www.pueblo.gsa.gov**

To order booklets, use the **bold** item number found at the end of each listing.

Don't forget—the $2.00 service still applies even if you order only free booklets!

Free Legal Services

Getting Free Legal Help

If you have a legal problem and can't afford to pay a small fortune for an attorney, you can now get free legal assistance thanks to funding from the U.S. Government. To help you get the kind of legal help you need but can not afford, Congress has given close to 300 million dollars to The Legal Services Corporation. They in turn provide funds for 262 local Legal Services offices throughout the U.S. to give you legal assistance. The funding is used to help over 4 million low-income individuals in civil cases. To find out about the free Legal Services in your area check the listings below or contact Legal Services Corporation directly.

LEGAL SERVICES CORPORATION
750 FIRST ST., N.E.
WASHINGTON, DC 20002
(202) 336-8800

You can also get the information you need about local Legal Services programs in your area by visiting their Internet site at:
www.lsc.gov

Directory of Free Legal Help

In addition to the legal services funded by the federal government, there are hundreds of what are called 'pro bono' (in other words ... 'free') programs which are staffed by attorneys who volunteer their time and services to insure that you get the legal representation you deserve. The following is a listing of these programs. Simply call the program closest to your home for legal assistance.

Alabama

Alabama State Bar Volunteer Lawyers Program
Phone: 334-269-1515

Legal Services Corporation of Alabama
(334) 264-1471

Legal Services of North-Central Alabama
(205) 536-9645

Legal Services of Metro Birmingham
(205) 328-3540

Alaska

Alaska Legal Services Corporation
(907) 276-6282

Alaska Pro Bono Program
Phone: 901-272-9431

Arizona

Pinal & Gila Counties Legal Aid Society
(520) 723-5326

Community Legal Services
(602) 258-3434 x 230

Papago Legal Services
(520) 383-2420

Southern Arizona Legal Aid
(520) 623-9465

DNA-People's Legal Services
(520) 871-4151

Affordable Housing Law Program
Arizona Commnunity Service Legal Assistance
Phone: 602-340-7372

Disability Claim Service
Phone: 602-256-9673

Directory of Free Legal Help

Arkansas

Arkansas Volunteer Lawyers for the Elderly
Phone: 501-376-9263

Ozark Legal Services
(501) 442-0600

Legal Services of Northeast Arkansas
(870) 523-9892

Western Arkansas Legal Services
(501) 785-5211

East Arkansas Legal Services
(870) 732-6370

Center for Arkansas Legal Services
(501) 376-3423

California

California Indian Legal Services
(510) 835-0284

Greater Bakersfield Legal Assistance
(805) 325-5943

Central California Legal Services
(209) 441-1611

Legal Aid Foundation of Long Beach
(562) 435-3501

Legal Aid Foundation of Los Angeles
(213) 801-7990

Legal Aid Society of Alameda County
(510) 451-9261

Channel Counties Legal Services Association
(805) 487-6531

San Fernando Valley Neighborhood Legal Services
(818) 834-7509

Legal Services for Pasadena & San Gabriel-Pomona Valley
(909) 620-5547

Legal Aid Society of San Mateo County
(415) 365-8411

Contra Costa Legal Services Foundation
(510) 233-9954

Inland Counties Legal Services
(909) 683-5841 x429

Legal Services of Northern California Inc.
(916) 551-2150

Legal Aid Society of San Diego
(619) 262-5557 x320

Directory of Free Legal Help

California Rural Legal Assistance
(415) 777-2752

San Francisco Neighborhood Legal Assistance
(415) 982-1300

Legal Aid of Marin
(415) 492-0230

Community Legal Services-San Jose
(408) 283-3844

Legal Aid Society of Orange County
(714) 571-5233

Legal Aid Society of the Central Coast
(408) 724-2253

Redwood Legal Assistance
(707) 445-0866

The State Bar of California
Office of Legal Services
555 Franklin St.
San Francisco, CA 94102

Disability Rights Education and Defense Fund
Phone: 510-644-2555

Colorado

Pikes Peak/Arkansas River Legal Aid
(719) 471-0380

Colorado Rural Legal Services
(303) 534-5702

Legal Aid Society of Metropolitan Denver
(303) 866-9399

Colorado Bar Association Pro Bono Project
Phone: 303-860-1115

Connecticut

Connecticut Bar Association Law
Phone: 800-722-8811

AIDS Legal Network for CT
Phone: 860-541-5000

Delaware

Legal Services Corporation of Delaware
(302) 575-0408

Delaware Volunteer Legal Services
Phone: 302-478-8680

District of Columbia

Neighborhood Legal Services Program of DC
(202) 682-2720

American Association of Retired Persons
Phone: 202-434-2120

Directory of Free Legal Help

Catholic Archdiocesan Legal Network
Phone: 202-628-4265

Asylum & Refugee Rights Law Project of DC
Phone: 202-835-0031

DC Bar Public Services Activities Corporation
202-737-4700 ext. 290

Florida

Central Florida Legal Services
(904) 255-6573

Legal Aid Society of Broward County
(954) 764-8957 x223

Florida Rural Legal Services
(941) 688-7376

Jacksonville Area Legal Aid
(904) 356-8371

Legal Services of Greater Miami
(305) 576-0080 x501

Legal Services of North Florida
(904) 385-9007

Greater Orlando Area Legal Services
(407) 841-7777

Bay Area Legal Services
(813) 232-1222 x137

Withlacoochee Area Legal Services
(352) 629-0105

Three Rivers Legal Services
(352) 372-0519

Northwest Florida Legal Services
(850) 432-1750

Gulfcoast Legal Services
(813) 821-0726

Florida Association for Community Action
Phone: 352-378-6517

Georgia

Atlanta Legal Aid Society
(404) 614-3990

Georgia Legal Services Program
(404) 206-5175

The Pro Bono Project of the State Bar of Georgia
Phone: 404-527-8762

Hawaii

Native Hawaiian Legal Corporation
(808) 521-2302

Legal Aid Society of Hawaii
(808) 536-4302

Hawaii Lawyers Care
808-528-7046

Directory of Free Legal Help

Idaho
Idaho Legal Aid Services
Phone: 208-336-8980

Idaho Volunteer Lawyers Program
Phone: 208-334-4510

Illinois
Cook County Legal Assistance Foundation
(708) 524-2600

Legal Assistance Foundation of Chicago
(312) 341-1070

Land of Lincoln Legal Assistance Foundation
(618) 462-0036 x13

West Central Illinois Legal Assistance
(309) 343-2141

Illinois Pro Bono Center
Phone: 217-359-6811

Lawyers for Creative Arts
Phone: 312-944-2787

Indiana
Legal Services of Maumee Valley
(219) 422-8070

Legal Services of Northwest Indiana
(219) 886-3161

Legal Services Organization of Indiana
(317) 631-9410

Legal Services Program of Northern Indiana
(219) 234-8121

Iowa
Legal Services Corporation of Iowa
(515) 243-2151

Legal Aid Society of Polk County
(515) 282-8375

Iowa State Bar Association
Volunteer Lawyers Project
Phone: 515-244-8617

Kansas
Kansas Bar Foundation
Phone: 913-234-5696

Kentucky
Access to Justice Foundation
Phone: 606-255-9913

Louisiana
Louisiana Bar Association
Phone: 504-566-1600

New Orleans Eighth Coast Guard District Legal Office
Phone: 504-589-6188

Directory of Free Legal Help

Maine
Maine Volunteer Lawyers Project
Phone: 207-828-2300

Maryland
Advocates for Children & Youth
Phone: 410-547-9200

Massachusetts
American Civil Liberties Union of Massachusetts
Phone: 617-482-3170

Michigan
Legal Services of S.E. MI
(734) 665-6181

Legal Services Organization of Southcentral Michigan
(616) 965-3951

Wayne County Neighborhood Legal Services
(313) 962-0466

Legal Services of Eastern Michigan
(810) 234-2621

Legal Aid of Central Michigan
(517) 485-5418 x235

Lakeshore Legal Services
(810) 469-5185

Oakland Livingston Legal Aid
(248) 456-8888

Berrien County Legal Services
(616) 983-6363

Legal Services of Northern Michigan
(616) 347-8115

Legal Aid of Western MI
(616) 774-0672

Legal Aid Bureau of Southwestern Michigan
308 Kalamazoo County Administration Building
201 West Kalamazoo Ave.
Kalamazoo, MI 49007-3777

Michigan Indian Legal Services
(616) 947-0122

State Bar of Michigan
517-372-9030 ext. 6317

Minnesota
Legal Aid Service of Northeastern Minnesota
(218) 726-4800

Judicare of Anoka County
(612) 783-4970

Directory of Free Legal Help

Central Minnesota Legal Services
(612) 332-8151

Legal Services of Northwest Minnesota Corporation
(218) 233-8585

Southern Minnesota Regional Legal Services
(612) 228-9823

Anishinabe Legal Services
(218) 335-2223

Minnesota Volunteer Attorney Program
Phone: 612-673-6331

Mississippi
Central Mississippi Legal Services
(601) 948-6752

North Mississippi Rural Legal Services
(601) 234-8731

South Mississippi Legal Services
(228) 374-4160

E. Mississippi Legal Services Corporation
(601) 693-5470

Southeast Mississippi Legal Services
(601) 545-2950

Southwest Mississippi Legal Services Corporation
(601) 684-0578

Mississippi Volunteer Lawyers
Phone: 601-948-4476

Missouri
Southwest Missouri Legal Services
(573) 683-3783

Meramec Area Legal Aid
(573) 341-3655

Legal Aid of Western Missouri
(816) 474-6750

Legal Services of Eastern Missouri
(314) 534-4200

Mid-Missouri Legal Services
(573) 442-0116

Legal Aid of Southwest Missouri
(417) 862-1100

St Joseph Paralegal Farm Project
Phone: 816-364-2325

Montana
Montana Legal Services Association
(406) 442-9830

Directory of Free Legal Help

State Bar of Montana Pro Bono Project
Phone: 406-252-6351

Nebraska
Legal Services of Southeast Nebraska
(402) 435-2161

Legal Aid Society
(402) 348-1060

Western Nebraska Legal Services
(308) 632-4734

Nebraska State Bar Association
Phone: 402-475-7091

Nevada
Nevada Legal Services
(702) 386-1070

New Hampshire
New Hampshire Legal Services
(603) 224-5723

The Pro Bono Referral of the New Hampshire Bar
Phone: 603-224-6942

New Jersey
Cape-Atlantic Legal Services
(609) 348-4200

Warren County Legal Services
(908) 475-2010

Camden Regional Legal Services
(609) 964-2010 x233

Union County Legal Services Corporation
(908) 354-4340

Hunterdon County Legal Service
(908) 782-7979

Bergen County Legal Services
(201) 487-2166

Hudson County Legal Services
(201) 792-6363

Essex-Newark Legal Services
(973) 624-4500

Middlesex County Legal Services
(732) 249-7600

Passaic County Legal Aid
(973) 345-7171

Somerset-Sussex Legal Services
(908) 231-0840

Ocean-Monmouth Legal Services
(732) 341-2727

Directory of Free Legal Help

Legal Aid Society of Mercer County
(609) 695-6249

Legal Aid Society of Morris County
(973) 285-6911

New Mexico

Legal Aid Society of Albuquerque
(505) 243-7871

Southern New Mexico Legal Services
(505) 541-4800

Northern New Mexico Legal Services
(505) 982-2504

Indian Pueblo Legal Services
(505) 867-3391

NM Lawyers Care Pro Bono Project
Phone: 505-797-1640

New York

Legal Aid Society of N.E. New York
(518) 462-1672 x304

Legal Aid for Broome & Chenango
(607) 723-7966

Buffalo Neighborhood Legal Services
(716) 847-0650

Chautauqua County Legal Services
(716) 483-2116

Chemung County Neighborhood Legal Services
(607) 734-1647

Nassau/Suffolk Law Services Committee
(516) 292-8100

Legal Aid Society of Rockland County
(914) 634-3627

Legal Services for NYC
(212) 431-7200

Niagara County Legal Aid Society
(716) 284-8831

Monroe County Legal Assistance
(716) 325-2520

Legal Services of Central NY
(315) 475-3127

Legal Aid Society of Mid-NY
(315) 732-2131

Westchester/Putnam Legal Services
(914) 949-1305

North County Legal Services
(518) 563-4022

Directory of Free Legal Help

Southern Tier Legal Services
(607) 776-4126

Asian American Legal Defense-NYC
Phone: 212-966-5932

Covenant House Legal Services Office
460 West 41st St., Suite 715
New York, NY 10036

American Civil Liberties Union
Phone: 212-549-2500

Department of Pro Bono Affairs
Phone: 518-487-5641

The Door's Legal Services Center-NYC
212-941-9090 ext. 233

Prisoners' Legal Services of New York
Phone: 212-513-7373

US Court of Appeals for the Second Circuit Pro Bono Panel
212-857-8800

Volunteer Lawyers for the Arts-NYC
212-319-2787

North Carolina
Legal Services of North Carolina
(919) 856-2564

Legal Services of Southern Piedmont
(704) 376-1600

North Central Legal Assistance Program
(919) 688-6396

Legal Aid Society of Northwest NC
(336) 725-9166

North Carolina Bar Foundation
919-677-0561

Land Loss Prevention Project Of Durham
Phone: 919-682-5969

North Dakota
Legal Assistance of North Dakota
(701) 222-2110

North Dakota Legal Services
(701) 627-4719

North Dakota State Bar Association
701-255-1404

Ohio
Western Region Legal Services
(330) 535-4191

Directory of Free Legal Help

Stark County Legal Aid Society
306 Market Ave. North, Ste 730
Canton, OH 44702-1423

Legal Aid Society of Cincinnati
(513) 241-9400

The Legal Aid Society of Cleveland
(216) 687-1900

The Legal Aid Society of Columbus
(614) 224-8374

Ohio State Legal Services
(614) 299-2114

Legal Aid Society of Dayton
(937) 228-8088

Legal Aid Society of Lorain County
(440) 323-8240

Butler-Warren Legal Assistance Association
(513) 894-7664

Allen County-Blackhoof Area Legal Services
(419) 224-9070

Advocates for Basic Legal Equality
(419) 255-0814

The Toledo Legal Aid
(419) 244-8345

Wooster-Wayne Legal Aid
(330) 264-9454

Northeast Ohio Legal Services
(330) 744-3196

Rural Legal Aid Society of West Central Ohio
(937) 325-2809

Columbus Ohio Legal Assistance
Phone: 614-752-8919

Oklahoma
Oklahoma Indian Legal Services
(415) 840-5255

Legal Services of Eastern Oklahoma
(918) 584-3211

Legal Aid of Western Oklahoma
Phone: 405-521-1302

Oregon
Oregon Legal Services
(503) 224-4094

Lane County Legal Aid
(541) 342-6056

Multnomah County Legal Aid
(503) 224-4086

Marion-Polk Legal Aid
(503) 581-5265

Directory of Free Legal Help

Oregon State Bar Foundation
Phone: 503-620-0222, x323

Pennsylvania
Philadelphia Legal Assistance
(215) 981-3800

Gettysburg Legal Services
(717) 334-7623

Delaware County Legal Assistance
(610) 874-8421

Bucks County Legal Aid
(215) 781-1111

Laurel Legal Services
(724) 836-2211

Southern Alleghenys Legal Aid
(814) 536-8917

Central Pennsylvania Legal Services
(717) 236-8932

Pittsburg Neighborhood Legal Services
(412) 644-7450

Northern PA Legal Services-Scranton
(717) 342-0184

Keystone Legal Services-State College
(814) 234-6231

Southwestern PA Legal Aid
(724) 225-6170

Legal Aid of Chester County
(610) 436-9150

Legal Services of Northeastern PA
(717) 825-8567

Susqeuhanna Legal Services
(717) 323-8741

Northwestern Legal Services
(814) 452-6949

Lehigh Valley Legal Services
(610) 317-8757

Montgomery County Legal Aid Service
(610) 275-5400

Pennsylvania Bar Association
Phone: 717-238-6807

Puerto Rico
Community Law Office-San Juan
(787) 751-1600

Puerto Rico Legal Services
(787) 728-9561

Directory of Free Legal Help

Rhode Island

Rhode Island Legal Services
(401) 274-2652

Legal Services for the Elderly Pro Bono Program
Phone: 401-421-7758

South Carolina

Neighborhood Legal Assistance -Charleston
(803) 722-0107

Palmetto Legal Services
(803) 799-9668

Carolina Regional Legal Aid Services
(803) 667-1896

Legal Services of Western Carolina
(864) 467-3248

Piedmont Legal Services
(864) 582-0369

South Carolina Bar Pro Bono Program
Phone: 803-799-4015

South Dakota

Black Hills Legal Services
(605) 342-7171

East River Legal Services
(605) 336-9230

Dakota Plains Legal Services
(605) 856-4444

Southeast Tennessee Legal Services
(423) 756-4013

Legal Services of Upper East TN
(423) 928-8311

Knoxville Legal Aid
(423) 637-0484

Memphis Area Legal Services
(901) 523-8822

Legal Aid Society of Middle TN
(615) 780-7123

Rural Legal Services of TN
(423) 483-8454

West Tennessee Legal Services
(901) 423-0616

Legal Services of South Central TN
(931) 381-5533

Texas

Legal Aid of Central Texas
(512) 476-7244

Coastal Bend Legal Services
(512) 883-3667 x143

Directory of Free Legal Help

Legal Services of North Texas
(214) 748-1234

El Paso Legal Assistance Society
(915) 544-3022

West Texas Legal Services
(817) 877-0609

Gulf Coast Legal Foundation
(713) 652-0077

Bexar County Legal Aid Association
(210) 227-0111

Heart of Texas Legal Services-Waco
(254) 756-7944

Texas Rural Legal Aid
(956) 968-6574

East Texas Legal Services
(409) 560-1850

AIDS Legal Resource Project-Austin
512-479-8473

Next Lawfirm Pro Bono Project-Longview
903-758-9123

Pro BAR-Harlingen
Phone: 210-425-9231

Austin Women's Advocacy Project
Phone: 512-476-5377

Utah
Utah Legal Aid Services
(801) 328-8891

Utah State Bar Association
Pro Bono Project
801-531-9077

Vermont
Vermont Volunteer Lawyer's Project
802-863-7153

Virgin Island
Legal Services of the Virgin Islands
(340) 773-2626

Virginia
Legal Services of Northern Virginia
(703) 534-4343

Rappahannock Legal Services
(540) 371-1105

Southwest Virginia Legal Aid
(540) 783-6576

Peninsula Legal Aid
(757) 827-5078

Directory of Free Legal Help

Central Virginia Legal Aid Society
(804) 648-1012

Legal Aid Society of New River Valley
(540) 382-6157

Legal Aid Society of Roanoke Valley
(540) 344-2088

Tidewater Legal Aid Society
757-627-5423

Virginia Legal Aid Society
(804) 528-4722

Southside Virginia Legal Services
(804) 862-1100

Blue Ridge Legal Services
(540) 433-1830

Client Centered Legal Services of S.W. VA
(540) 762-5501

Piedmont Legal Services
(804) 296-8851

Virginia State Bar-Richmond
804-775-0522

Washington
Northwest Justice Project
(206) 464-1519

West Virginia
WV Legal Services Plan
922 Quarrier St., Suite 550
Charleston, WV 25301

Appalachian Research & Defense Fund
Phone: 304-344-9687

Pro Bono Referral -Legal Aid of Charlestown
Phone: 304-343-4481
(304) 343-3013 x28

Wisconsin
Legal Action of Wisconsin
(414) 278-7777

Wisconsin Judicare
(715) 842-1681

Legal Services of Northeastern WI
(920) 432-4645

Western Wisconsin Legal Services
(608) 935-2741

State Bar of WI-Delivery of Legal Services
Phone: 608-250-6177

Wyoming
Wind River Legal Services
(307) 332-6626

Nationwide Directory Of Consumer Protection Offices

Check Out A Company Before Doing Business With Them

It is always smart before doing business with any company you have questions about to check with your local Better Business Bureau. They will be able to tell you whether other consumers have reported any problems they have had with this company.

Usually you can find the address and phone number of the Bureau nearest you in your local phone book but some of the Better Business Bureaus are serviced by bureaus in adjoining states. To locate the bureau nearest you, you can also check with the U.S. National Headquarters listed below or use the zip code search or state directory at:
http://www.bbb.org/bureaus/index.html.

UNITED STATES-NATIONAL HEADQUARTERS
Council of Better Business Bureaus
4200 Wilson Blvd., Suite 800
Arlington, VA 22203
703-276-0100
http://www.bbb.org

Directory of Consumer Protection Agencies

Don't Be The Victim Of Consumer Fraud

As a general rule, once it's clear that you are not going to get satisfaction directly from the company you are having a dispute with, the first place to call for help with a consumer problem is your local consumer protection office. It is their job to protect you, the consumer against unfair and illegal business practices.

Listed here are consumer protection offices throughout the country. If you have a complaint, check this directory for your state, city or county and call the office nearest you.

If you are having a problem with a business outside your state, however, contact the consumer office in the state in which you made the purchase.

When you call the consumer protection or Attorney General's office, simply ask to be connected to the person in charge of consumer complaints.

Alabama
Consumer Protection / 800-392-5658

Alaska
The Consumer Protection Section in the Office of the Attorney General has been closed. Consumers with complaints are being referred to the Better Business Bureaus in Anchorage and Fairbanks, small claims court, and private attorneys.

Arizona-State Offices
Phoenix Consumer Protection / 800-352-8431
Tucson Consumer Protection / 602-628-6504

Directory of Consumer Protection Agencies

Arizona-County Offices
Apache County / 602-337-4364
Cochise County / 602-432-9377
Coconino County / 602-779-6518
Gila County / 602-425-3231
Graham County / 602-428-3620
Greenlee County / 602-865-3842
La Paz County / 602-669-6118
Mohave County / 602-753-0719
Navajo County / 602-524-6161
Pima County / 602-740-5733
Pinal County / 602-868-5801
Santa Cruz County / 602-281-4966
Yavapai County / 602-771-3344
Yuma County / 602-329-2270

Arizona-City Office
Tucson Consumer Affairs / 602-791-4886

Arkansas-State Office
Consumer Protection / 501-682-2341

California-State Offices
California Consumer Affairs / 916-445-1254 (consumer information)
Attorney General's Office / 916-322-3360
California Bureau of Automotive Repair / 916-366-5100

California-County Offices
Alameda County / 415-530-8682
Contra Costa County / 415-646-4500
Fresno County / 209-488-3156
Kern County / 805-861-2421
Los Angeles County / 213-974-1452
Marin County / 415-499-6190
Consumer Protection / 415-499-6450
Mendocino County District / 707-463-4211
Monterey County / 408-755-5073

Directory of Consumer Protection Agencies

Napa County / 707-253-4059
Orange County / 714-541-7600
Orange County / 714-541-7600
Riverside County / 714-275-5400
Sacramento County / 916-440-6174
San Diego / 619-531-3507 (fraud complaint line)
San Francisco County / 415-552-6400 (public inquiries)
415-553-1814 (complaints)
San Joaquin County / 209-468-2419
San Luis Obispo County / 805-549-5800
San Mateo County / 415-363-4656
Santa Barbara County /805-568-2300
Santa Clara County / 408-299-7400
Santa Clara County / 408-299-4211
Santa Cruz County /408-425-2054
Solano County / 707-421-6860
Stanislaus County / 209-571-5550
Ventura County / 805-654-3110
Yolo County / 916-666-8424

California-City Offices
Los Angeles / 213-485-4515
Santa Monica / 213-458-8336

Colorado-State Offices
Consumer Protection Unit / 303-620-4500
Consumer and Food Specialist / 303-239-4114

Colorado-County Offices
Archuleta, LaPlata, and San Juan Counties / 303-247-8850
Boulder County / 303-441-3700
Denver County / 303-640-3555 (inquiries) / 303-640-3557 (complaints)
El Paso and Teller Counties / 719-520-6002
Pueblo County / 719-546-6030
Weld County / 303-356-4000 ext. 4735

Directory of Consumer Protection Agencies

Connecticut-State Offices
Department of Consumer Protection / 203-566-4999 / 800-538-2277 (CT only)
Antitrust/Consumer Protection / 203-566-5374 / 800-538-2277 (CT only)

Connecticut-City Office
Middletown / 203-344-3492

Delaware-State Offices
Division of Consumer Affairs / 800-443-2179

District of Columbia
Consumer Affairs / 202-727-7000

Florida-State Offices
Division of Consumer Services / 904-488-2226 / 800-327-3382 (FL only)
Consumer Litigation Section / 904-488-9105
Office of the Attorney General / 305-985-4780

Florida-County Offices
Broward County / 305-357-6030
Metropolitan Dade County Consumer Protection / 305-375-4222
Dade County / 305-324-3030
Hillsborough County / 813-272-6750
Orange County / 407-836-2490
Palm Beach County / 407-355-3560
Palm Beach County / 407-355-2670
Pasco County / 813-847-8110
Pinellas County / 813-530-6200
Seminole County / 407-322-7534
Titusville Consumer Fraud Unit / 407-264-5230

Florida-City Offices
City of Jacksonville / 904-630-3667
Lauderhill / 305-321-2450

Directory of Consumer Protection Agencies

Tamarac / 305-722-5900

Georgia-State Office
Governors Office of Consumer Affairs / 404-651-8600 / 800-869-1123 (toll-free in GA only)

Hawaii-State Offices
Office of Consumer Protection / 808-586-2630
Hilo Office of Consumer Protection / 808-933-4433
Lihue Office of Consumer Protection / 808-241-3365
Honolulu Office of Consumer Protection / 808-586-2630

Idaho-State Office
Consumer Protection Unit / 208-334-2424 / 800-432-3545 (ID only)

Illinois-State Offices
Governors Office of Citizens Assistance / 217-782-0244 / 800-252-8666 (IL only)
Chicago Consumer Protection / 312-814-3580
Springfield Consumer Protection / 217-782-9011 / 800-252-8666 (IL only)
Chicago Department of Citizen Rights / 312-814-3289

Illinois-Regional Offices
Carbondale Regional Office / 618-457-3505
Champaign Regional Office / 217-333-7691 (voice/TDD)
East St. Louis Regional Office / 618-398-1006
Granite City Regional Office / 618-877-0404
Kankakee Regional Office / 815-935-8500
LaSalle Regional Office / 815-224-4861
Mount Vernon Regional Office / 618-242-8200 (voice/TDD)
Peoria Regional Office / 309-671-3191
Quincy Regional Office / 217-223-2221 (voice/TDD)
Rockford Regional Office / 815-987-7580
Rock Island Regional Office / 309-793-0950
Waukegan Regional Office / 708-336-2207
West Frankfort Regional Office / 618-937-6453

Directory of Consumer Protection Agencies

West Chicago Regional Office / 708-653-5060 (voice/TDD)

Illinois-County Offices
Cook County / 312-443-4600
Madison County / 618-692-6280
Rock Island County / 309-786-4451, ext. 229

Illinois-City Offices
Wheeling Township / 708-259-7730 (Wed. only)
Chicago Department of Consumer Services / 312-744-4090
Des Plaines Consumer Protection / 708-391-5363

Indiana-State Office
Consumer Protection / 317-232-6330 / 800-382-5516 (IN only)

Indiana-County Offices
Consumer Protection / 219-755-3720
Marion County / 317-236-3522
Vanderburgh County / 812-426-5150

Indiana-City Office
Gary Office of Consumer Affairs / 219-886-0145

Iowa-State Office
Consumer Protection / 515-281-5926

Kansas-State Office
Consumer Protection / 913-296-3751 / 800-432-2310 (KS only)

Kansas-County Offices
Johnson County / 913-782-5000
Sedgwick County / 316-268-7921
Shawnee County / 913-291-4330

Directory of Consumer Protection Agencies

Kansas-City Office
Topeka Consumer Protection / 913-295-3883

Kentucky-State Offices
Consumer Protection / 502-564-2200
Louisville Consumer Protection / 502-588-3262 / 800-432-9257 (KY only)

Louisiana-State Office
Consumer Protection / 504-342-7373

Louisiana-County Office
Consumer Protection / 504-364-3644

Maine-State Offices
Consumer Credit Protection / 207-582-8718 / 800-332-8529
Office of the Attorney General / 207-289-3716

Maryland-State offices
Consumer Protection / 301-528-8662 / 800-969-5766
Motor Vehicle Administration / 301-768-7420
Consumer Affairs Specialist
Office of the Attorney General / 301-543-6620
Western Maryland / 301-791-4780

Maryland-County Offices
Hamard County / 301-313-7220
Montgomery County / 301-217-7373
Prince Georges County / 301-925-5100

Massachusetts-State Offices
Consumer Protection / 617-727-8400
Executive Office of Consumer Affairs / 617-727-7780
Western Massachusetts Consumer Protection / 413-784-1240

Directory of Consumer Protection Agencies

Massachusetts-County Offices
Franklin County / 413-774-5102
Hampshire County / 413-586-9225
Worcester County / 508-754-7420

Massachusetts-City Offices
Boston Mayor's Office of Consumer Affairs / 617-725-3320
Springfield Action Commission / 413-737-4376 (Hampton and Hampshire counties)

Michigan-State Offices
Consumer Protection / 517-373-1140
Michigan Consumers Council / 517-373-0947
Bureau of Automotive Regulation / 517-373-7858 / 800-292-4204 (Michigan only)

Michigan-County Offices
Bay County / 517-893-3594
Macomb County / 313-469-5350
Washtenaw County / 313-971-6054

Michigan-City Office
Detroit Department of Consumer Affairs / 313-224-3508

Minnesota-State Offices
Office of Consumer Services / 612-296-2331
Duluth Consumer Services / 218-723-4891

Minnesota-County Office
Hennepin County / 612-348-4528

Minnesota-City Office
Minneapolis Consumer Services / 612-348-2080

Mississippi -State Offices
Consumer Protection / 601-354-6018
Department of Agriculture & Commerce / 601-354-7063
Gulf Coast Regional Office / 601-436-6000

Directory of Consumer Protection Agencies

Missouri-State Offices
Office of the Attorney General / 314-751-3321 / 800-392-8222 (MO only)
Office of the Attorney General-Trade Offense Division / 314-751-3321 / 800-392-8222 ((toll-free in MO only)

Montana-State Office
Consumer Affairs / 406-444-4312 / 800-332-2272

Nebraska-State Office
Consumer Protection / 402-471-2682

Nebraska-County Office
Douglas County / 402-444-7040

Nevada-State Offices
Las Vegas Commissioner of Consumer Affairs / 702-486-7355 / 800-992-0900 ((toll-free in NV only)
Reno Consumer Affairs / 702-688-1800 / 800-992-0900 (Nevada only)

Nevada-County Office
Washoe County / 702-328-3456

New Hampshire-State Office
Consumer Protection / 603-271-3641

New Jersey-State Offices
Consumer Affairs / 932-648-4010 / 800-242-5846
Department of the Public Advocate / 609-292-7087 / 800-792-8600 (toll-free in NJ only)
New Jersey Division of Law / 973-648-7579 / 800-242-5846

New Jersey-County Offices
Atlantic County / 609-345-6700
Bergen County / 201-646-2650
Burlington County / 609-265-5054

Directory of Consumer Protection Agencies

Camden County / 609-757-8397
Cape May County / 609-463-6475
Cumberland County / 609-453-2202
Essex County / 973-678-8071/8928
Gloucester County / 609-853-3349
Hudson County / 201-795-6295
Hunterdon County / 908-236-2249
Mercer County / 609-989-6671
Middlesex County / 732-324-4600
Monmouth County / 732-431-7900
Morris County / 973-285-6070
Parsippany Consumer Affairs / 973-263-7011
Perth Amboy / 732-826-0290, ext. 61
Plainfield Action Services / 908-753-3519
Secaucus Consumer Affairs / 201-330-2019
Union Township / 908-688-6763
Wayne Township / 973-694-1800
Weehawken Consumer Affairs / 201-319-6005
West New York Consumer Affairs / 201-861-2522

New Mexico-State Office
Consumer Protection / 505-827-6000 / 800-432-2070 (in New Mexico only)

New York-State Offices
New York State Consumer Protection / 518-474-8583
Bureau of Consumer Frauds & Protection / 518-474-5481
NY State Consumer Protection Board / 212-417-4908 (complaints) / 212-417-4482 (main office)
Bureau of Consumer Frauds & Protection / 212-341-2345

New York-Regional Offices
Binghamton Regional Office / 607-773-7877
Buffalo Regional Office / 716-847-7184
Plattsburgh Regional Office / 518-563-8012
Poughkeepsie Regional Office / 914-485-3920
Rochester Regional Office / 716-546-7430
Suffolk Regional Office / 516-231-2400
Syracuse Regional Office / 315-448-4848

Directory of Consumer Protection Agencies

Utica Regional Office / 315-793-2225

New York-County Offices
Broome County / 607-778-2168
Dutchess County / 914-471-6322
Eric County / 716-858-2424
Nassau County / 516-535-2600
Orange County / 914-294-5151
Orange County / 914-294-5471
Putnam County / 914-621-2317
Rockland County / 914-638-5282
Steuben County / 607-776-9631 (voice andTDD)
Suffolk County / 516-360-4600
Ulster County / 914-339-5680
Westchester County Fraud Bureau / 914-285-3303
Westchester Consumer Affairs / 914-285-2155

New York-City Offices
Babylon Consumer Protection Board / 516-422-7636
Town of Colonie Consumer Protection / 518-783-2790
Mt. Vernon Consumer Affairs / 914-665-2433
New York City Consumer Affairs / 212-487-4444
Bronx Consumer Affairs / 718-579-6766
Brooklyn Consumer Affairs / 718-636-7092
Queens Consumer Affairs / 718-261-2922
Staten Island Consumer Affairs / 718-390-5154
Oswego Consumer Affairs / 315-342-8150
Ramapo Consumer Protection / 914-357-5100
Schenectady Consumer Protection / 518-382-5061
White Plains Dept. of Weights & Measures / 914-422-6359
Yonkers Consumer Protection / 914-377-6807

North Carolina-State Office
Consumer Protection / 919-733-7741

North Dakota-State Offices
Office of the Attorney General / 800-472-2600 (toll-free in ND only)

Directory of Consumer Protection Agencies

North Dakota-County office
Quad County / 701-746-5431

Ohio-State Offices
Consumer Frauds and Crimes Section / 614-466-4986 (complaints) / 800-282-0515 ((toll-free in OH only)
Office of Consumers' Counsel / 614-466-9605 (voice/TDD) / 800-282-9448 ((toll-free in OH only)

Ohio-County Offices
Franklin County / 614-462-3555
Lake County / 800-899-5253 (Ohio only)
Montgomery County / 513-225-5757
Portage County / 216-296-4593
Summit County / 216-379-2800

Ohio-City Offices
Cincinnati Office of Consumer Services / 513-352-3971
Youngstown Consumer Affairs / 216-742-8884

Oklahoma-State Offices
Attorney General / 405-521-4274
Department of Consumer Credit / 405-521-3653

Oregon-State Office
Financial Fraud / 503-378-4320

Pennsylvania-State Offices
Consumer Protection / 717-787-9707 / 800-441-2555 (PA only)
Consumer Advocate-(Utilities Only) / 717-783-5048
Pennsylvania Public Utility Commission / 717-787-4970 / 800-782-1110 ((toll-free in PA only)

Pennsylvania- Branch Offices
Allentown Consumer Protection / 215-821-6690
Erie Consumer Protection / 814-871-4371

Directory of Consumer Protection Agencies

Harrisburg Consumer Protection / 717-787-7109 / 800-441-2555 (PA only)
Ebensburg Bureau of Consumer Protection / 814-949-7900
Philadelphia Consumer Protection / 215-560-2414 / 800-441-2555 (PA only)
Pittsburg Consumer Protection / 412-565-5394
Scranton Consumer Protection / 717-963-4913

Pennsylvania-County Offices
Beaver County / 412-728-7267
Bucks County / 215-348-7442
Chester County / 215-344-6150
Cumberland County / 717-240-6180
Delaware County / 215-891-4865
Montgomery County / 215-278-3565
Philadelphia District Attorney / 215-686-8750

Rhode Island-State Offices
Consumer Protection / 401-277-2104 / 800-852-7776 (RI only)
Rhode Island Consumers' Council / 401-277-2764

South Carolina-State Offices
Consumer Protection Office / 803-734-9452 / 800-922-1594 (in SC only)
State Ombudsman / 803-734-0457

South Dakota-State Office
Consumer Affairs / 605-773-4400

Tennessee-State Offices
Consumer Protection / 615-741-2672
Consumer Affairs / 615-741-4737 / 800-342-8385 ((toll-free in TN only)

Texas-State Offices
Dallas Consumer Protection / 214-742-8944
El Paso Consumer Protection / 915-772-9476
Houston Consumer Protection / 713-223-5886

Directory of Consumer Protection Agencies

Lubbock Consumer Protection / 806-747-5238
McAllen Consumer Protection / 512-682-4547
San Antonio Consumer Protection / 512-225-4191
Austin Consumer Protection / 512-322-4143

Texas-County Offices
Dallas County / 214-653-3820
Harris County / 713-221-5836

Texas-City Office
Dallas Dept. of Environmental & Health Services / 214-670-5216

Utah-State Offices
Consumer Protection / 801-530-6601
Assistant Attorney General for Consumer Affairs / 801-538-1331

Vermont-State Offices
Office of the Attorney General / 802-828-3171
Consumer Assurance / 802-828-2436

Virginia-State Offices
Richmond Branch of Consumer Affairs / 804-786-2042 / 800-552-9963 ((toll-free in VA only)
Northern Virginia Branch of Consumer Affairs / 703-532-1613

Virginia-County Offices
Arlington County / 703-358-3260
Fairfax County / 703-246-5949
Prince William County / 703-792-7370

Virginia-City Offices
Alexandria Citizens Assistance / 703-838-4350
Norfolk Consumer Affairs / 804-441-2821
Roanoke Consumer Protection / 703-981-2583
Virginia Beach Consumer Affairs / 757-426-5836

Directory of Consumer Protection Agencies

Washington-State Offices
Seattle Consumer Services / 206-464-6431 / 800-551-4636 (WA only)
Spokane Office of the Attorney General / 509-456-3123
Tacoma Office of the Attorney General / 206-593-2904

Washington-City Offices
Department of Weights and Measures / 206-259-8810
Seattle Prosecuting Attorney / 206-296-9010
Seattle Department of Licenses & Consumer Affairs / 206-684-8484

West Virginia-State Offices
Consumer Protection / 304-348-8986 / 800-368-8808 ((toll-free in WV only)
Division of Weights and Measures / 304-348-7890

West Virginia-City Office
Charleston Consumer Protection / 304-348-8172

Wisconsin-State Offices
Madison Consumer Protection / 608-266-9836 / 800-422-7129 (in WI only)
Altoona Consumer Protection / 715-839-3848 / 800-422-7128 (in WI only)
Green Bay Consumer Protection / 414-448-5111 / 800-422-7128 (in WI only)
Milwaukee Consumer Protection / 414-257-8956
Madison Department of Justice / 608-266-1952 / 800-362-8189
Milwaukee Department of Justice / 414-227-4948 / 800-362-8189

Wisconsin-County offices
Marathon County / 715-847-5555
Milwaukee County / 414-278-4792
Racine County / 414-636-3125

Directory of Consumer Protection Agencies

Wyoming-State Office
Office of Attorney General / 307-777-7874

American Samoa
Consumer Protection / 011-684-633-4163/64

Puerto Rico
Secretary of Consumer Affairs / 809-721-0940
Department Of Justice / 809-721-2900

Virgin Islands
Commissioner & Consumer Affairs / 809-774-3130

Free & Low Cost Dental Programs

Throughout the U.S. professional dental care is available at a reduced rate or even absolutely free depending upon their income and circumstances to people living on a limited budget. This care is offered through a wide variety of programs including dental clinics, dental colleges, and through dentists who volunteer their time and service without charge or at a greatly reduced rate. You will get the finest professional dental care from licensed dentists with many years of experience.

To get free or low cost dental care, check the listing below for your state. Call the phone number listed for each of the organizations listed and explain that you are looking for a low cost dental program. In some instances you will be referred to an agency in your local area that will assist you in getting the dental care you need. If the organization you call does not have the particular kind of care you need, always ask them to refer you to another organization that does provide the care.

In addition to the listings below, if you are a senior citizen be sure to check with your **STATE'S OFFICE OF THE AGING**. (check the white pages of the phone book for their number). They often will have access to special programs not available anywhere else.

Directory of Dental Programs

Alabama
Alabama Dental Association
836 Washington St.
Montgomery, AL 36104
334-265-1684
800-489-2532

University of Alabama
School of Dentistry
1919 Seventh Avenue, S.
Birmingham, AL 35294
205-934-2700

Alaska
Alaska Dental Society
3305 Arctic Blvd., Suite 102
Anchorage, AK 99503-4975
907-563-3009

Anchorage Neigthborhood Health Center
1217 East 10th Ave.
Anchorage, AZ 99501
907-257-4600

Senior Citizen Discounts
Anchorage Dental Society
3400 Spenard Rd., Suite 10
Anchorage, AK 99503
907-279-9144

Arizona
Arizona Dental Association
4131 N. 36th St.
Phoenix, AZ 85018
602-957-4777
800-866-2732

Department of Health Services
Office of Dental Health
1740 West Adams St.
Phoenix, AZ 85007
602-542-1866

Arkansas
Arkansas State Dental Association
2501 Crestwood Drive, Suite 205
North Little Rock, AR 72116
501-771-7650

California
Senior Dent Program
California Dental Association
P.O. Box 13749
1201 "K" Street
Sacramento, CA 95853
916-443-0505
800-736-8702

Loma Linda University
School of Dentistry
11092 Anderson St.
Loma Linda, CA 92350
909-824-4675

University of California at Los Angeles
School of Dentistry
10833 LeConte Ave.
Los Angeles, CA 90095
310-206-3904

Directory of Dental Programs

University of Southern California
School of Dentistry Rm. 203
University Park, MC 0641
Los Angeles, CA 90089
213-740-2800

University of California
School of Dentistry
513 Parnassus Ave., S-630
San Francisco, CA 94143
415-476-1891

University of the Pacific
School of Dentistry
2155 Webster Street
San Francisco, CA 94115
415-929-6400

Colorado

Colorado Dental Association
3690 S. Yosemite, Suite 100
Denver, CO 80237
303-740-6900
800-343-3010
Ask for Senior Discount referrals

State Health Dept. Oral Health Department
4300 Cherry Creek Dr. South
Denver, CO 80246
303-692-2360

University of Colorado Medical
School of Dentistry
4200 E. 9th Ave., Box A095
Denver, CO 80262
303-270-8751

Connecticut

Connecticut State Dental Association
62 Russ Street
Hartford, CT 06106
860-278-5550

The University of Connecticut
School of Dental Medicine
263 Farmington Avenue
Farmington, CT 06032
203-679-3400

Delaware

Delaware State Dental Society
1925 Lovering Ave.
Wilmington, DE 19806
302-654-4335

Division of Public Health Department of Dentistry
501 W. 14th Street
Wilmington, DE 19801
302-428-4850

Nemours Health Clinic
1801 Rockland Rd
Wilmington, DE 19803
800-292-9538
302-651-4400

Ministry of Caring Dental Program
1410 N. Claymont St
Wilmington, DE 19802
302-594-9476

Directory of Dental Programs

District Of Columbia

District of Columbia Dental Society
502 C Street N.E.
Washington, DC 20002
202-547-7613

Howard University
College of Dentistry
600 "W" Street, N.W.
Washingon, DC 20059
202-806-0100

Florida

Florida Dental Association
1111 E. Tennessee St.
Tallahassee, FL 32308
904-681-3629 / 800-877-9922

Department of Health & Rehabilitative Services
Public Health Dental Program
1317 Winewood Blvd
Tallahassee, FL 32399
850-487-1845
Ask for referral to a clinic near you

Nova Southeastern University
College of Dental Medicine
3200 S. University Drive
Fort Lauderdale, FL 33328
954-262-7500

University of Florida
College of Dentistry
P.O. Box 100405
Gainesville, FL 32610-0405
904-392-4261

Georgia

Georgia Dental Association
2801 Buford Highway, Suite T-60
Atlanta, GA 30329
404-636-7553
800-432-4357

West End Medical Center
868 York Ave
Atlanta, GA 30310
404-752-1443

Ben Massell Dental Clinic
18 7th St., NE
Atlanta, GA 30308
404-881-1858

Southeast Health Center
1039 Ridge Ave.
Atlanta, GA 30315
404-688-1350 ext 305

Medical College of Georgia
School of Dentistry
1459 Laney Walker Blvd.
Augusta, GA 30912-0200
706-721-2696

Hawaii

Hawaii Dental Association
1345 S. Beretania St. Ste. 301
Honolulu, HI 96814
808-593-7956

Department of Health
Dental Health Division

Directory of Dental Programs

1700 Lanakila Ave. Room 202
Honolulu, HI 96817
808-832-5710

Idaho
Idaho State Dental Association
1220 W. Hays St.
Boise, ID 83702
208-343-7543
800-932-8153
Ask for a referral to your local Community Health Center

Senior Care Program
Boise City/Ada County
3010 W. State St. Suite 120
Boise, ID 83703
208-345-7783

Illinois
Illinois State Dental Society
P.O. Box 376
Springfield, IL 62705
217-525-1406

Southern Illinois University
School of Dentistry Medical Bldg 273
2800 College Avenue - Room 2300
Alton, IL 62002
618-474-7000

University of Illinois at Chicago
College of Dentistry
801 South Paulina Street
Chicago, IL 60612
312-996-7558

Northwestern University
Dental School
240 East Huron Street
Chicago, IL 60611
312-908-5950

Indiana
Senior Smile Dental Care Program
Indiana Dental Association
401 W. Michigan Street
Indianapolis, IN 46206
317-634-2610
800-562-5646

Indiana University
School of Dentistry
1121 West Michigan Street
Indianaplis, IN 46202
317-274-3547

Iowa
Iowa Dental Association
505 5th Ave. #333
Des Moines, IA 50309
515-282-7250
800-828-2181

The University of Iowa College of Dentistry
Dental Building
Iowa City, IA 52242
319-335-7499

Directory of Dental Programs

Kansas
Senior Access Program
Kansas Dental Association
5200 SW Huntoon St.
Topeka, KS 66604
800-432-3583

Kentucky
Kentucky Dental Association
1940 Princeton Drive
Louisville, KY 40205
502-459-5373
800-292-1855

Jefferson County Dental Park Duval Community Health Facility
1817 South 34th St.
Louisville, KY 40211
502-774-4401

University of Kentucky
College of Dentistry
800 Rose Street - Medical Ctr.
Lexington, KY 40536-0084
606-323-6525

University of Louisville
School of Dentistry
Health Sciences Center
Louisville, KY 40292
502-852-5096

Louisiana
Louisiana Dental Association
7833 Office Park Blvd.
Baton Rouge, LA 70809
504-926-1986

Louisiana State University
School of Dentistry
1100 Florida Ave., Bldg. 101
New Orleans, LA 70119
504-947-9961

Maine
Senior Dent Program
Maine Dental Association
P.O. Box 215
Manchester, ME 04351
800-369-8217

Maryland
Maryland State Dental Association
6450 Dobbin Road
Columbia, MD 21045
410-964-2880
800-766-2880

University of Maryland
Baltimore College of Dental Surgery
666 West Baltimore Street
Baltimore, MD 21201
410-706-5603

Massachusetts
Massachusetts Dental Society
83 Speen Street
Natick, MA 01760
508-651-7511
800-342-8747

Directory of Dental Programs

Boston Univsity
School of Dental Medicine
100 East Newton Street
Boston, MA 02118
617-638-4671

Harvard School of Dental Medicine
188 Longwood Avenue
Boston, MA 02115
617-432-1423

Tufts University
School of Dental Medicine
1 Kneeland Street
Boston, MA 02111
617-956-6547

Michigan
Michigan Dental Association
230 N. Washington Square #208
Lansing, MI 48933
517-372-9070
800-589-2632

The University of Michigan
School of Dentistry
1234 Dental Building
Ann Arbor, MI 48109-1078
734-763-6933

University of Detroit Mercy
School of Dentistry
8200 W. Outer Drive, PO Box 98
Detroit, MI 48219-0900
313-494-6600

Minnesota
Minnesota Dental Association
2236 Marshall Avenue
St. Paul, MN 55104
612-646-7454

University of Minnesota
School of Dentistry
515 S.E. Delaware Street
Minneapolis, MN 55455
612-625-8400

In Minnesota also contact:
Neighborhood Health Care Network
612-489-2273

Senior Link Line
1-800-333-2433

"First Call For Help"
612-224-1133

Mississippi
Mississippi Dental Association
2630 Ridgewood Road
Jackson, MS 39216
601-982-0442

The University of Mississippi
School of Dentistry - Med. Ctr.
2500 North State Street
Jackson, MS 39216-4505
601-984-6155

Directory of Dental Programs

Missouri

Missouri Dental Association
230 W. McCarty Street
Jefferson City, MO 65102
573-634-3436
800-688-1907

University of Missouri
School of Dentistry
650 East 25th Street
Kansas City, MO 64108
816-235-2100

Montana

Montana Dental Association
P.O. Box 1154
Helena, MT 59624
406-443-2061 / 800-257-4988

Donated Dental Services
PO Box 1154
Helena, MT 59624
406-449-9670

Cooperative Health Dental Clinic
1930 Ninth Ave.
Helena, MT 59601
406-443-2584

Nebraska

**Senior Dent Program
Nebraska Dental Association**
3120 "O" Street
Lincoln, NE 68510
402-476-1704
800-234-3120

University of Nebraska Medical Ctr.
College of Dentistry
40th & Holdrege Street
Lincoln, NE 68583-0740
402-472-1333

Creighton University
School of Dentistry
2500 California Street
Omaha, NE 68178
402-280-2865

Nevada

Nevada Dental Association
6889 W. Charleston Blvd. #B
Las Vegas, NV 89117
702-255-4211
800-962-6710

New Hampshire

New Hampshire Dental Society
P.O. Box 2229
Concord, NH 03302
603-225-5961
800-244-5961

New Jersey

New Jersey Dental Association
One Dental Plaza
North Brunswick, NJ 08902-6020
732-821-9400

Directory of Dental Programs

**University of Medicine & Dentistry
New Jersey Dental School**
110 Bergen Street
Newark, NJ 07103-2425
201-982-4300

New Mexico

New Mexico Dental Association
3736 Eubank Blvd. N.E.
Suite C-1
Albuquerque, NM 87111
505-294-1368

New York

Dental Society of the State of New York
7 Elk Street
Albany, NY 12207
518-465-0044
800-255-2100

State University of New York
School of Dental Medicine
325 Squire Hall
Buffalo, NY 14214
716-829-2720

Columbia University
School of Dental & Oral Surgery
640 West 168th Street
New York, NY 10032
212-305-5665

New York University
College of Dentistry
345 E. 24th Street
New York, NY 10010
212-998-9800

State University of New York
School of Dental Medicine
South Campus
Stony Brook, NY 11794-8700
516-632-8974

North Carolina

North Carolina Dental Society
P.O. Box 4099
Cary, NC 27519
919-677-1396

University of North Carolina
School of Dentistry
104 Brauer Hall, 211 H
Chapel Hill, NC 27599-7450
919-966-1161

North Dakota

North Dakota Dental Association
Box 1332
Bismarck, ND 58502
800-795-8870

Ohio

**Oral Health Access Coordinator
Bureau of Oral Health Services**
246 North High St.
Columbus, OH 43266-0118

614-466-4180
In Ohio: 1-888-765-6789
Provides access to over 90 dental programs throughout the state

Ohio Dental Association
1370 Dublin Road
Columbus, OH 43215
800-MY-SMILE 1-800-69-76453)
or Options Program: 1-888-765-6789

Case Western Reserve Univ.
School of Dentistry
2123 Abington Road
Cleveland, OH 44106
216-368-3200

Ohio State University
College of Dentistry
305 West 12th Avenue
Columbus, OH 43210
614-292-2751

Oklahoma
Senior Dent/Care-Dent Programs
Oklahoma Dental Association
629 West Interstate 44, Service Rd.
Oklahoma City, OK 73118
405-848-8873
800-876-8890

University of Oklahoma Health Science Center
College of Dentistry
P.O. Box 26901
Oklahoma City, OK 73190
405-271-6056

Oregon
Oregon Dental Association
17898 S.W. McEwan Rd.
Portland, OR 97224
503-620-3230 / 800-452-5628

Department of Health Dental Health Division
Community Access Programs
800 NE Oregon St.
Portland, OR 97232
503-731-4098

Senior Smile Dental Service
Multnomah Dental Society
1618 SW First Ave.
Portland, OR 97201
503-223-4738

Donated Dental Services
CDRC
PO Box 574 Room 2205
Portland, OR 97207
503-248-3816

The Oregon Health Services University
School of Dentistry
Sam Jackson Park
611 S.W. Campus Drive
Portland, OR 97201
503-494-8867

Pennsylvania

Pennsylvania Dental Association
P.O. Box 3341
Harrisburg, PA 17105
717-234-5941 / 800-692-7256

Dental Care For Senior Citizens
Access To Care Program
3501 North Front St.
Harrisburg, PA 17110
717-234-5941

Temple University
School of Dentistry
3223 North Broad Street
Philadelphia, PA 19140
215-707-2900

University of Pennsylvania
School of Dental Medicine
4001 West Spruce Street
Philadelphia, PA 19104
215-898-8961

University of Pittsburgh
School of Dental Medicine
3501 Terrace Street
Pittsburgh, PA 15261
412-648-8760

Puerto Rico

Colegio de Cirujanos Dentistas
Avenida Domenech #200
Hato Rey, PR 00918
787-764-1969

University of Puerto Rico
School of Dentistry
G.P.O. Box 5067
San Juan, PR 00936
787-555-1212

Rhode Island

Rhode Island Dental Association
200 Centerville Place
Warwick, RI 02886
401-732-6833

Department of Public Health
Oral Health Division
3 Capital Hill
Providence, RI 02908
401-222-2588

South Carolina

Senior Care Dental Program
South Carolina Dental Association
120 Stonemark Lane
Columbia, SC 29210
803-750-2277
800-327-2598

Medical University of South Carolina
College of Dental Medicine
171 Ashley Avenue
Charleston, SC 29425
803-792-2611

Directory of Dental Programs

South Dakota

South Dakota Dental Association
330 South Poplar
Pierre, SD 57501
605-224-9133

Tennessee

Tennessee Dental Association
2104 Sunset Place
Nashville, TN 37212
615-383-8962

Tennessee Department of Dentistry
Cordell Hull
425 Fifth Ave. North
Nashville, TN 37247
615-532-5073

University of Tennessee
College of Dentistry
875 Union Avenue
Memphis, TN 38163
901-448-6257

Meharry Medical College
School of Dentistry
1005 Dr. D.B. Todd Blvd.
Nashville, TN 37208
615-327-6669

Texas

Texas Dental Association
P.O. Box 3358
Austin, TX 78764
512-443-3675

Texas A&M University System
Baylor College of Dentistry
3302 Gaston Ave.
Dallas, TX 75266-0677
214-828-8100

The University of Texas
Health Science Center
Dental Branch
6516 John Freeman Avenue
Houston, TX 77030
713-792-4056

The University of Texas
Health Science -Dental School
7703 Floyd Curl Drive
San Antonio, TX 78284-7914
210-567-3222

Utah

Department of Health
Dental Health Division
1365 West 1000 North
Salt Lake City, UT 84116
801-328-5756

Utah Dental Association
1151 E. 3900 S., Suite B160
Salt Lake City, UT 84124
800-662-6500

Vermont

Island Pond Health Center
Dental Program
PO Box 425
Island Pond, VT 05846
802-723-4300

Directory of Dental Programs

Vermont State Dental Society
100 Dorset Street Suite 12
South Burlington, VT 05403
802-864-0115

Virginia
Virginia Dental Association
P.O. Box 6906
Richmond, VA 23230
804-358-4927 / 800-552-3886

Health Department
Dental Division
1500 E. Main
Richmond, VA 23219
804-786-3556

Virginia Commonwealth Univ.
MCV-School of Dentistry
P.O. Box 566
Richmond, VA 23298
804-828-9095

Washington
Elderly and Disabled Washington State Dental Assn.
2033 6th Ave., Suite 333
Seattle, WA 98121
206-448-1914
800-448-3368

University of Washington
School of Dentistry
Health Science Blvd. SC-62
Seattle, WA 98195
206-543-5830

West Virginia
West Virginia Dental Association
2003 Quarrier Street
Charleston, WV 25311
304-344-5246

West Virginia University
School of Dentistry
The Medical Center
P.O. Box 9400
Morgantown, WV 26506-9400
304-598-4810

Wisconsin
Wisconsin Dental Association
111 E. Wisconsin Avenue, Ste 1300
Milwaukee, WI 53202
414-276-4520
800-364-7646

Dane County Public Health Division
Dental Health Program
1202 Northport Drive
Madison, WI 53704
608-242-6510

Marquette University
School of Dentistry
604 North 16th Street
Milwaukee, WI 53233
414-288-6500

Wyoming

Wyoming Dental Association
P. O. Box #1123
Cheyenne, WY 82003
307-634-5878
800-244-0779

State Health Department
Dental Division
Hathaway Building, 4th Floor
Cheyenne, WY 82002
307-777-7945

Nationwide Helplines

Alliance for Aging Research 202-293-2856
Alzheimer's Association 800-272-3900
Alzheimer's Disease Education and Referral Center 800-438-4380
American Association of Retired Persons (AARP) 800-424-3410
American Assoc. of Homes & Services for the Aging 202-783-2242
    For publications call 800-508-9442
American Cancer Society Response Hot Line 800-227-2345
American Council for the Blind 800-424-8666
American Diabetes Association 800-342-2383
American Diabetes Foundation 800-232-3472
American Heart Association 800-242-8721
American Institute For Cancer Research 800-843-8114
American Lung Association 800-586-4872
Arthritis Foundation Information Line 800-283-7800
Bell Atlantic LifeLine Service 800-555-5000
Brookdale Center on Aging 800-647-8233
Cancer Care 800-813-4673
Cancer Information Service. 800-4-CANCER
Eldercare Locator 800-677-1116
Equal Employment Opportunity Commission 800-669-4000
Family Violence Information 800-537-2237
Gray Panthers 800-280-5362
Grief Recovery Institute 800-445-4808
Help for Incontinent People 800-252-3337
Hill-Burton Hot Line (if you need help with hospital costs) . 800-492-0359

Directory of Nationwide Helplines

Leukemia & Lymphoma Society 800-955-4572
Lighthouse Center for Vision and Aging 800-334-5497
Medicare Hotline 800-638-6833
National AIDS Hot Line 800-342-2437
National Alliance of Breast Cancer Organizations 888-806-2226
National Alliance for the Mentally Ill 800-950-6264
National Breast Cancer Coalition 202-296-7477
National Cancer Institute 800-422-6237
National Caregiving Foundation 800-930-1357
National Center on Elder Abuse 202-682-2470
National Citizens' Coalition for Nursing Home Reform 202-332-2275
National Clearinghouse for Alcohol & Drug Info. 800-729-6686
National Committee to Preserve Social Security & Medicare 202-822-9459
National Council of Senior Citizens 301-578-8800
National Diabetes Information Clearinghouse 301-654-3327
National Digestive Disease Clearinghouse 301-654-3810
National Eye Care Project Helpline 800-222-3937
National Health Information Center 800-336-4797
National Hospice Organization 800-658-8898
National Institute on Aging 800-222-2225
National Institute on Deafness & Other Communication
    Disorders Information Clearinghouse 800-241-1044
National Institute of Mental Health 800-421-4211
National Institute of Neurological & Stroke Disorders 800-352-9424
National Insurance Consumer Helpline 800-942-4242
National Kidney & Urological Disease Clearinghouse 301-654-4415
Parkinson's Disease Foundation 800-457-6676
Y-ME National Breast Cancer Organization 800-221-2141